# COUNTDOWN TO VALKYRIE

Count Claus Schenk von Stauffenberg, as a captain of the 6th Panzer Division.

# COUNTDOWN TO VALKYRIE

## The July Plot to Assassinate Hitler

## Nigel Jones

FRONTLINE BOOKS, LONDON

*For Liam, Tom, Alfie and Milena.*

FRONTLINE BOOKS, LONDON

*Countdown to Valkyrie: The July Plot to Assassinate Hitler*

This edition published in 2008 by Frontline Books, an imprint of Pen and Sword
Books Ltd, 47 Church Street, Barnsley, S. Yorkshire, S70 2AS
www.frontline-books.com

Copyright © Nigel Jones, 2008

ISBN: 978-1-84832-508-1

*CIP data records for this title are available from the British Library and the Library of
Congress*

For more information on our books, please visit
www.frontline-books.com, email info@frontline-books.com
or write to us at the above address.

Printed by the MPG Books Group in the UK

# Contents

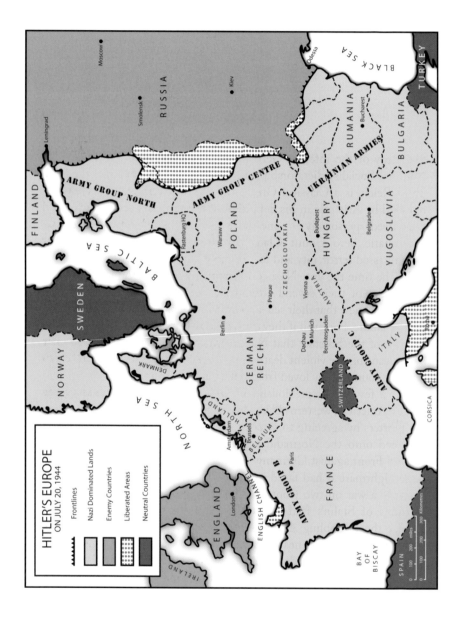

HITLER'S EUROPE
ON JULY 20, 1944

Frontlines
Nazi Dominated Lands
Enemy Countries
Liberated Areas
Neutral Countries

miles 0 100 200 300
Kilometers 0 100 200 300

MOSCOW

RUSSIA

Smolensk

Kiev

Odessa

BLACK SEA

ARMY GROUP NORTH

ARMY GROUP CENTRE

UKRAINIAN ARMIES

RUMANIA

Bucharest

BULGARIA

TURKEY

Leningrad

FINLAND

BALTIC SEA

Rastenburg HQ

Warsaw

POLAND

CZECHOSLOVAKIA

Budapest

HUNGARY

Belgrade

YUGOSLAVIA

SWEDEN

Prague

Vienna

AUSTRIA

Berlin

Dachau

Munich

Berchtesgaden

ARMY GROUP C

ITALY

NORWAY

DENMARK

GERMAN REICH

SWITZERLAND

CORSICA

NORTH SEA

HOLLAND

Amsterdam

Brussels

BELGIUM

Paris

FRANCE

ARMY GROUP B

ENGLISH CHANNEL

IRELAND

ENGLAND

London

BAY OF BISCAY

SPAIN

# Introduction

The story of the internal German resistance to Adolf Hitler and his National Socialist dictatorship, the hideous regime that he called the Third Reich, is a Classical Greek tragedy, containing all the elements required by Aristotle in his definition of the term. Its actors performed their deeds personally – none more so than its legendary leader, the charismatic hero Count Claus Schenk von Stauffenberg – and it encompassed terror, pity and fear in more than full measure.

By the time the anti-Nazi conspirators carried out the last and most spectacular of their several attempts to assassinate Hitler on 20 July 1944, they knew that their self-appointed mission was doomed to almost certain failure. For, even if they succeeded in outwitting the all-pervasive security of the SS state that Nazi Germany had become and hit their target, causing the violent death of the dictator, it was already too late to save the country they loved from defeat and destruction.

Just a few weeks previously, on D-Day, 6 June, the armies of the Anglo-American western allies, who previously had refused to encourage the plotters by agreeing to a separate peace deal excluding Russia, had swarmed onto the Normandy beaches and opened the long-awaited Second Front against Germany. The Fatherland was now living out the same nightmare it had faced in the First World War just twenty years before – a war on two fronts. In the east, the seemingly inexhaustible divisions of Stalin's Red Army were hurling themselves relentlessly against the crumbling defences of Hitler's realm. Each passing day brought their columns nearer to the heartland of the Reich, and by late July they were just a hundred miles away from Hitler's personally chosen eastern headquarters; the Wolf's Lair at Rastenburg, tucked away among the brooding, swampy forests of the East Prussian/Polish marches.

Almost every day and night now, fleets of American and British heavy bombers, virtually unopposed by the depleted remnants of Germany's once-mighty Luftwaffe, droned overhead and pounded the cities of the Reich, gradually grinding them into rubble. The news from the fronts – moving ever closer – that was brought to Hitler's twice-daily conferences with his military staff was almost uniformly bad. The perimeters of the Reich were shrinking, the losses of his armies could not be repaired or replaced, his remaining allies were searching for ways to desert him, and the inescapable truth was staring even the meanest intelligence in the face: Hitler's war was irretrievably lost.

But even though no move of theirs could affect the inevitable outcome of the war, the leading conspirators were more determined than ever that action should be taken. As one of the most clear-headed among them, General Henning von Tresckow, put it: 'The assassination must be attempted at all costs . . . what matters now is not the practical purpose of the coup, but to prove to the world and for the records of history that the men of the resistance movement dared to take the decisive step. Compared to this objective, nothing else is of consequence.' In other words, it was not so much the 'practical purpose' of an assassination and an associated putsch to overthrow the regime that mattered any longer: an assassination attempt was necessary to redeem the honour of the once-proud German army, a quality that had been surrendered on the snow-covered killing fields of Russia and eastern Europe long before.

Though opposition to Hitler and the barbaric policies he embodied long predated the outbreak of war and even his arrival in power in 1933, it was the actual murderous realisation of Nazi racial doctrines on the vast Russian steppes and hidden in the dense forests east of Warsaw that spurred some – including Stauffenberg himself – from mere grumbling into active anti-Nazi conspiracy. This radicalisation of the resistance was most marked among army officers who witnessed such atrocities as the massacre of Jewish communities and the slaughter of Slav 'sub-humans', both civilians and Soviet prisoners, and who gradually became aware of similar Nazi crimes inside Germany itself, including the euthanasia of the mentally and physically handicapped. Such flagrant trampling on the Christian ethics that had traditionally underpinned German society profoundly shocked the Prussian officer corps.

An activist minority of such men, however obedient to the head of state they may have been taught to be, held a higher loyalty to the laws of God, the teachings of Christ, or merely to codes of simple human decency. To restore the primacy of such higher commands, and to return Germany to the rule of law and the path of Christian civilisation, seemed to them the highest duty of all, outweighing soldierly concepts like obedience to their superiors' orders and even the defence of their country's borders against the enemy in wartime.

With military courage, determination and energy – alas, not always matched by military efficiency – the conspirators set about a final attempt to murder Adolf Hitler, the man to whom they had all pledged a compulsory oath of loyalty as their Führer, a leader combining the three posts of Commander-in-Chief of the armed forces, head of the government and head of state. In doing so, they were fully aware of what was at stake, and what they were putting at mortal risk. Failure would mean that the full fury of Nazi vengeance would be unleashed against them, with all that that entailed: arrest, imprisonment, cruel and prolonged torture, a humiliating public trial and a lonely, degrading death. Perhaps hardest of all to bear would be the reproaches of those of their fellow Germans, in whose name they claimed to be acting, who would accept the Nazis' caricature of them as traitors who had stabbed their country in the back in its hour of greatest need. In the words of the Irishman Roger Casement, hanged for treason in the First World War, and equally revered in some quarters as a hero and reviled in others as a traitor: 'It is a cruel thing to die with all men misunderstanding.'

Notwithstanding the high price that might have to be paid, the men of the resistance went ahead with the near-hopeless plan that was concealed under the codeword 'Valkyrie'. The plan was for the simultaneous assassination of Hitler and a Reich-wide military putsch; a *coup d'état* aimed at arresting the SS and loyalist Nazis, not only in Germany itself but also in countries still occupied by Germans – France, Czechoslovakia, Austria and Norway – and replacing Hitler's rule with that of a mixed civilian-military government dedicating to supplanting National Socialism with a *Rechtsstaat*. This would be a Germany where the rule of law once again reigned supreme, and German citizens would no longer tremble in dread at the sound of a midnight knock on their doors ushering them into the terrors of '*Nacht und Nebel*', night and fog.

What happened during the course of that dramatic day forms the core of this book. But 20 July 1944 was the climax to years of plotting, and abortive attempts to arrest and/or assassinate Hitler (whether it was morally right to kill Hitler, or merely to detain him and bring him to trial was the subject of agonised debate among the conspirators). While concentrating on the military conspiracy that reached its final, tragic culmination in the last summer of the war, I have also told the stories of other plots against the Führer's life, and other centres of opposition to Nazi rule, since these were inextricably intertwined with the long-meditated military plot that reached its final, fatal fruition on 20 July. Inevitably the story centres on the main actor on that fateful day: the shining personality of Claus von Stauffenberg, who – just as Hitler was the ungodly trinity of Nazi rule – embodied in his single dynamic personality the head, hands (or rather hand, since Stauffenberg had lost one of his) and heart of the conspiracy.

Stauffenberg was the man who, entering the conspiracy relatively late in the day, quickly assumed the leadership of the whole tangled enterprise, infusing the plot with his own unquenchable drive, energy and enthusiasm. He reinvigorated more senior officers: generals like Tresckow, Beck and Olbricht, who, frustrated by the repeated failure of their previous attempts to eliminate the evil that Hitler represented, had lapsed into a state of near fatalistic resignation. I will examine the factors that formed Stauffenberg's remarkable character: his family, upbringing, military career, the evolution of his quasi-mystical religious and political philosophy, and his transformation from an elitist nationalist with more than a sneaking sympathy for the Nazi *Weltanschauung*, into the Hitler regime's most implacable and convinced opponent.

The form that seems most convenient for telling this story is that of a timeline. The story forms a chronological narrative that begins with Stauffenberg's youth and the Nazi rise to power, takes on momentum as the regime tightens its grip and embarks on the road to war and genocide, and reaches its shattering climax as Hitler's increasingly desperate internal enemies reluctantly wrestle with their own Christian convictions forbidding them to kill the man they know is leading their people – and the world – into the abyss.

In telling their story, I hope that – without sparing criticism of the resistance where it is justified – I can make their actions comprehensible and admirable to readers unfamiliar with German history in general, and in particular to all those lucky enough never to have lived under a ruthless, cruel and ultimately utterly insane dictatorship. The men of the resistance were genuine heroes and the world still needs their unconquerable spirit. It is a spirit that made one of the few of them who survived, the jurist Fabian von Schlabrendorff, when asked how he had endured the fiendish tortures of the Gestapo, write:

> We all made the discovery that we could endure far more than we had ever believed possible. The two great polar forces of human emotions, love and hate, together formed a supporting structure on which we could rely when things became unbearable. Love, the positive force,

included our faith in the moral worth of our actions, the knowledge that we had fought for humanity and decency, and the sense of having fulfilled a higher duty. Those among us who had never prayed learned to do so now, and discovered that in a situation such as ours prayer, and prayer alone, is capable of bringing comfort and lending almost superhuman strength. One also finds that love in the form of prayers by relatives and friends on the outside transmits currents of strength.

Hate, the negative force, was just as important in sustaining us. The consuming, unqualified hatred, made up of equal parts of revulsion, contempt, and fury which we felt for the evil of Nazism, was so powerful a force that it helped us endure situations which otherwise would have been intolerable.

Thanks to Schlabrendorff and his colleagues in the resistance who refused to endure the intolerable situation that was Nazi rule, the flame of humanity they lit in the darkness of Hitler's Reich was never entirely extinguished. They may have failed to kill Hitler, but in the mere fact of making the attempt these brave men snatched the soul of their tortured country from the pit – and saved it.

# Prologue
## High Summer in the Wolf's Lair

## 20 July 1944: Rastenburg

Thursday 20 July dawned like many another high summer's day at Rastenburg, Adolf Hitler's chosen Field Headquarters deep on the north Polish plain, in a region enclosed by gloomy forests of birch, beech and oak, and dotted with hundreds of small lakes. Despite its proximity to the Baltic coast, barely a breath of sea air penetrated the dark woods surrounding the complex of concrete bunkers and electrified fences housing the nerve centre of the Führer's once formidable but now faltering war machine.

Rastenburg, a small German town in the east Prussian enclave around the ancient port of Königsberg, the birthplace of philosopher Immanuel Kant, had been chosen as a military site as early as 1940, after the victorious conclusion of the German campaign to conquer Poland. A landing strip was constructed on the edge of the Gorlitz forest, and the Karlshof Café – once a gathering place for the local people – was requisitioned by the SS. That November, Dr Fritz Todt, Germany's chief military engineer, whose name would become synonymous with the construction of the Atlantic Wall and other defensive fortifications using slave labour, chose the forest as the perfect place to build Hitler's eastern headquarters. The Führer, turning away from the west after his humbling of France and his less successful attempt to batter Britain into submission, was already planning what he saw as the triumphant fulfilment of his political and military mission: the smashing of Stalin's Russia, and the conversion of its inhabitant into a race of semi-educated helots serving the *Herrenvolk*.

The code name chosen for the site was 'Wolfschanze' (Wolf's Lair); a conceit on the part of a man usually marked by his modest, even austere

Hitler exercises his Alsatian Blondi in the open meadow east of the Wolfschanze, probably in August 1943.

style. The Führer's forename, Adolf, was a corruption of *Adelwolf* (Noble Wolf) and his other wartime headquarters were the 'Wolfschlucht' (Wolf's Gorge) in the Ardennes for the Battle of France, and his forward headquarters at Vinnitsa in the Ukraine, 'Werwolf' (Werewolf). Vinnitsa was the scene of the first serious – if abortive – attempt to assassinate Hitler by officers of the Army Group Centre in 1943; a year earlier, in 1942, it had been the place where Hitler's path first crossed that of his would-be nemesis, Count Claus von Stauffenberg.

It was Colonel von Stauffenberg who was expected at Rastenburg on this broiling day in late July to report personally to Hitler on the state of readiness of the Reserve Home Army, of which he had been appointed Chief of Staff the previous autumn. The haemorrhaging of manpower on the Eastern Front – more than fifteen hundred Wehrmacht soldiers were killed daily – had, since D-Day the previous month, been boosted by a similar rate of attrition on the Normandy Front. The human resources of the Reich were being worn down ever more rapidly, and the unpalatable scraping of the manpower barrel had begun that would see old men and young boys donning ill-fitting uniforms and flung into the furnace that was consuming Germany's future.

Even at dawn, the day promised to be a fine if muggy one, although there would be few opportunities to enjoy the sunshine. Already before the war news began to turn grim, the atmosphere here had always been oppressive. The dark forest provided a sombre backdrop to increasingly gloomy events, and the brooding menace of the place was not lightened by the ubiquitous camouflage netting, strung everywhere on tall poles in an effort to conceal the complex from Russian aerial attack; the once-distant Red Army was now only 150 kilometres away. Fear of attack was all-pervading at Rastenburg – the whole five-acre complex was protected by three concentric rings of electrified fencing, with SS sentries accompanied by savage, snarling *Schaferhund* guard dogs posted every thirty metres. The bunkers themselves were made of reinforced concrete, some six metres thick, making them almost impervious to even a direct hit, but rendering the living-space inside excessively cramped, adding to the oppressive atmosphere hanging heavily on the place.

Work on the complex was still proceeding, three and a half years after it had begun under the transparent cover name of the Askania Chemical Works. Hitler's own block was still under construction, and so whenever

The Wolfschanze's Führerbunker, which measured 37 metres across, with the east and west wings adding another 25 metres. The height was estimated at over 13.5 metres. This photograph was taken in 1974.

he came to Rastenburg he stayed at the guesthouse bunker, one of a collection of buildings inside the innermost and most closely guarded section of the complex, the Sperrkreis 1. For his most recent visit he had arrived from the Berghof, his Bavarian mountain retreat in southern Germany a few days earlier, on 14 July. As well as the Führer's quarters, this inner area also held a number of structures, including offices of the Wehrmacht, Luftwaffe and naval liaison staff attached to the Führer, and the briefing room, its windows flung wide open in the July heat. This was where Stauffenberg would deliver his report during Hitler's customary midday situation conference.

Also inside Sperrkreis 1 were the quarters of the SS guards, drivers, stenographers and secretaries; garages and personal bunkers for the falling and rising stars of the Reich. These included the Luftwaffe overlord Hermann Goering; Hitler's personal Chief of Staff and gatekeeper, the self-effacing but increasingly powerful intriguer Martin Bormann; and Hitler's favourite technocrat, the architect turned munitions minister and industrial chief Albert Speer. Here too were located the fortified underground bunkers where the Wolfschanze's staff would retreat from the threat of air raids, and where military conferences were sometimes held. There was room for buildings catering to the limited leisure hours of Hitler and his staff: a cinema, a sauna, and a tea house where the food faddist Führer would sip his herbal infusions and munch through endless sickly Austrian cream

Goering and Luftwaffe General Karl Bodenschatz walk with Hitler at the Wolf's Lair, with Casino I in the background, in the spring of 1942.

cakes, an incorrigible appetite for which he had acquired in the Vienna of his youth. All the while he would regale his bored minions with his table talk: the interminable monologues – meticulously recorded by hidden stenographers on Bormann's orders – setting out his views on history, politics, war and race, and tales from earlier, happier days of the *Kampfzeit*: his own rise to supreme power. Within a few yards of these buildings was Rastenburg's signals centre: the hub of Hitler's communications with his armies and the rest of the Reich, commanded by General Erich Fellgiebel, a colleague of Stauffenberg's in the conspiracy, who would play a crucial role in the day's events.

Stauffenberg was not the only visitor expected in Rastenburg that day. Although the colonel did not yet know it, the midday situation conference would be brought forward by an hour so that Hitler could prepare for the arrival of his fellow dictator, Italy's fallen Fascist leader, Benito Mussolini. Il Duce's train was due to pull into the sidings at Gorlitz, the Wolf Lair's own rail station, where three trains were kept with their steam up on permanent standby. From being Hitler's idol in his early years as an apprentice dictator, Mussolini had fallen to the status of junior follower, failed brother-in-arms and finally deposed dictator after he had been unseated and arrested by his own Fascist colleagues a year earlier, in July 1943. Daringly rescued in an audacious raid on his secret mountain jail in the Apennines by German special forces, Mussolini, by now only a sawdust Caesar, had been propped back on the seat of power as puppet ruler of German-controlled northern Italy, the so-called Italian Social Republic. But although he was treated by Hitler with all the warmth of former times, nothing could conceal the brute fact that the once strutting Duce was now a German-controlled marionette, a broken man who had backed the wrong horse.

Even though the writing was now on the wall for the Nazi and Fascist causes for all to read, within his rapidly receding realm the realities of power – and its trappings – were still held in Hitler's palsied, shaking hands; the grimmer the tidings from all fronts, the shriller became his insistence that he would still win the war: there must be no retreat, no going back. Anyone in the Wehrmacht who raised their voice in protest, no matter how mildly, knew that they would be unceremoniously silenced. The roll call of those who had crossed Hitler and paid for their defiance was a steadily lengthening one, and the worse the news grew, the more his paranoid suspicion of his own generals increased.

From the regime's earliest days, the field marshals and generals who had dared defy the Führer's implacable will had followed each other one by one into enforced retirement and semi-disgrace. Field Marshal Werner von Blomberg, the war minister responsible for the Wehrmacht's supine acquiescence to Hitler's assumption of power, had, despite his loyalty to the regime, been unceremoniously dumped in 1938 for marrying a young typist who turned out to be a former prostitute. At the same time General Werner von Fritsch, the pre-war army commander who opposed Hitler's march to war, had been implicated by the Nazis in a trumped-up homosexual scandal; disgraced and out of sheer disgust, he had voluntarily gone to his death in the Polish campaign. Also in 1938, General Ludwig Beck, the Chief of the General Staff whose hatred for Hitler and Nazism had been enough for him to contemplate a coup against the regime even before the war, had resigned in horror, and had since devoted himself full-time to the conspirators' cause. Beck had been joined in the anti-Nazi conspirators' ranks by two other senior commanders fatally bruised by their encounters with Hitler's mania: Field Marshal Erwin von Witzleben, an outspoken anti-Nazi who had been all for arresting Hitler before the war, and had been retired by the Führer in 1941 on the grounds of ill-health; and General Erich Hoepner, a tank commander sacked for his alleged failures on the Russian Front.

Beck's successor, General Franz Halder, who had presided over the Battle of France, had shared his predecessor's alarm that Hitler's reckless foreign policy would lead Germany into a war with the Western Allies, and become so disillusioned with Hitler that he had wanted to produce a pistol at one of their regular meetings and personally execute him. Scorning Halder as an old woman who lacked the aggressive spirit, Hitler had fired him in September 1942.

Field Marshal Walther von Brauchitsch, appointed with Halder to head the Wehrmacht, had only lasted until December 1941, when Hitler heard that he had been secretly discussing tactical withdrawals with his generals after the first Russian reverses. Telling Goebbels that Brauchitsch was a 'vain, cowardly wretch', Hitler had summarily dismissed him. Even the brilliant Erich von Manstein, a favourite of the Führer's ever since his bold *Sichelschnitt* plan for a surprise attack on France through the unguarded Ardennes hills had opened the way for the fall of France, had seen his hitherto glittering career consumed by the explosive mixture of the unwinnable war in Russia and Hitler's increasingly unstable temperament. Manstein, along with another field marshal, the tank commander Kleist, had been summoned to Hitler's mountain retreat the previous March – decorated with the prestigious Knight's Cross with Oak Leaves and Swords to sugar the pill – and

Hitler talks with Generaloberst Richthofen in front of Casino I, with the Keitelbunker in the distance on the left. SS-Obersturmführer Hans Pfeiffer, SS adjutant, is behind Hitler, and the latter's chief servant, SS-Untersturmführer Heinz Linge, is just behind Richthofen.

sacked. Hitler told them that their tactical talents were of no use to him any more: in the endgame that was fast approaching in Russia, he needed convinced National Socialist soldiers with the fibre to stick it out no matter how tough things became. Even the latest Chief of Staff, General Kurt von Zeitzler, tired of the Führer's endless temper tantrums, had recently left Rastenburg on what proved to be permanent sick leave.

Just as Hitler's Russian folly – his stubborn refusal to yield a metre of territory once it had been taken – had consumed the cream of his troops, so his cavalier treatment of his senior commanders meant that he was now rapidly running out of generals too. Disaster was looming fast in the east, but if anything the news from France, where the newly opened Western Front was fast approaching Paris, was even worse. Just three days previously, on 17 July, Germany's most charismatic soldier, Field Marshal Erwin Rommel, had been shot up from the air in Normandy by an Allied fighter, flying free now that the Luftwaffe had been knocked out of the skies. Rommel had suffered serious head wounds and, even if he lived, was unlikely to resume his command in the near future. Besides, there were disquieting rumours afoot at Rastenburg suggesting that even the hitherto loyal 'Desert Fox' had deserted his master's side. It was said that Rommel, the simple Swabian soldier, saw clearly that the war was lost now that the Anglo-American forces had established their bridgehead in France, and had bluntly advised Hitler to make peace with the west while he still had the chance before Germany suffered any more useless destruction. If there was any substance to these reports, then the future looked bleak indeed: if the wider German public learned that even the spirited Rommel wanted to throw in the towel, then it looked very much as if it was all over.

Of the other top commanders, Field Marshal von Leeb had quit as early as January 1942, appalled like so many of his comrades by Hitler's blank refusal to contemplate strategically essential troop withdrawals in the east. Field Marshal von Bock, the man whose advance into Russia had been stopped at the gates of Moscow in December 1941, had gone the same way in July 1942 for similar reasons. Field Marshal Siegmund List had also resigned that September, at the same time as Halder, when his offensive in the Caucasus had ground to a halt as a result of lack of supplies. The frozen furnace that was the Russian Front had consumed two more field marshals in 1943: Friedrich von Paulus, who had surrendered along with what was left of his decimated Sixth Army in February after being surrounded in Stalingrad thanks to Hitler's crazed 'No withdrawal' orders, and Maximilian von Weichs, sacked in Russia and transferred to the Balkans to deal with the increasingly troublesome resistance of Marshal Tito's Yugoslav partisans. Rommel's nominal superior in France, Field Marshal Gerd von Rundstedt, was aged and uninspiring and moved in and out of retirement as Hitler's whims took him. Rommel's recently appointed successor in Normandy, Günther von Kluge, was, like Halder, a half-hearted anti-Nazi who knew in his heart and head that the war was lost, but lacked the courage and will to stand up to Hitler.

Now the generals' larder was almost bare: almost the only commanders available and acceptable to Hitler were the yes-men surrounding him at Rastenburg – Wilhelm Keitel and Alfred Jodl, and die-hard Nazis like the monocled Walter Model, the savagely cruel Ferdinand Schoerner, the brilliant tank tactician Heinz Guderian and the former street fighter turned brutally efficient Waffen SS general, 'Sepp' Dietrich. Even the loyal Guderian had been known to growl out rumbles of dissent. Hitler, the First World War veteran who had never risen higher in rank than a humble corporal, had always hated and distrusted the stiff-necked Prussian officer corps, with their arrogant hauteur, their snobbish rituals. He saw the barely concealed sneers contorting their thin lips when they explained in lofty terms their objections to his grand strategic plans; he heard – or thought he heard – the disloyal whispers, glimpsed the eyebrows raised in disdain at his micro-managing interventions. And time after time they had let him down: failing to take Moscow or Leningrad, failing to hold Stalingrad or the Crimea. Since Paulus's shameful surrender – the first capitulation by a German field marshal since the time of Napoleon – the Russian campaign had turned into one long retreat.

Coupled with their blundering incompetence was rank disloyalty, even treason. Paulus had led the way: instead of committing suicide as any officer of honour would, the foxy-faced Prussian had meekly entered Soviet captivity from where he had begun broadcasting treasonable appeals on Moscow Radio. Stalin had set up something called the Committee of Free German Officers who were calling on their comrades to desert Hitler and turn their guns on the Nazis. No, Hitler was done with the Prussians: he needed new blood.

Perhaps this tall colonel who was coming from the Reserve Army would have some ideas. At least he was a Swabian rather than a Prussian, even if he still had a title and a 'von' before his name. Everyone spoke well of him – said he was the most brilliant staff officer of his generation. The fact that he had lost an eye and an arm at the fighting front only increased Hitler's admiration. He hated desk warriors and defeatists. Yes, he would see what Stauffenberg could do . . .

# A Good German
## The Early Life of Count Claus von Stauffenberg

**Jettingen, 15 November 1907**: boy twins are born to Caroline, Countess von Stauffenberg, at one of the family's several country properties in the province of Swabia in south-western Germany. Very unusually, this is the second set of male twins that the countess has borne her husband, Count Alfred von Stauffenberg, Lord Chamberlain to the king and queen of the small state of Württemberg. Just over two years before, on the Ides of March 1905, one year after their marriage, and on the anniversary of Julius Caesar's assassination, she had presented

(Left to right) Countess Caroline Schenk von Stauffenberg with Alexander, Berthold and Claus, c.1910.

her husband with another pair: Alexander and Berthold. As they grew up, Alexander would be merry and musical, but smaller in stature and academically less gifted than his brilliant twin. Berthold, whose salient physical feature was his luminous, penetrating eyes, would grow up closer to his younger brother Claus in their good looks, keen intellects and in their courageous, mystically chivalrous temperaments.

Sadly, of Countess Stauffenberg's second set of twins, only one survived: Konrad died the day after his birth, but Claus grew to be the family's favoured Benjamin: tall, dark and handsome, with a natural ease of manner and grace that charmed almost all those who entered his circle. The Stauffenbergs were a noble family who had lived among the rolling wooded hills of Swabia for centuries, and traced their ancient lineage, and family name – Schenk – back to the Middle Ages.

The first record of a Stauffenberg – the name derives from a long-vanished Swabian fortress on a conical hill near Hechingen – is of a certain 'Hugo von Stophenberg' in 1262. From 1382, the family can be traced in an unbroken line of descent. The Stauffenbergs followed professions suitable to their status: there were many soldiers, including warriors who served on Germany's ever restive eastern borders with the Teutonic Knights or the Knights of St John. Other family members, however, showed more spiritual than temporal inclinations, and the family produced a number of clerics and university scholars. In Claus von Stauffenberg the two strains – worldly and mystic, military and

(Left to right) Alexander, Claus and Berthold in the garden of Lautlingen Castle, c.1918.

Alexander, Claus
and Berthold in
the Old Castle,
Stuttgart.

ecclesiastic – united in one commanding, towering personality, just as
he inherited his handyman father's practical capability, alongside his
mother's contrasting dreamy literary tendencies.

In 1698 one Stauffenberg became a hereditary baron, and a century
later in 1791, to reward the staunchly Catholic family's loyalty to the
Habsburg Holy Roman Emperors who reigned in Vienna, another
Stauffenberg was promoted to become a hereditary imperial count
(Graf). Claus von Stauffenberg's title of count had been granted to his
great-grandfather, Baron Franz von Stauffenberg, by Ludwig II, the
unstable, castle-building king of Bavaria, in 1874. Over the centuries
the family had acquired extensive estates on the borders of Bavaria and
Swabia, including Claus's birthplace, Jettingen, and the 'castle' (Schloss)
– in reality a small manor house at Lautlingen in the 'Swabian Alps' hills
– where the brothers would do much of their growing up. Their early
childhood was spent at the Alte Schloss (Old Castle), an ancient royal
residence in the heart of the Swabian capital Stuttgart, long the seat of
their royal masters, the monarchs of Württemberg.

The boys' father, Alfred, was appointed Lord Chamberlain in 1908,
a year after Claus's birth. Valued for his practical, no-nonsense skills
in running the royal estates as well as his own – he was not above

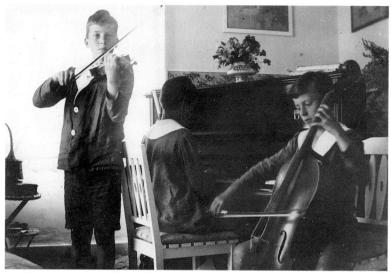

Family concert in Lautlingen: Berthold (with violin); Alexander (piano) and Claus (cello), 1917.

wallpapering a room, or taking the family gardens in hand personally – Alfred's position gave his family the run of the royal residences and a familiarity with casually superior aristocratic ways that were to become second nature to them. The boys affected a casual, even eccentric style of dress that in Claus's case would lead to charges of slovenliness when he joined the army. The attitude of not caring what others thought extended to the family table, where guests were astonished by their habit of communicating in growls and grunts rather than words, a private language they called 'signalling'.

Countess Caroline was a complete contrast to her gruff, unsentimental husband, both in her background and in her unworldly, languorous character. Where he was a south German and Catholic in religion, she was a Lutheran Protestant from Germany's harsh north-eastern coast. Born Caroline Üxküll-Gyllenbrand, she was descended from the notable soldier Field Marshal August von Gneisenau, who had galvanised Prussian resistance to Napoleon. Fluent in French and English, the countess loved art and the theatre, and enthused her three sons with her passion for literature and languages. All the boys were precocious learners, though their interests diverged: Alexander was silent, sedate and philosophical; Berthold fiercely intellectual and academic; while

Claus was the fearless warrior: riding horses and scrambling up rocks from an early age. When confronted with a problem Claus always sought a solution, even if it was a 'quick fix'. All three brothers loved the outdoor pursuits that came with their cultivation of the family estates: haymaking, riding, skiing and walking the high Alpine pastures came as easily to them as knocking on doors and running away did to city boys.

**Lautlingen, 31 July 1914**: the Stauffenberg family were enjoying their annual summer holidays at Schloss Lautlingen when the news came through that would disrupt their rural idyll – and that of the rest of Europe – forever. Germany was mobilising for war. Already, her forces were moving according to pre-arranged timetables, crowding onto trains carrying them across the Rhine into Belgium and France, an invasion that would bring Britain into the conflict, and turn a European struggle into the First World War. In the east huge Russian armies were moving into the Teutonic heartland of east Prussia – the area of the Masurian Lakes around Rastenburg that Claus von Stauffenberg would one day come to know all too well.

The following day, **1 August 1914**, Countess von Stauffenberg decided to follow her husband back to the family apartments on the second floor of the Old Castle in Stuttgart. An air of excitement, even hysteria had swept over the nation. Even the sleepy Swabians, a people mocked by other Germans for their placid, cautious nature, were caught up in the prevailing excitement.

Within days came the first news of the fighting: on **13 August 1914** a cousin, Clemens von Stauffenberg, was reported killed; and on **28 August** there was an air-raid alarm over Stuttgart. The boys were infected by the war: young Claus – just seven years old – dissolved into a flood of tears at the thought that the war would almost certainly be over before he was old enough to fight in it. All the brothers wrote poems hymning the successes of German arms; Berthold showed a particular interest in the Kaiser's High Seas Fleet that would one day blossom into a naval career.

The Stauffenberg family felt the war's depredations like all other Germans: in March 1917 Alfred von Hofacker, the boys' cousin, fell at Verdun. Alfred's brother Casar, a future close collaborator of Claus in the conspiracy against Hitler, was taken prisoner by the French in October 1918, and remained in captivity until 1920.

The British naval blockade bit hard, forcing Countess von Stauffenberg to abandon her regular tea stall at Stuttgart station for lack of supplies. In 1917 the boys shouldered scythes and went out into the fields around

Lautlingen to help bring the harvest home in place of the men who were away at war. Caroline's sister, Countess Alexandrine von Üxküll, head of the Württemberg Red Cross, returned from Russia after a nightmare nine-month journey by train and sledge to bring supplies and solace to German prisoners of war shivering in remote Siberian camps. She told tales of a vast country in the throes of revolution, where atrocities and spreading inhumanity were but a foretaste of the terrible decades to come.

Russia's withdrawal from the war early in 1918 came too late to stave off Germany's defeat. After the failure of the last-gasp German spring 1918 offensives in the west, the collapse came quickly. Squeezed by the blockade and subsisting on a diet largely composed of turnips and ersatz food, the working classes were in an angry, resentful mood, and ready to listen to the revolutionary message coming out of Russia. As German armies reeled back at the front, the country's rulers asked for an armistice, only to find the spectre of red revolution stalking the Fatherland too.

**Stuttgart, 9 November 1918**: throughout German history 9 November is a date that recurs like a tolling bell. In 1989, it was the day that the Berlin Wall came down, reuniting the nation sundered by the Second World War. In 1938 as the storm clouds of that war gathered, it was the date of the infamous *Reichskristallnacht* – the most blatant display of the Hitler regime's murderous hostility towards the Jews – when mobs inspired by the authorities had torched synagogues, trashed shops, looted property and beaten and arrested hundreds of Germany's Jews in naked displays of toxic hate that shocked and horrified the world. In 1918, 9 November was the day when revolution engulfed Germany.

King Wilhelm II of Württemberg – not to be confused with Kaiser Wilhelm II of all Germany, whose abdication and flight to Holland occurred on this fateful day – had already given orders, as strikes and disorders erupted across even previously peaceful Swabia, that no one should attempt to defend Württemberg's local monarchy with arms. The king had always enjoyed a cosy, typically Swabian intimacy with his subjects, and now, as always, he walked alone and unguarded through Stuttgart's streets, despite the flying of red flags and noisy demonstrators calling for peace and revolution. At the request of his ministers, the king called an assembly to devise a new republican constitution. At 11 a.m., a mob invaded the royal palace, and Count Alfred von Stauffenberg was one of the loyal servants who prevented the intruders from gaining access to the royal apartments. Even so, a red flag was hoisted above the palace and the king – accompanied by Count Stauffenberg – left the city for his hunting lodge at Bebenhausen. Stauffenberg senior took charge of the subsequent negotiations between the king and the new republican authorities, and the monarch abdicated on 30 November.

Meanwhile, on **11 November 1918**, the armistice ending the war had come into force. Claus von Stauffenberg spent his eleventh birthday on **15 November** in tears; he had resented the king's refusal to defend the monarchy by force, and did not want, he said, to 'celebrate the saddest birthday in my short life'. During the next few months the Stauffenbergs, staying largely at Lautlingen while a new town flat in Stuttgart's Jagerstrasse was prepared for them, experienced vicariously Germany's chaotic political events.

A Communist revolution, spearheaded by the Spartacus League led by Karl Liebknecht and Rosa Luxemburg, was crushed by the paramilitary Freikorps – remnants of the old Imperial Army and young right-wing volunteers – employed by, but hostile to, the new Social Democratic government of Friedrich Ebert. The Spartacus rising in January 1919 in Berlin was bloodily suppressed, and Liebknecht and Luxemburg were murdered. In Germany's second city, Munich, a 'Soviet republic' led at first by German anarchists, then by professional revolutionaries sent by Lenin, was similarly crushed by the Freikorps. This left Bavaria, Swabia's neighbour, a happy hunting ground for right-wing extremists who found the atmosphere of the Bavarian capital more tolerant of their constant anti-republican conspiracies than 'red' Berlin.

Swabia was largely spared such disorders, and the Stauffenberg brothers continued their education at the Eberhard Ludwig Gymnasium, one of Stuttgart's most prestigious schools. In their spare time the brothers often visited the theatre, though their father refused to set foot in Stuttgart's former Royal Theatre since it had fallen into the hands of republicans. They relished the classic giants of the German stage – Goethe, Schiller and Hölderlin (the latter two were fellow Swabians) – and themselves acted in a production of Shakespeare's tragedy about the assassination of a tyrant, *Julius Caesar*.

Also to their father's disapproval, the brothers fell under the influence of Germany's *Jugendbewegung* – the youth movement known as the *Wandervogel* (Wandering Birds). This had originated before the war in which many of its young members had sacrificed themselves, and was much given to long hikes through Germany's fields and forests. At night the *Wandervogel* would camp out and recite poetry or strum songs on their guitars around the camp fire. Owing something to Britain's Boy Scouts, and resembling the later Beatniks, the *Wandervogel* were generally nationalist in their political views, although some dabbled in idealistic socialist notions too. There was also a strong streak of mysticism in the movement, a semi-pantheist identification with the 'soul' of Germany. The group joined by the Stauffenbergs – the 'New Pathfinders' – were particularly influenced by the ideas of the poet Stefan George.

Now largely forgotten, George was then a hugely influential figure in Germany. An aloof, austere man who affected a late nineteenth-century 'decadent' artists' style of dress – long hair, floppy beret, smock, with an expression of mocking disdain on his chiselled features – George was famous for his peripatetic lifestyle. Disdaining a permanent home, he travelled constantly to stay at the residences of his devoted young – and exclusively male – disciples. His privately published poetry was not widely known, but to the self-appointed elite who followed him, his verses were guiding stars.

Homosexual in tone, and heavy with portentous symbolism, George's poetry prophesied the coming of a 'New Reich' (the title of one of his works). Like many writing in the apocalyptic atmosphere of post-

Stefan George with Claus and Berthold in Berlin, November 1924.

war chaos in Germany, such as Oswald Spengler in his monumental *Untergang des Abendlands* (Decline of the West) or Wagner's English-born son-in-law Houston Stewart Chamberlain, George voiced a vague longing for a new Führer-figure to rescue the Fatherland from decadence and terminal decline. Above all, he called for a new elite to inculcate lofty spiritual and artistic ideals into German life. He seemed to find the germ of this elite among his own besotted circle of followers, and entry into this George-Kreis (George Circle) was much prized and jealously guarded and fought over.

Heidelberg, **Spring 1923**: Alexander and Berthold von Stauffenberg joined the George-Kreis early in 1923 when they left school and started their studies at the ancient Swabian University of Heidelberg. Introduced to the poet by one of their professors, they soon brought along their handsome and talented younger brother to meet the Master. Claus, then still a sixteen-year-old schoolboy, was instantly besotted by George's mystique. The importance of George's influence on the life of Claus and his brothers can hardly be exaggerated. All three brothers addressed poems to the Master, which he carried around and often read. He returned their adoration, and while he made his customary suggestions as to how his new disciples, Alexander and Berthold, could improve their attitudes and character, he made no such edicts for Claus: the youngest Stauffenberg, he pronounced, was already perfectly moulded and could not be improved upon.

The ideas that Claus imbibed from the poet would govern the course of the rest of his life. As his friend and fellow George disciple Ludwig Thormaelen confirmed, 'For Claus von Stauffenberg George's environment and his relationship with the poet remained the decisive factor in his life.' The concept of a 'hidden' or 'secret' elite whose noble spirituality would set the tone for the whole nation would inform Stauffenberg's thinking from then on. It was not by chance that he suggested that the name for the anti-Hitler conspiracy should be 'Secret Germany'. He met George as often as he could, while he meditated on which course to choose for his own career. Although he suffered from frequent bouts of ill-health as a child, and was clearly of a spiritual and artistic bent, callings as a priest or academic did not appeal: Stauffenberg's primary drive was as a man of action. He toyed at first with music or architecture, rejecting both on the grounds that while he was sure he could attain competence in them, he did not have the ability for a major 'achievement' in either field. The rejection of mediocrity and the idea that he was destined to rise above the common run of mankind in whatever capacity he chose seemed uppermost in his thinking. In the end, he surrendered to the inevitable and opted for a military career.

Meanwhile, for the first time, the Stauffenbergs heard the name of Adolf Hitler. It came in 1923, again on that fateful day **9 November**. On that date, the young street-corner politician and beerhall orator, whose rise to prominence as leader of the National Socialist German Worker's Party (NSDAP or 'Nazis') had been accomplished in Munich in the space of four years, launched a serious armed attempt to seize power. It came in Bavaria, which he planned to use as a springboard for seizing the German state as a whole. The Beerhall Putsch came to a bloody end after a thin line of Munich police opened fire on the marching Nazi column, killing sixteen putschists, but sparing Hitler, who survived to

Count Alfred von Stauffenberg with his sons Berthold, Claus and Alexander, c. 1925.

turn the tables on the authorities at his subsequent trial, getting off with a lenient year in jail for his attempt to overthrow the state.

While Hitler languished in the fortress of Landsberg, and his movement stagnated without his driving hand, Germany in 1924 was emerging from economic (hyper-inflation) and political (the French occupation of the Ruhr industrial area to 'encourage' the payment of war reparations) crises to what briefly seemed like a brighter future.

**Stuttgart, 5 March 1926**: Claus von Stauffenberg passed his *Abitur* exam. Claus's decision to opt for an army career surprised his family. Although he numbered several distinguished soldiers among his own ancestors, he did not seem to be ideal army material. How would he cope with the physical demands of service life, or its discipline? His health had never been robust, his dress inclined to the casually untidy; he did not suffer fools gladly, even if – or especially if – they were in a superior position; and his sensitive nature would surely recoil from the raw brutalities of war. Besides, his father did not consider service in the truncated, often despised 100,000-strong army of the Weimar Republic an honourable profession for his son. But Claus was adamant.

Stauffenberg as a young officer in Bamberg.

Stauffenberg (left) leading a mortar platoon in Bamberg, 1933.

If he had become an architect, he said, he would have dealt only with things. In the army he would be dealing with people, and, as he told Karl Schefeld, a friend who had tried to involve him more deeply in the *Jugendbewegung*, from henceforth, people were to be his ruling passion: 'I do not follow ideas, but people.'

What Claus really meant – in line with the teaching of his idol Stefan George – was that he would not be following people, but leading them.

Claus joined the 17th Cavalry Regiment garrisoned in the small cathedral city of Bamberg on **1 April 1926**. There were family connections – his uncle Berthold had served with the Regiment in the First World War – and his skill as a horseman, coupled with his aristocratic birth, made the choice of an elite cavalry unit a natural one. As he told his father in a letter a month after joining up: 'It is not easy for our kind to play the common man for any length of time.'

The first few years of basic training were strenuous. Although Stauffenberg excelled in equitation and tactics, he drew criticism for his sometimes slapdash style of dress. In his limited leave time, he mingled with local aristocratic acquaintances and kept up his connections with the Stefan George circle, albeit in secret. His new friends in the army knew nothing of his membership of George's 'Secret Germany' group. In Germany's army, perhaps more than most military organisations, artistic and intellectual interests tended to be derided and distrusted.

In **October 1927** Stauffenberg began a ten-month course at the Infantry School in Dresden, learning the mysteries of mortars, machine-guns and motor bikes. On **1 August 1928**, still an officer cadet, he was promoted to sergeant, and in **October 1928** attended the Hanover Cavalry School to complete his training.

In the final examination for an officer's commission Stauffenberg was awarded first place among the cavalry candidates, winning the Sword of Honour for his efforts. On **1 January 1930**, having returned to base at Bamberg, he was gazetted a Second Lieutenant: his glittering career as an army officer had begun.

Count Claus von Stauffenberg, c.1936.

# 2 Seizing the State
## The Irresistible Rise of Hitler's Nazis

After the chaotic early years of the Weimar Republic, Germany had, in the mid-1920s, settled into a state of precarious prosperity, in which the fragile freedoms established at such high cost after the postwar period of near civil war, of revolution and counter-revolution, of strikes, demonstrations, political assassinations, plots, putsches and murderous conspiracy, were briefly enjoyed by a majority of Germans. Appearances, however, were deceptive. Although Weimar governments were dominated by parties of the centre and moderate left, the forces of extremism were quiescent, rather than subdued; many – perhaps most – conservative Germans regarded the republic, the bastard child of defeat and revolution, as a necessary evil at best, to be grudgingly tolerated until a more suitable form of government appeared.

On the right, conservatives and nationalists fondly harked back to the days of the Kaiser, to order, military pride and keeping the working classes firmly in their place at the bottom of the social heap. On the left, the fathers of the republic, the majority Social Democratic Party (SPD), remained in government, in coalition with other parties such as the Catholic Centre Party and the Liberal Democrats. The SPD were, however, always menaced by the German Communist Party (KPD) on their far left. The KPD had never forgiven their SPD rivals for their complicity in the Freikorps' murder of their founders, Liebknecht and Luxemburg. Now fierce rivals for Germany's working-class vote, the two socialist parties, with their different versions of Marxism – the gradualist and the Leninist – expended more energy in attacking each other than they did their 'bourgeois' rivals. The Communists, true to the party line dictated from Stalin's Moscow, suicidally regarded their true enemy to be the 'social fascism' of the SPD rather than Nazism, which they saw as a passing phenomenon: this was to prove a fatal error. Although Communist Red Front fighters battled the Nazi Brownshirts on the streets, they had much in common with their proletarian political opposite numbers, including a taste for violence and thuggery, a fondness for uniforms and an aggressive hostility to bourgeois respectability in all its forms. But the greatest threat to the frail republic lay on the right. Although the Nazi Party was still weak outside its Bavarian birthplace – the First World War hero General Erich von Ludendorff had won less than 2 per cent of the vote when he stood on the Nazi ticket against his old comrade-in-arms, Paul von Hindenburg, in the 1925 presidential elections – the Nazis had built the skeleton of a national organisation. They received a further boost in 1929 when Hitler appointed a propagandist of genius, the mesmeric 'poison dwarf' Josef Goebbels, to head the party organisation in Berlin and wrest the capital away from its allegiance to the 'Reds'.

The Wall Street crash of **October 1929** was the storm signal that gave the Nazis their chance. The global depression that followed the crash was particularly severe in Germany, which had barely recovered from the debilitating inflation of the mid-1920s. To the embitterment of the middle class, who had lost both their savings and psychological security in the chaos that had followed the war, was added the fury of a resentful working class as unemployment climbed steadily towards six million. Benefits were slashed to the bone by the bankrupt state, presided over by the Catholic politician Heinrich Brüning, appointed chancellor by Hindenburg in March 1930. Brüning's own parliamentary backing in the Reichstag was so shaky that he had to rule by decree, which hardly did much to increase his already negligible popularity.

In these conditions Hitler's intoxicating message – a heady brew mixing hatred with hope, bawled out hoarsely and repetitiously by the Nazi leader from a thousand public platforms – found a ready, even eager response from a demoralised public desperate for order, stability and vengeance on the world of enemies that had laid Germany low. Hitler demonised such enemies: the Marxists who had plunged their knife into Germany's prostrate body as she waged her life-or-death struggle in 1918; the traitorous politicians – the 'November criminals' – who had ridden to power on the back of Communist revolution and then made a treacherous peace with the Allies; above all, the Jews, whose 'money power' lay at the root of all the Fatherland's myriad of woes. But there was also hope in Hitler's impassioned, vengeful rhetoric: identify Germany's enemies, rub them out, and all might yet be well. Once the Marxist republic and the venal men of Weimar had been pulled down and all power given to the Führer and his cohorts, work would return, the criminals would be put in their place, and a shining future would open for all racially purged and pure sons and daughters of the true *Volk*.

Hitler's message of German national resurgence held a strong appeal, even for aristocratic families such as the Stauffenbergs, who might have been expected to look askance at the vulgar street brawling and violent criminality that were the thuggish hallmarks of the Nazi Brownshirts or Sturmabteiling (SA). The writings of Stefan George had certainly called for the coming of a Führer-figure to save the country from dissolution, and if the almost absurd, common, gesticulating figure of Hitler was some way from the ideal knight as envisaged by the George-Kreis, at least he might represent a move in the right direction.

That was certainly the view of Stauffenberg's cousin, Casar von Hofacker, later a courageous and central figure in the anti-Hitler resist-

Stauffenberg's cousin, Lieutenant-Colonel Casar von Hofacker in the Second World War.

ance who would suffer torture and death at the hands of the regime, but who in 1922/3 helped to found the first SA group at Göttingen University. Ten years later, in March 1933, in the last elections before the National Socialists clamped their shackles around Germany, Hofacker was campaigning for the Nazis, publicly demanding that the people must empower the government 'to do away with elections once and for all, and to replace the Reichstag by a dictatorship'.

The reactionary politician Franz von Papen and the wily General Schleicher (both later destined to suffer – Schleicher fatally – during the Night of the Long Knives purge) succeeded each other as chancellor, and jostled for the ear of the rapidly fading President Hindenburg. After this complex game of political musical chairs, the ageing president was bamboozled into doing what he had sworn he would never do: call for the man he called a 'Bohemian Corporal' – Hitler – to become chancellor. Although Hitler's first cabinet was a coalition in which the Nazis held only a minority of posts, and conservatives like Papen were convinced that they could master and manipulate the insignificant little Austrian, it was Hitler who turned the tables on them. In giving him the keys to the Reichs Chancellery, Papen and the others had boarded a train they could not stop. On **30 January 1933** Hitler was appointed chancellor.

It is more difficult – because hard evidence is lacking – to gauge Claus von Stauffenberg's attitude towards Hitler and the Nazis in their early days in power than it is to perceive the views of other members of his circle. Apart from Hofacker, those who initially threw their support behind the new government but who later became passionate Hitler-haters and prominent in the resistance included Hans Oster, Henning von Tresckow, Mertz von Quirnheim and Helmut Stieff. There is one unsubstantiated – and unlikely – report that, on the night of 30 January, as joyful Nazis lit beacons all across Germany, Stauffenberg, in full uniform, placed himself at the head of a spontaneous celebratory column of enthusiastic Nazi supporters in Bamberg. His own explanation was that he had been swept up willy-nilly by the mob, and had simply walked along with them. As he told fellow officers who reproached him in the Mess later that evening, the soldiers of the Prussian national revolution against Napoleon, including his own ancestor Gneisenau, would certainly have had a more sympathetic attitude towards this new and latter-day revolution than Hitler's critics did.

It does not detract from Stauffenberg's later heroic role in the resistance to concede that, like most of his brother officers in the army, he adopted a wait-and-see attitude towards the new regime that was broadly sympathetic towards the avowed Nazi aims of national renewal, economic reconstruction and strengthening the armed forces. The army – from its chief Blomberg downwards – was unanimous that rearmament and a reclaiming of Germany's standing through throwing off the chains imposed by the Versailles Treaty were essential if the nation was to regain the world's regard and its own self-respect. It took several years before the officer corps learned the hard way that what they first dismissed as Nazism's 'excesses' were in fact the very essence of a criminal regime.

Besides, Stauffenberg had other things to think about. On **1 May 1933** he was promoted to full Lieutenant. Four months later, on **26 September 1933** he married a fellow aristocrat, Baroness Nina von Lerchenfeld. The social backgrounds of the couple were almost identical. Like his mother,

Nina Freiin von Lerchenfeld and Claus von Stauffenberg, 1931.

Claus von Stauffenberg and his bride Nina outside St Jakob's Church in Bamberg after their wedding on 26 September 1933.

Stauffenberg's bride came from a mixed Baltic and Bavarian background and was a Lutheran Protestant. Her father, like Alfred von Stauffenberg, had also been a royal chamberlain – in his case to the Bavarian court in Munich. Nevertheless, despite Nina's Protestantism, the wedding took place in Bamberg's St Jakob's Catholic Church, and the couple's children would be brought up in their father's Catholic faith.

The match seems to have been more of a career move than a grand passion. Stauffenberg quoted a comment made by the homosexual Prussian king Frederick the Great to his future mother-in-law when he said that for an officer a wife was 'a necessary evil'. Aged twenty-six himself, Claus told his seventeen-year-old fiancée that he had chosen her because she would make a good mother for his children. They had met in Bamberg at her father's house in 1930 and swiftly became engaged, albeit secretly because of Nina's youth. Stauffenberg married in full uniform – including steel helmet – and they honeymooned in Mussolini's Italy.

While the young couple had been sunning themselves and seeing the ancient sites of Italy, momentous events were occurring in their Fatherland. The **March 1933** elections, which had hardly been free or fair as there had been heavy Nazi pressure and intimidation thanks to the party's control of the police and organs of propaganda, including the radio, had still failed to return an absolute majority for Hitler, his party gaining 43 per cent of the vote. Even before the elections, though, the Nazis had been moving with increasingly bold steps to take over the German state.

In **February 1933** the Reichstag, the German parliament in central Berlin, had been destroyed in a suspicious fire. A young Dutch Communist, Marinus van der Lubbe, had been arrested inside the building with combustible material in his possession, but the fire had spread with astonishing rapidity; there were many who suspected the Nazis themselves had torched the place. At any rate, alleging that there was a Communist conspiracy to take control in a coup, the Nazis banned the party and arrested many of its functionaries.

The SA street fighters stepped up their thuggery: arresting, beating up, torturing and imprisoning opponents in scores of private jails. The first of many concentration camps for those who dared to speak out against Hitler was opened at Oranienburg, fifty miles from Berlin. Thanks to Goebbels's increasingly tight control of the press and radio, Hitler's image and his ranting, raving voice were seen and heard in every corner of the country. As soon as the election results were in, on **23 March 1933** the remnants of the Reichstag, meeting in Berlin's Kroll Opera House, were pressured, persuaded, bribed and bullied into passing an Enabling Act giving Hitler's government the power to pass any law it saw fit – without reference to parliament or indeed to the German Constitution itself, which could be bypassed by Special Courts, against whose decisions there was to be no right of appeal. Only the SPD voted against the law, its last action before being banned itself. Its Parliamentary leader Otto Wels courageously told Hitler, '*Wir sind wehrlos, aber nicht ehrlos*' ('We are defenceless, but not without honour'). At a stroke, the Weimar Republic had committed suicide, and German democracy had sleepwalked into a dictatorship.

# 3 Rule of the Outlaws

Within an astonishingly short space of time, the Nazi dictatorship fixed its immovable clutches around the country's throat. In a ruthless process known as *Gleichschaltung* (coordination) all institutions and individuals in Germany were subordinated to the new regime: free trade unions and employers' organisations were submerged into Nazi-run 'Fronts'; all political parties except the NSDAP were banned.

For young people, membership of the Hitler Youth and its female equivalent, the Bund Deutsche Mädel (BDM) became all but compulsory. A range of repressive new laws made criticism of the regime and its Führer a criminal offence punishable by a spell in one of the feared new concentration camps, where beatings, torture, starvation and hard labour became the order of the day. For millions of Germans, fear of the midnight knock on the door became all-pervasive; the shorthand name for the regime's secret police – the 'Gestapo' (*Geheime Staatspolizei* – secret state police) entered the language. By **July**, Hitler was able to proclaim his national revolution complete. After the Stauffenbergs returned from their honeymoon, plebiscites in **November 1933** returned 96 per cent rates of approval for the new policies.

There is little evidence one way or the other on Stauffenberg's attitude to the demise of the republic whose armed forces he had joined. Under its compliant leader, Field Marshal Werner von Blomberg, the army tamely submitted to the new order, benignly viewing the Hitler government as a reliable bulwark against Bolshevism, and rejoicing at the new chancellor's evident ambition to expand and rearm the armed forces – the Luftwaffe and navy as well as the army – in order to reassert Germany as a major player on the world stage. Meanwhile, Stauffenberg was continuing with the serious business of becoming a soldier. In a progress report of **October 1933** on the somewhat priggish but popular officer, Stauffenberg's squadron leader, Hans Walzer, noted in the credit column that he was 'reliable, independent minded, highly intelligent and of above average ability, both tactically and technically'. Walzer described his handling of both horses and men as 'exemplary'. After this glowing praise, however, Walzer listed on the debit side that Stauffenberg, as well as the old complaint about being 'somewhat sloppy in dress', was also too well aware of his superior intellect and was liable to 'adopt a somewhat overbearing attitude towards his fellow officers, frequently evidenced by sarcasm'.

In **December 1933** Stauffenberg had suffered a loss so great that it amounted to a close family bereavement: his Master and mentor, Stefan George, died in Swiss exile at the age of sixty-five. George's attitude to the coming of the Third Reich had been ambiguous. On the one hand, he specifically refused a Nazi invitation to join the Prussian Academy of Arts after it had been purged of anti-Nazi writers such as Thomas Mann. On the other hand, he disowned two of his Jewish followers who had spoken out against the increasingly vicious anti-Semitism of the regime, although some of his disciples who stated that the Third Reich was indeed the ideal Germany that George had been calling for were not similarly disavowed. His departure for Switzerland was not a flight into exile on political grounds: he was on holiday there when overtaken by his fatal illness, and there is no evidence that he did not intend to return to Germany. All three Stauffenberg brothers would continue to revere the poet and seek to live by his precepts for the rest of their lives.

The year 1934 was dominated by the showdown between the army and the SA. The swaggering, bullying, brown-shirted storm troopers under their beefy Chief of Staff, Ernst Röhm, had been an important – if blunt – instrument in opening up Hitler's path to power. Once that power had been attained, however, the SA became simply an embarrassment. The Nazi *Kampfzeit* – 'time of struggle' – had been marked by street brawls, beerhall battles and gun and knife fights as the SA took on their Communist and Socialist opponents. Their vulgarity and brutality had always appalled the German middle and upper classes; and now these were the very groups that Hitler needed to cement his grip on the levers of state.

Moreover, the old soldier Röhm seemed unable to grasp the realities of running a state. No sooner was Hitler in the Reichs Chancellery than the battered bruiser was making aggressive speeches calling for a 'second revolution' that would boot the hated stiff-necked, glassy-eyed Prussian officer corps out of power and substitute the storm troopers as Germany's new army. This was a threat to the Wehrmacht's role as the state's sole

Ernst Röhm in his
Brownshirt uniform
in the early 1930s.

bearer of arms; it was a threat that not even the army chief, war minister Werner von Blomberg, could ignore. Nicknamed '*Gummilowe*' ('Rubber Lion') for his normal stance of slavish subservience to Hitler, Blomberg left the new chancellor in no doubt that Röhm's insolent demands must be resisted, and that the menace that his rowdy, three million-strong paramilitary force posed to the order and stability of the new state must be crushed.

There was another issue too: a major reason why Röhm and his cohorts were detested by the army's conservative officer corps was his more-or-less open homosexuality. Not only were the pot-bellied SA leadership generally of rough-hewn proletarian origins, but many of them also shared Röhm's sexual tastes and were despised by the officer caste, who feared that the nation's soldierly spirit was about to be debauched by sexual degeneracy, just as the army would be swept away in a brown flood if Röhm's plans to merge the two forces into a new People's Army ever came to pass. Hitler himself felt torn as the storm clouds of the SA-versus-army conflict gathered. He was uneasily aware that it was the fists and boots of the SA that had propelled him into power. He also knew that it was Captain Röhm, his oldest party comrade, who had, as an intelligence officer in the post-war army, originally plucked him from the ranks when he recognised the gawky corporal's uncannily persuasive power as a demagogue. Moreover, Hitler shared in full measure Röhm's distrust for the snobbish, effete officer corps. On the other hand, he knew of Röhm's seething resentment of his own dominance. Jealous aides had reported Röhm's indiscreet jeers at what Röhm called 'this ridiculous corporal's' newly acquired airs and graces, and Hitler was determined that now power had fallen into his hands he would not let it go: had he not pledged that once inside, the only way that he would be removed from the Berlin Chancellery would be as a corpse? Even so, throughout the long brooding spring and summer of 1934 Hitler dithered, waiting for someone to show their hand, waiting for the right moment, waiting for the fruit to ripen and fall rotten from the branch.

It was then that the personal jealousies that always bedevilled the Nazi hierarchy came into play. Hermann Goering, First World War flying ace turned flamboyant Nazi paladin, and Heinrich Himmler, the deceptively mild-mannered, bespectacled former chicken farmer who now headed the SS (the black-uniformed party security service), were united in little more than deep personal animosity. Yet on one subject they both agreed: the loathsome Röhm was a danger to their ambitions and he had to go. As the overlord of Prussia's police, Goering had the legal power to gather surveillance reports on the drunken boasts and threats uttered by Röhm and his cohorts. Himmler had always wished to supplant the inefficient brutishness of the SA with his own elite force of young, tough, ruthless Aryan recruits. Himmler, whose crackpot racism even outdid that of Hitler, was in the early stages of building the SS into the core of the Nazi state: a Praetorian Guard responsible for policing the population and eliminating threats – real and imagined – to Nazi rule. Removing Röhm would be a giant step towards his goal.

Goering and Himmler put their heads together in a rare show of co-operation, and set about drenching Hitler's already suspicious mind with poison about his old comrade. Röhm was planning a putsch, they whispered. The SA had always been an undisciplined rabble, and now they were threatening to undermine the smooth Nazi takeover of the state and to eliminate Röhm's rivals physically. The threat had to be nipped in the bud. Only by striking first and with ruthless violence could they thwart Röhm's wild ambitions, reassure the broad mass of the public – and cow it into submission. Hitler allowed himself to be persuaded and as June turned into July he struck, lashing out not only at Röhm, but at a host of other enemies too.

Hitler travelled to one of his favourite hotels, the Dreesen at Bad Godesberg on the Rhine, ostensibly to attend the nearby wedding of Essen's Nazi Gauleiter, Joseph Terboven. From there, he flew south through the night of **30 June 1934** to Munich. There, the accumulated tension burst: the first SA man that he saw was arrested after a furious tirade from Hitler in which he accused the hapless man of treason. Hitler, accompanied by Goebbels and a group of armed SS men, then drove out of Munich to Bad Weissee on the Tegernsee, the lakeside resort where Röhm and a group of his closest cronies were taking the cure for their various dissipations. The official Nazi line that the SA chief was planning a putsch is disproved by the fact that Röhm had just stood his legions down and sent the entire SA on a month's leave.

Hitler arrived at the hotel, the Pension Hanselbauer, soon after 6 a.m. and stormed into the lobby. Röhm received a rude awakening; Edmund Heines, SA commander in Silesia, after being found in bed with a boy, was summarily shot in the hotel's grounds along with his unlucky partner. Röhm himself and the other SA leaders were arrested and packed into Munich's Stadelheim prison, where most were shot in the prison yard. Goebbels sent a pre-arranged signal 'Colibri' ('Hummingbird') for the slaughter to begin in Berlin. Here SS men, provided with arms by the army, set about their work. Firing squads killed scores in the SS barracks at Lichterfelde, while other victims were shot in their own homes by death squads. During a long weekend's bloodletting, many old scores were settled. Not only was the entire leadership of the SA eliminated, but Hitler also put to death those who had at some point impeded his path to power. His memory went back a long way.

Gustav von Kahr, the Bavarian Regent who had gone back on his promise – extracted by Hitler at pistol point – to support the Nazi Beerhall Putsch in November 1923, paid dearly for his *volte face*. Though aged seventy-two, and long since retired from politics, he was abducted from his home by SS thugs, hacked to death with pickaxes, and his body thrown into a swamp near Dachau, soon to become the site of the most notorious of the Nazi concentration camps. Others who had deviated from the path of unquestioning obedience to Hitler suffered similar fates: Gregor Strasser, once the head of the Nazis' national organisation and who had extended the party from its Bavarian birthplace across the whole Reich, was, like Röhm, a Nazi who took the 'socialism' of the party's title seriously. In the late 1920s Strasser had challenged Hitler's control of the movement and now he paid the price for his temerity. He was gunned down through his cell window, the same fate that would befall Röhm himself after Hitler had finally been persuaded to authorise the killing of his old comrade. General Kurt von Schleicher, the creepy intriguer who had become Weimar's last pre-Nazi chancellor and had plotted with Strasser to keep Hitler out of office, was shot down at his study table. His wife, who opened the door to her husband's killers and tried to stop their bloody work, died in the same hail of fire. One of Schleicher's closest colleagues, the army general Ferdinand von Bredow, was also killed: he was bludgeoned to death in a police van and his body slung into a ditch.

Hitler's vice-chancellor, Franz von Papen, the conservative who had preceded Schleicher as chancellor, and then successfully manoeuvred to put Hitler into power in his place, miscalculating that he could control the new chancellor and corral him in a safely conservative direction, only narrowly escaped death himself. He was held under house arrest in his own office for three days as Hitler – enraged by a speech Papen had given at Marburg University in mid-June in which he had called for an end to Nazi lawlessness and excesses – debated whether to have him killed. In the end he was satisfied by having Papen's three closest associates in Catholic conservative circles, including his secretary, and the man who had written his Marburg speech, murdered. Papen himself was demoted to become Germany's ambassador to Austria, charged with the task of smoothing the way to Hitler's early takeover of his homeland. Shaken by the slaughter of his closest aides, Papen would make sure that he never again uttered a squeak of dissent. The illusion that he could manage and manipulate Hitler had been brutally shattered.

At the close of that long summer weekend of blood and terror Hitler himself admitted that seventy-four victims were dead, though unofficial tallies point to a death toll of four hundred or more. Hitler had struck to his left and right, eliminating the SA, Nazi 'socialists' and reactionary generals and conservatives alike in one fell swoop. He had left no one – within Germany or in the wider world – in any doubt that he had taken on the role of judge, jury and executioner. Reaction in the army was mixed: Field Marshal Erwin von Witzleben, always an implacable opponent of Hitler and destined to be nominated as the new army

Field Marshal Erwin
von Witzleben.

Commander-in-Chief by the July plotters in 1944, cried 'Splendid!' when he heard that the SA leadership had been shot. While Witzleben's delight that the SA enemies had been eliminated was widely shared in the army – an act facilitated a couple of days before the purge by the army's formal expulsion of Captain Röhm from its ranks – more perceptive officers were aware that the lawless executions, and especially the insensate violence with which they had been carried out, were the hallmarks of a viciously barbaric regime that had buried the rule of law in the graves of its victims. As they looked ahead with foreboding, several far-sighted officers feared that in associating themselves with Hitler's first public act of mass murder the army had irretrievably forfeited its honour, staining itself with the blood of its own members, Generals Schleicher and Bredow. They had unleashed a beast they could not halt.

These early stirrings of unease among the army's leadership were shared by Stauffenberg, who nonetheless welcomed the purge as 'a clean-up'. Two incidents, both from early in 1934, show the seeds of Stauffenberg's later moral revulsion at the Nazi regime. Both events centre on the unsavoury figure of Julius Streicher. Streicher was the notorious Jew-baiting Gauleiter of Franconia: a grotesque figure whose manic anti-Semitic ravings in his gutter weekly *Der Stürmer* invariably

Julius Streicher,
c.1933.

revolved around his own psycho-sexual pathology. In the first incident Stauffenberg attended a Nazi party rally in Bamberg as a representative of the army. Streicher was the guest speaker and launched into his usual pornographic tirades, despite the blushing presence of teenage BDM girls around the podium. Appalled, Stauffenberg and his colleague staged a public walkout. In the second incident, in **March 1934**, Stauffenberg publicly leapt to the defence of his idol Stefan George, after the poet was accused by Streicher in the pages of *Der Stürmer* of being Jewish and his poetry damned as 'Jewish Dadaism'. Stauffenberg wrote to Goebbels's Propaganda Ministry – responsible for licensing Streicher's rag – complaining about the Gauleiter's rant, which, he told his brother Berthold, was the work of 'inferior National Socialists'. Stauffenberg still made a distinction between 'good' and 'bad' Nazis.

Hitler followed up his gruesome triumph in the Blood Purge by making his victory over the army explicit. On **2 August 1934** the aged President Hindenburg, in whose name the purge had been officially approved, finally died. Immediately Hitler moved to make his absolute dictatorship official, by combining the posts of president, chancellor and chief of the armed forces – head of state and of government – in his own person as a single, all-powerful 'Führer'. To underline his supremacy, every member of the armed forces, from Blomberg down to the humblest private, was obliged to take a personal oath of loyalty to Hitler. 'I swear before God this sacred oath: I will render unconditional obedience to Adolf Hitler, the Führer of the German nation and people, supreme Commander of the armed forces, and will be ready as a brave soldier to risk my life at any time for this oath.' Many officers later made their fealty to this oath a convenient reason for not joining the anti-Hitler conspiracy.

Another institution of the German state feeling an icy breeze that would become a raging tornado was the Christian Church. Both the Catholic and Protestant denominations recognised early on that in the ideology of National Socialism, Germany's Christian traditions faced a mortal rival, and that the battle between the two incompatible faiths would be a fight to the death. As Roland Freisler, the savage judge of the Nazi People's Court, would tell Helmuth von Moltke, a member of the Christian resistance, at his trial in 1944: 'National Socialism and Christianity have this in common: we both demand the whole man.'

As early as September 1933, one of Germany's best-known Protestant pastors, Martin Niemöller, would found a *Pfarrernotbund* or Pastors' Emergency League of fellow Evangelical ministers, deeply concerned at the direction in which Hitler was taking Germany. At first sight, Niemöller was an unlikely opponent of the Nazis: a staunch nationalist, in the patriotic traditions of Prussia's Lutheran faith, he had been commander of a U-boat in the First World War and, after wreaking huge damage on Allied shipping in the Mediterranean, he had been awarded Germany's highest decoration, the Pour le Mérite medal. Niemöller was from a deeply conservative background, and while he was a theology student at Münster University he had raised his own Freikorps and helped put down the Red Rising in the Ruhr that followed the 1920 Kapp Putsch. At first sympathising with Hitler's avowed aim of restoring Germany's greatness, and sharing the anti-Semitism that had traditionally disfigured Lutheranism, Niemöller had nevertheless been disturbed by what he perceived as the movement's paganism, and sought a meeting with Hitler to allay his doubts.

As a pastor in the fashionable Berlin suburb of Dahlem in 1933, Niemöller became increasingly concerned by what he saw as a false and Godless ideology, and attracted some six thousand pastors – roughly one-third of all Protestant clergy – to his Emergency League. The following year Niemöller and like-minded ministers broke away from the official Lutheran Church, which under Bishop Ludwig Müller had warmly welcomed Hitler's advent to power, to found the Confessing Church at Ulm on **22 April 1934**. The new Church was explicit in its condemnation of the 'mortal danger' posed by Nazism, with its false claim to be a 'new religion'. The Catholic Church, too, registered its disapproval of the Nazi takeover of faith schools and its assault on church youth movements, which were forcibly incorporated in the Hitler Youth and the BDM. Catholic bishops issued memoranda to Hitler on the subject, a foretaste of battles to come.

In 1935 and 1936, as Stauffenberg ascended through the army's ranks, successfully rode and jumped in equitation tournaments, learned English and even made a brief visit to England, the Nazis tightened their remorseless hold on German life. A huge portion of Hitler's regeneration of German industry was devoted to rearmament. Mechanisation of the army meant that Stauffenberg's regiment abandoned their beloved horses in favour of tanks and other armoured vehicles. In **March 1935**, Hitler delightedly tore up the disarmament clauses of the hated Treaty of Versailles forbidding Germany more than token armed forces, and stridently proclaimed what was already an open secret: Germany was rearming, fast and strong. At the same time, compulsory conscription was introduced. The new German air force – the Luftwaffe – would become the most Nazified of the three services, and would absorb the lion's share of the substantial military budget. The new service was Goering's baby, and he relinquished his control of the police and Gestapo to Himmler's SS, which was quietly augmenting the power it had accrued since the Röhm purge. In a taste of things to come, also in **March**, the SS were permitted to form an armed wing – the Waffen SS – which would one day challenge the army as the weapons bearer of Hitler's new state.

At the same time, the regime's anti-Semitism became codified law with the passing in **November** of a National Citizenship Law that limited full German citizenship to pure-blooded 'Aryans'. Jews, or those with one Jewish parent – *Mischlinge* – were denied the right to hold public office, and marriage between Aryans and Jews or *Mischlinge* was officially forbidden. Jews were now second-class citizens in their own country. The serpent was laying its poisoned eggs.

# 4 Hitler's March to War

Having established unquestioned dominance within the Reich, Hitler's regime began to flex its expanding muscles abroad, although its slowly escalating step-by-step approach at first effectively disguised these ambitions from the anxious eyes of the outside world. There was, moreover, a strong feeling among foreign observers that by moving into the Saar – a coal-rich region administered since the First World War by the League of Nations – and a year later, in **March 1936** into the Rhineland, Germany was merely reoccupying its own backyard. The outbreak of the Spanish Civil War in **July 1936** gave the Nazis an unlooked-for opportunity to test their growing armed might. Junkers 52 transport aircraft were used to ferry the Nationalist rebel General Franco's Army of Africa from Morocco to the Spanish mainland, and, as the Civil War became an international conflict, Goering's Luftwaffe formed a Condor Legion of planes and pilots to fight on Franco's side. The Condor Legion's most notable exploit was the destruction of the ancient Basque capital of Guernica – a dry run for the future bombing of many another European city by the Luftwaffe.

**Moabit, Berlin**, **6 October 1936**: Stauffenberg had by now been marked down by his superior officers and contemporaries alike as an exceptional soldier with a glittering future ahead of him. In the autumn of 1936, he was selected to attend Berlin's War Academy in the Moabit district for training as a potential General Staff officer. In the capital, Stauffenberg was among both family and friends. His two eldest sons, Berthold and Heimaren had been born in 1934 and 1936 respectively, and his brother Berthold lived nearby in Wilmersdorf, along with his cousin Casar von Hofacker. Other friends and future conspirators were also in the neighbourhood, including a circle of fellow aristocrats among whom were numbered Fritz-Dietlof, Count von Schulenburg, a fellow officer; the intellectual diplomat Adam von Trott zu Solz; Count Ulrich von Schwerin; another Stauffenberg cousin, Count Peter Yorck von Wartenburg; and their maternal uncle Count Nikolaus von Üxküll-Gyllenbrand.

These men represented the cream of the old Prussian aristocracy, with lines of ancestors distinguished by their military services to the state. The younger ones were members of a discussion group that came to be known as the Kreisauer-Kreis (Kreisau Circle) after the country estate of the group's informal leader, Count Helmuth von Moltke, where they sometimes met.

The bluest of Prussian blue blood ran through Moltke's veins. Descended from two other Helmuth von Moltkes – the 'Elder', who had won the Franco-Prussian War of 1870–1, and the 'Younger', who had notably failed to win the replay against France in 1914 – the current Helmuth was, like Stauffenberg, a thoughtful intellectual whose distinguished mind, sweetness of nature and commanding height gave him the leading position in any gathering. Unlike Claus, however, and despite his martial ancestry and his job as a legal adviser to the army, Moltke was a pacifist who loathed violence. Half-English and a convinced Christian, he strove to see the good in everybody, even the Nazis. His refusal to countenance any sort of armed action, including the assassination of Hitler, against the dictatorial regime he abhorred was a fatal handicap dooming the Kreisau Circle to political impotence, and Moltke personally, along with most of his friends, to death on the gallows.

These were early days for the Kreisau Circle, however, and as yet the overthrow of the regime did not figure in their discussions. They represented the younger generation among the conservative and aristocratic opposition to Hitler. Moltke, Yorck, Trott and their spiritual adviser, the Jesuit priest Father Alfred Delp, were much concerned with the future of Germany and Europe after the demise of Nazism. They envisaged Germany as the centre of a united Europe, a state based on Christianity and the rule of law. Although from society's upper echelons, they were in favour of social justice and made contact with former social democratic labour and party leaders. Stauffenberg, who was often in their company, certainly imbibed their heady notions of remaking Germany in a more ideal image; as a man of action as well as ideas, though, he would never be content with their purely intellectual theorising.

Colonel Albrecht
Ritter Mertz von
Quirnheim.

Stauffenberg's contemporaries at the War Academy included two other future conspirators: balding, bespectacled Ritter Mertz von Quirnheim, an impulsive, daring and sarcastic officer who had recanted his early enthusiasm for Nazism by rebounding into bitter opposition, denouncing the officially sponsored boycott of Jewish shops and businesses in 1933 as 'a disgrace'. Also in the same study hall was a fellow Swabian, Eberhard Finckh, quiet but clever and determined, and fated to play a key role in the events of 20 July in Paris. Surrounded by such sympathetic colleagues, Stauffenberg enjoyed his two years at the War Academy – participating in military manoeuvres in the ancestral heartlands of east Prussia, and viewing the 1914 battlefields of Tannenberg and the Masurian Lakes with a professional soldier's eye. He was not to know that he would achieve his life's tragic apotheosis in the same haunted region.

The papers that Stauffenberg delivered to his fellow General Staff candidates reflected the contradictory impulses of his character. One, on defences against paratroop landings, was forward looking – indeed, it was the first on the topic ever mooted by a German officer. The other, on the future of cavalry in warfare, reflected the romantic nostalgia that was also an integral part of his personality. On a visit to the river Rhine, the traditional barrier guarding western approaches to the Fatherland, Stauffenberg delivered an impromptu lecture in which he pictured the great waterway as the site for a mighty decisive battle in the future: but what, he wondered, if the enemy came from the east – from the vast fastnesses of Soviet Russia?

On **1 January 1937**, Stauffenberg was promoted to the rank of Captain. At the conclusion of his course in June of the following year, he passed out first in his class. His final report was glowing, referring to his 'Tireless industry, tactical ability, [and] great organisational talent'. He was, it concluded, an 'above average' officer. As these words were being written, the army to which Stauffenberg had decided to dedicate his life was passing through the greatest crisis since the Röhm Putsch. It was a crisis that was to end in the complete subordination of the last vestiges of army independence to a criminal regime; it set a fatal course that Stauffenberg would eventually pledge himself to reversing – even, if necessary, at the cost of his life and of those who thought as he did.

On **5 November 1937**, Hitler summoned his top commanders and ministers to a conference to hear his proposals for the armed forces over the coming year. Present were Goering, Foreign Minister Konstantin von Neurath, War Minister Field Marshal Werner von Blomberg; the Commander-in-Chief of the army, General Werner von Fritsch; and the head of the newly created Kriegsmarine (the navy), Grand Admiral Erich Raeder. What they heard from the Führer was truly explosive. He planned, he announced, to conquer Czechoslovakia before 1938 was out, using the plight of the young state's large German minority in the Sudetenland as a pretext for the takeover. Hitler had a very Austrian contempt for the Czechs, and wiping their hated state from the map would enhance Germany's military might through the acquisition of the giant Skoda armaments works. Blomberg swallowed hard. He had already suffered two severe shocks to his fragile nervous system with the takeover of the Rhineland in **March 1936** and the intervention in Spain, both of which he had opposed, fearing that the army was not yet ready for such dangerous adventures. Indeed, so terrified had he been that France and Britain would stop the reoccupation of the Rhineland by armed force, that he panicked halfway through the operation and demanded a German withdrawal. A furious Führer had called Blomberg a 'hysterical woman' for his reaction. As far as Hitler was concerned, the Rubber Lion's card was marked.

Field Marshal Werner von Blomberg, Hitler's pliable army chief.

As his derisive nickname indicated, despite the Pour le Mérite medal that twinkled at his throat, Blomberg was physically brave, but a moral coward. He soon overcame his own objections to the coming occupation of Czechoslovakia and obediently set Hitler's plans in train, much to the disgust of Commander-in-Chief Fritsch and Fritsch's bitterly anti-Nazi Chief of Staff, General Ludwig Beck. It was in vain: the Führer would not forget the war minister's cold feet and his revenge would soon follow.

On **15 December 1937** a 'highly excited' Blomberg set out for a week's holiday at the Thuringian winter sports resort of Oberhof. The sixty-year-old widower's anticipation was understandable: his companion on the ski slopes would be a twenty-four-year-old Fraulein Marguerite (also known as Erna or Eva) Gruhn. Gruhn's day job was as a typist at the Reich's Egg Marketing Board, but she moonlighted by night as an 'escort girl' in Berlin's more louche clubs and bars, which is presumably where the lonely field marshal, who had been widowed in 1932, had met her. Travelling from Oberhof to Munich, on **22 December 1937**,

Blomberg delivered the funeral oration for Ludendorff, Germany's First World War overlord who had died in grumpy retirement after garnering a derisory vote in the 1927 presidential election, when he stood as the Nazi candidate against his old chief Hindenburg. While there Blomberg took the opportunity to have a quiet word with a fellow mourner, Goering.

His ticklish problem, he explained, was that he wished to marry Fraulein Gruhn, but he was not sure that the Führer would view the young stenographer – younger than his own four children – as an ideal match for Germany's top soldier. Young as she was, Blomberg admitted sheepishly, Erna was a woman with a past. Nonsense, Goering guffawed. That would be no problem at all. In the new Germany, he assured the field marshal, such absurd and outmoded snobbery had no place. Fraulein Gruhn was doubtless a good daughter of the German *Volk* and Blomberg was to be congratulated for winning her.

Here Blomberg admitted a second problem – he had a younger rival who was dancing attendance on Erna. No problem at all, the Reichsmarschall declared again: he would send the man on a long foreign trip, a very long one: all the way to a plum job with a German firm in Argentina. Why, he would even intercede with Hitler and make sure that no difficulties were placed along Blomberg's path to wedded bliss.

Much relieved, Blomberg met Hitler in Munich later that day to formally request permission from his boss to marry a social inferior young enough to be his daughter (Erna's mother was a laundress, a profession which, lowly as it was, was at least respectable: her other job was manageress of a massage parlour). Not only did Hitler give the field marshal his blessing, but he also promised that he and Goering would be guests of honour at the nuptials too. Having won the Führer's permission to wed, Blomberg, an old man in a hurry, did not hang around. Barely a fortnight later, on **12 January 1938**, he married the petite blonde Erna. Although, on Goebbels's orders, there was no publicity – still less wedding pictures – Hitler and Goering kept their promise and attended the ceremony, and the newly weds left for Leipzig on the first stage of their Italian honeymoon.

Despite the publicity ban, rumours about the field marshal's *més-alliance* were rife in Berlin. The wife of a police official named Curt Hellmuth Müller mentioned them to her husband. The name of the field marshal's bride rang a bell in the bureaucrat's brain, and the next day Müller checked his files. Sure enough, with the ink hardly dry on Blomberg's wedding certificate, a clutch of pornographic pictures tumbled out showing the new Frau Blomberg performing oral sex on a shaven-headed Czech Jew named Lowinger. Erna Gruhn had a police record as a prostitute and she and her pimp had been prosecuted for selling porn. Aghast, Müller passed the explosive dossier up the police chain of command until it reached the desk of the chief of Berlin police, Count Wolf Heinrich von Helldorf.

The police president was a deeply ambiguous figure: an opportunist who always sought to be on the winning side, he had fought with the Freikorps, and had fled into exile after taking part in the 1920 Kapp Putsch. As police president, he would extort money from wealthy Jews to procure them passports to safety, and, riding two horses, was a member of both the SS and the SA. Destined to join the anti-Nazi resistance, albeit late in the day, he would suffer torture and execution for his pains. Now, the Blomberg dossier presented him with a dilemma. Strictly speaking, he should have passed it to his superior, Heinrich Himmler, the head of the SS. But, knowing that Himmler would use it to weaken further the army and the officer caste, Helldorf – bearing in mind that he too, an ex-Hussar, was a member of the Prussian officer corps – took the material instead to his former Freikorps colleague,

Hitler and (left to right) Field Marshal Keitel, Colonel-General Halder, Field Marshal Brauchitsch.

General Wilhelm Keitel, head of the Wehrmachtamt (Army Office) and effectively Blomberg's office manager. Despite the fact that his son was married to Blomberg's daughter, and that he owed his position entirely to the field marshal, Keitel did not agree to Helldorf's suggestion that they destroy the file. Yet another moral coward – a character trait that ideally fitted him for his future job as Hitler's army hatchet man – Keitel proposed instead that they forward the document to Goering, although even a man of his strictly limited intelligence must have known that this would give the Reichsmarschall the ammunition he needed to fulfil his ambition to destroy Blomberg's career and run the armed forces himself.

On Saturday, **22 January 1938** Helldorf submitted the dossier to the Luftwaffe chief. In great glee, Goering rushed to Hitler's mountain retreat at Berchtesgaden and acquainted the Führer with the unsavoury facts. Hitler, mindful of Blomberg's past services to him in making the army acquiescent in the Nazi takeover of the German state, professed reluctance to dismiss the field marshal, but Goering insisted. The entire officer corps was outraged by Blomberg's reckless marriage, he said: he had to go. Without further ado, Hitler summoned Blomberg back from honeymoon and, although the ever-compliant war minister obediently offered to divorce his damaged bride, Hitler insisted on his dismissal. He let him down gently: he would receive a full pension, retain his rank, and the scandal, as far as possible, would be hushed up. Moreover, he added, when – not if – war came, Blomberg would be recalled to command. This pledge would not be honoured.

In a second interview, Hitler asked Blomberg's advice on his successor. Not knowing of the Luftwaffe overlord's role in his downfall, the disgraced field marshal suggested Goering as a suitable replacement. Hitler dismissed his Number Two's ambitions with something approaching contempt – Goering was too lazy. In that case, suggested Blomberg, obsequious to the last, how about Hitler personally taking charge? The idea was music to Hitler's ears – even if he had not already considered it. And if that happened, who should transmit his orders to the army, he wondered. Blomberg shrugged. 'Who ran your office?' Hitler demanded. Blomberg named Keitel, but added that he did not really have a first-class mind. 'That's exactly the man I'm looking for,' Hitler exclaimed. And so the deed was done: within a week Hitler, the former corporal, had been named Supreme Commander of the Armed Forces. And to head the newly created Oberkommando des Wehrmachts (OKW), the colourless Wilhelm Keitel was promoted far, far beyond his own abilities. The mediocre Keitel was supreme in one respect only: no one outdid him in supine obedience to his master's will. Not for nothing was he nicknamed '*Lakeitel*' ('Lackey') or '*Nickesel*' ('Nodding Donkey').

As for Blomberg, he and the bride who had caused him so much grief left for Capri on an interrupted honeymoon that would turn into an extended round-the-world cruise to let the scandal blow over. Secure in the illusion that he was indispensable, and happy in the enjoyment of Erna's charms, Blomberg departed. He would never be recalled, and by some sort of irony would retire with Erna to a chalet at Bad Weissee, the self-same resort where Röhm and his SA cohorts had had their own final encounter with Hitler. Blomberg, his faith in Hitler unshaken, survived the war to give evidence at the Nuremberg Tribunal. Despised by the army he adored, he became ill and died of cancer in American captivity in 1946. Erna returned to her Berlin roots, dying alone and forgotten in a bedsit in 1978 – forty years after the match that had made her notorious and set the final seal on Hitler's mastery of the army.

Blomberg's downfall gave the ever-ambitious Himmler an undreamed-of opening for his long-term strategy: to weaken the army and replace it with his own SS. His sinister deputy and ruthless hatchet man, Reinhard Heydrich, suggested the satanic means: that a similar sexual scandal could be manufactured to bring down Werner von Fritsch, Commander-in-Chief of the army. Fritsch was a notable drag on the Nazi Party's drive to dominate Germany's armed forces. An exceptionally able soldier, but decidedly professional and non-political, Fritsch was an officer of the old school, and markedly less amenable than Blomberg had been to Hitler's insatiable will. Heydrich reminded his boss of the existence of a police file on Fritsch's alleged sexual proclivities.

The file alleged that the austere bachelor Fritsch had been caught red-handed in 1935 in an illegal homosexual encounter near Potsdam railway station with a well-known rent-boy, known in his Berlin low-life haunts as 'Bavarian Joe'. They had been observed by a professional blackmailer named Hans Schmidt, who had followed Fritsch home and successfully extorted money from him. The file had already been shown to Hitler, who had rightly perceived what Himmler and Heydrich knew perfectly well: the documents impugning Fritsch were a tissue of lies. Schmidt's true victim was not the Commander-in-Chief, but an obscure retired cavalry officer named Frisch. The file was a clumsy attempt to frame Fritsch, which the Führer saw through, scorned and even ordered to be destroyed. The wily Heydrich, however, had hung on to it against the rainy day that had now arrived. Himmler took the dossier to Goering.

Werner von Fritsch, Commander-in-Chief of the army.

Once again, as they had during the Röhm purge and the Blomberg affair, Himmler and Goering overcame their mutual loathing for the greater good of doing down their enemies. Goering, in his accustomed role as the postman of chaos, once more brought the dodgy dossier to Hitler. This time, well knowing that Fritsch opposed his plans for an *Anschluss* (union) with Austria and an annexation of Czechoslovakia, Hitler was more than ready to listen. A hasty meeting was arranged at the Chancellery on **26 January 1938** at which the wretched Schmidt confronted Fritsch and accused him of being the elderly officer whose activities he had witnessed. The Commander-in-Chief was too humiliated and dumbfounded to speak, and taking his silence for guilt, Hitler abruptly terminated the meeting, sending an outraged Fritsch on indefinite leave – and effectively terminating his career. To add insult to injury, just as he had done with Blomberg, Hitler asked Fritsch who should succeed him. Fritsch promptly recommended his own deputy, Chief of Staff General Ludwig Beck, a known and outspoken critic of Nazism whom Hitler rejected out of hand, favouring instead one of the army's rare militantly pro-Nazi commanders, the unpopular General Reichenau. In a rare moment of dissent from his Führer's wishes, Keitel, the newly appointed head of the OKW, murmured that the army would not stand for such a political general after the double shock of the Blomberg and Fritsch scandals.

**Berlin, 27 January 1938**: by the end of January, Berlin was alive with rumours as to what was afoot. Senior officers who were opposed to Nazism or lukewarm in their loyalty to Hitler looked at each other with horror as they wondered what further abominations the dictator had in store for their beloved army. Stauffenberg, nearing the end of his staff course at the War Academy, was one of those who heard the rumours of what was happening behind the scenes, via his friend Count von der Schulenberg, Helldorf's deputy as vice-president of the Berlin police. Courageously, he stood up in his classroom and demanded to know the real reason for Fritsch's dismissal. Privately, he also expressed dismay that the generals had accepted the underhand intrigue behind the Commander-in-Chief's fall without a squeak of protest.

But further up the chain of command there was serious disquiet. In his office at the old War Ministry, General Beck met with Lieutenant-Colonel Hans Oster, director of operations for the Abwehr, Germany's military intelligence department, headed since 1935 by Oster's direct

Lieutenant-Colonel
Hans Oster.

superior, Admiral Wilhelm Canaris. Beck and Oster were at this time the most convinced anti-Nazis in influential positions. Aghast at the actions and lawlessness already committed by the Hitler regime, and appalled by the prospect of further such offences, they were, unlike many critics, prepared to go beyond grumbling and put an end to Nazi rule if they possibly could.

Colonel-General Ludwig Beck.

Oster in particular was an uncompromising opponent of Hitler. Tall, elegant and an officer of the old school, his dislike of the regime dated at least as far back as 1934 and the murder of General Schleicher, under whom he had once served. He had developed an unwavering hatred of the SS for killing his old superior, and even at that stage accepted that Hitler – whom he referred to contemptuously as 'the pig' or 'Emil' – would have to be killed to unseat his regime. Oster's strength was his clubbable charm and ease of manner. His job at the Abwehr allowed him to travel freely and meet whomever he pleased; he made full use of such opportunities. The problem was that, along with the Abwehr's legal adviser, his fellow conspirator Hans von Dohnanyi, Oster had an almost criminally lax attitude towards security. Bizarrely for a spymaster, he would meet contacts quite openly in cafés and restaurants and chat freely about their plans, no doubt to the education and delight of many listening ears. Dohnanyi even kept documents recording the crimes of the regime in his office safe. Given such elementary breaches in security it is hardly surprising that both Oster and Dohnanyi were destined to be arrested in 1943, before their conspiratorial plans had come to final fruition. What is more surprising is that they managed to conceive such an attempt before the doors of their Gestapo cells clanged shut behind them.

Admiral Wilhelm Canaris, chief of the Abwehr.

Canaris was also present at the meeting between Beck and Oster. His commitment to anti-Nazi

Colonel-General Franz Halder.

activity would always be ambivalent. A convinced anti-Communist and a staunch German nationalist, he had at first welcomed the arrival in power of a government committed to expanding the armed forces and reasserting Germany's power. Canaris had delighted in the shady world of espionage since his active service days in the navy in the First World War. In the turbulent post-war state he had even, as a naval judge, helped spring the military killers of the Communist leaders Liebknecht and Luxemburg from jail, and aided their escape abroad. As an old hand at such cloak-and-dagger tricks, the 'little Admiral' – he was just over five-foot in height – was less shocked by the Nazis' excesses than the rigidly moral Beck and Oster. But the blatant stitching up of Blomberg and Fritsch had severely shaken him and he was ready to hear what the two anti-Nazis proposed.

Oster knew the inside story of Fritsch's framing; he had been tipped off by Arthur Nebe, head of the criminal police and another senior police official who would, like Helldorf, become a future conspirator. As a soldier who had served under the fallen commander in the 1920s, Oster was especially outraged by the affair, rightly attributing it to the dirty tricks of Himmler and Heydrich. Even at this early date, Oster was determined that the regime could and should be removed by force, that the army should act before it was completely emasculated by the Nazis. Oster contacted leading provincial commanders – Generals Wilhelm Ulex in Hanover, Günther von Kluge in Munster and Siegmund von List in Dresden – in an attempt to persuade them to move. Even though Kluge turned 'white as ash' when he heard the details of the Fritsch framing, none of the generals were prepared to stand up to Hitler and insist on Fritsch's reinstatement. When another general, Franz Halder, stormed into Beck's office on **31 January 1938** and demanded to know what was going on, Beck remained silent. Why didn't he, insisted Halder, raid the Gestapo headquarters on Prinz Albrechtstrasse, which was surely the vipers' nest from where all the poison was emanating? 'Mutiny and revolution', replied the man who would commit both on 20 July 1944, '. . . are not words in the lexicon of a German officer.' The dithering and procrastination that were to become the abiding and fatal handicaps of the anti-Hitler resistance were already exercising their paralysing influence.

But the generals' foot-dragging becomes more comprehensible if we take into account the fact that even the victim himself seemed ready to swallow the injustice without protest. The un-political Fritsch was vaguely aware that he was the victim of a plot, but refused to accept that Hitler was a party to it. Silent and stiff-lipped, he awaited the verdict of his peers. A Court of Honour was established to look at the charges against Fritsch, but by the time it had reached the conclusion in March that the fallen Commander-in-Chief was entirely innocent, Hitler was riding high after the acclaimed and bloodless *Anschluss* with Austria; the caravan had moved on and the world had forgotten about poor Fritsch. The following year, given command of a mere corps in the Polish campaign, Fritsch deliberately exposed himself to enemy fire, was hit in the thigh by a splinter, and bled to death in a minute. Those who knew him best were sure that he no longer wanted to live.

On **4 February 1938** the Führer completed his takeover of the army. He issued a decree appointing himself the 'direct and personal' supreme commander of the Wehrmacht, with Keitel running the new OKW under him. At the same time he purged the Wehrmacht's upper ranks: no fewer than sixteen senior generals were compulsorily retired and forty-four others were transferred from their current jobs to posts of lesser importance. Among the victims who were retired were future field marshals whom Hitler was forced to reinstate after the Second World War began: Leeb, Kuechler, Weichs, Kluge and Witzleben. Fritsch's colourless successor as Commander-in-Chief under Hitler was to be Walther von Brauchitsch. Hitler also took the opportunity to reshuffle his cabinet, ridding himself of the non-Nazi foreign minister Neurath and the economics wizard Hjalmar Schacht in favour of the party toadies Ribbentrop and Funk.

The year 1938 would prove to be the most momentous since the advent of the Third Reich. With a government and army now entirely in his own image, and a country at his feet, Hitler was free to embark on the next step along his road to European domination: the annexation of his Austrian homeland. As with his earlier occupation of the Rhineland, this was not an event that attracted much condemnation abroad, even though the Versailles Treaty specifically forbade the unification of Germany and Austria. Most foreign observers believed that, once again, Hitler was merely strolling into his own backyard. The vast majority of Germans and Austrians, Stauffenberg included, also approved the move, seeing the division of ethnically, culturally and linguistically similar people into two states as an unnatural aberration. The *Anschluss*, however, was carried out by methods that were becoming the characteristic hallmark of Hitler's diplomacy: a mixture of violence, deceit and bullying bluster. The young Austrian chancellor, Kurt von Schuschnigg – whose predecessor, the diminutive Engelbert Dollfuss, had been callously murdered in a botched Nazi putsch in 1934 – had been summoned to Berchtesgaden on **12 February 1938** by Hitler and issued with an ultimatum: he must lift the ban on the Nazi Party, release all Nazis jailed after the 1934 putsch, and accept the Nazi leader, Seyss-Inquart, into his cabinet as minister of the interior in charge of the police and internal security. Although this would effectively mean the end of Austria's independence and its subordination to Germany as a Nazi satellite state, a bruised and browbeaten Schuschnigg accepted the demands.

However, on his return to Vienna he called a referendum on whether Austria should continue to exist as a free and independent nation. Enraged, Hitler ordered the Wehrmacht to mobilise and cross the Austrian border on **12 March 1938**, by uncanny coincidence or otherwise the same day that the Court of Honour belatedly exonerated Fritsch. Unopposed by the Austrian army and police, the Wehrmacht rolled across the frontier and were greeted by rapturous crowds of cheering, swastika-sporting Austrians. Hitler made a triumphal entry into Vienna, the city where in his impoverished youth he had experienced bitter years as a lonely vagrant. Addressing vast crowds, he proclaimed the incorporation of Austria into the greater Reich. The only people not rejoicing, it seemed, were the Austrian capital's large Jewish community, who were forced to endure such indignities as scrubbing anti-Nazi slogans off the pavements with toothbrushes: a mere foretaste of what was to come.

While the *Anschluss* was in full swing, an emissary of the nascent opposition was in London. It was not Carl Goerdeler's first visit to the British capital; he had been there already in **June 1937**, just one of twenty-two countries he travelled to in his tireless efforts to secure foreign support for the overthrow of the Hitler regime. Goerdeler knew that regime at first hand. A conservative economist and a sworn German nationalist, he had been mayor of Leipzig and price-control tsar under both Weimar and Hitler. An almost pathological optimist, Goerdeler believed right to the end in the power of persuasion and sweet reason to change men's minds. He tried at first to work with the Hitler regime, and it was only the evidence of the Nazis' savage anti-Semitism that swung him into the ranks of the opposition. He resigned as mayor of Leipzig after the Nazis insisted on removing a statue of the Jewish composer Mendelssohn, and thereafter devoted all his formidable energy as an indefatigable networker to galvanising the opposition.

In London, Goerdeler met with senior officials at the Foreign Office and with his customary volubility, pleaded with them to extend a

Carl Goerdeler as Mayor of Leipzig.

helping hand – if only an encouraging word – to the 'decent men' who he claimed were already working to supplant the Nazis. As before, he was listened to politely, but met the same stone wall he had the previous year. Diplomat, politician and journalist Harold Nicolson noted in his diary on **13 March** that Goerdeler had arrived travelling under an assumed name, on a Yugoslav passport and on a secret mission. 'He is a hero,' Nicolson added. That mission, though Nicolson did not say so, was to persuade Whitehall that the German army, disgusted by the framing and besmirching of Fritsch, was preparing a putsch against Hitler. Whitehall simply refused to believe it. Foreign Office mandarin Ivo Mallet noted that Goerdeler, whom he correctly characterised as 'over optimistic', exaggerated the possibility of an army coup.

Goerdeler's fruitless visit to London was made at the behest of Oster and Beck. The latter had at last been persuaded, probably by Oster's eloquence, that a move had to be made by the army, even if it fell short of a full-scale mutiny or putsch. Beck devised a clumsy slogan: 'For the Führer, against war, against rule by the bosses, for peace with the Church, freedom of speech, and an end to Cheka methods'. The last reference to the first brutal secret police set up in Bolshevik Russia was an unsubtle reference to the SS and their crimes. What Beck was proposing was a 'Generals' Strike' – a refusal by the military establishment to carry out Hitler's aggressive plans for foreign conquest without actually rising against him – although he was, he said, quite prepared to shoot at the SS. Beck's sudden determination was prompted by a deadline. He knew that the Führer had vowed to abolish the state of Czechoslovakia before the year was out. Lest there be any doubt on that score, Hitler had summoned the leading generals to another conference at the Chancellery on **28 May 1938** and had told them unambiguously: 'It is my unshakeable will that Czechoslovakia shall be wiped off the map.' He predicted that Britain and France would not go to war to defend Czech integrity: after all, they had stood aside when he occupied Austria. He told the generals to prepare to move against the Czechs by the end of September.

Beck's immediate tactic was to stall. He had already written memoranda to Hitler pointing out the weakness of the Wehrmacht, as evidenced during the *Anschluss* when many of the army's motorised vehicles had broken down on the road to Vienna. Now he stepped up his bombardment of memoranda, variously stressing the strength of the Czech army and its defensive formations; the weakness of Germany's only putative allies – Italy and Japan – and the likelihood that Britain and France would go to war. Hitler's reaction to this host of mantraps flung in his path was predictable: 'What kind of generals are those that I have to drag to war?' he wondered aloud. He added ominously, 'I do not require that my generals understand my orders – only that they obey them.'

Beck's next ploy was to approach the Western Powers to convince them that Hitler was serious about smashing Czechoslovakia – the next stage in his plan to bring all Europe under German domination. Only if the West stood up to Hitler now and drew a line in the sand along the Czech frontier, Beck's emissaries declared, would the Nazi Führer's insatiable appetite be checked. Then, and only then, would the German army move to thwart Hitler and replace him with a more 'civilised' and reasonable regime. Beck's first messenger was Erich Kordt, an Anglophile German diplomat who had been educated as a Rhodes Scholar at Oxford. Kordt had risen to be a close aide to the new German foreign minister, Joachim von Ribbentrop, during that former Champagne salesman's stint as ambassador to Britain. Ribbentrop – known as 'Brickendrop' in London for his lack of tact – valued Kordt for the knowledge of English society that he so painfully lacked himself. His regard was not returned, however, since Kordt despised his boss as

Joachim von Ribbentrop, Hitler's ambassador in London and foreign minister.

Hitler's toadying lackey, and firmly allied himself with Oster and Beck in their opposition.

On **3 July 1938** Kordt met T. Philip Conwell-Evans, a friend of his diplomat brother and fellow resister Theodor. Conwell-Evans was a socialite with contacts high in the British government. Erich Kordt's message to him was clear. On Beck's authority he told the Englishman that, so long as Britain made a firm declaration of support for Czech independence, then Beck would lead an army putsch to depose Hitler should he proceed with his plan to make war on Czechoslovakia. Conwell-Evans was non-committal but promised to pass the message on.

Beck followed up Kordt's visit a month later, on **4 August 1938** by convening a meeting of Germany's top generals in the Bendlerstrasse-block, the large brooding office block surrounding a wide central courtyard that housed the army's headquarters, and where the conspirators' efforts were destined to reach their final, tragic culmination almost exactly six years later. Beck had filled the intervening month by penning yet more memoranda pointing out the perils of the planned assault on the Czechs. He had also been badgering the army's chief, Walter von

The Bendlerstrasseblock, headquarters in Berlin of the Reserve Army, 1944.

Brauchitsch to support his projected generals' strike. The upshot of his efforts was this meeting in the Bendlerstrasse.

Beck addressed his fellow generals and demanded that they present Hitler with a united ultimatum demanding that he call off the Czech adventure scheduled to go ahead, as he reminded his audience, the following month. The risks were enormous, he stressed. Germany would find herself fighting not only France and Britain, but waiting in the wings were the Soviet Union and the United States, with their limitless economic and manpower resources. Beck was backed by General Wilhelm Adam, the elderly commander of Germany's barely fortified Western Front – the much trumpeted but barely begun Siegfried Line. Adam painted a black picture of an almost defenceless front that would be overrun within weeks, if not days. There were only two dissenting voices: General Busch and the Nazi-sympathising Reichenau, who lost no time in informing Hitler of what had been discussed. If Hitler did not know before how unenthusiastic his top military men were about his plans, he was in no doubt now.

Furious with the 'defeatism' of his senior generals, Hitler decided to skip a generation. On **10 August 1938** at the Berghof, he called a meeting of twenty of the younger commanders, predominantly the

Chiefs of Staff of their more timid seniors, and subjected them to a three-hour harangue. The burden of Hitler's song was the same as previous performances: he had always been proved right in his estimation of the weakness of his western adversaries, and he would also be correct over Czechoslovakia. When it came to questions, General Wietersheim, deputy to the sceptical General Adam, commander of the western wall, asked him how long the weak defences would stand up to an Anglo-French assault. 'I can assure you, Herr General,' Hitler hissed back, 'that the western wall will resist not just for three weeks – but for three years.' When it came to the defensive, the corporal who had learned his warfare on the static Western Front in the First World War remembered everything but had learned nothing.

On **15 August 1938** at Jüterbog, an artillery range south of Berlin, Hitler was at it again. This time he had called his commanders to a practical demonstration of the power of the German guns. The 15-centimetre howitzers crashed away, showing – at least to Hitler's satisfaction – that the much-vaunted Czech defences would be as matchwood in the face of a ferocious Wehrmacht assault. As soon as the guns fell silent, Hitler plunged in with another pep talk, once more pooh-poohing the possibility of western intervention. For an enraged Beck, the Jüterbog meeting was the final straw. On **18 August 1938** he submitted his resignation to Brauchitsch. 'If I wanted to preserve one spark of self-respect I could not do otherwise,' he told his friend General Kurt von Liebmann, commandant of the War Academy where Stauffenberg was completing his General Staff course. 'After all, I sat in the seat of Moltke and Schlieffen and had an inheritance to administer. I could not quietly observe how this band of criminals let loose a war.' When Brauchitsch broke the news that Beck had quit, the Führer was visibly relieved. With his uncanny intuition he had marked the general down as an enemy: 'The only man I fear is Beck,' he had told an aide, 'That man would be capable of acting against me.' Now, by honourably resigning over policy, Beck had saved him the trouble of manufacturing another Blomberg- or Fritsch-type scandal to get rid of him.

On the same day that Beck submitted his resignation, a second envoy acting for him and Oster – the ultra-conservative Pomeranian landowner Ewald von Kleist-Schmenzin – was in London to support the message that Kordt had delivered in July. Briefing Kleist-Schmenzin in Berlin before his trip, Beck had asked him to 'Bring me certain proof that England will fight if Czechoslovakia is attacked and I will put an end to this regime.'

With these words ringing in his ears, Kleist-Schmenzin, travelling under a false name and staying at Mayfair's exclusive Park Lane Hotel, began his round of contacts. He met Sir Robert Vansittart, the Foreign Office's German expert, and a passionate Germanophobe. Kleist-Schmenzin prefaced their discussion by telling Vansittart, with grim prescience, 'I come with a rope around my neck,' and then disclosed that Hitler intended to attack the Czechs on or by 27 September. Vansittart agreed that he was committing high treason, but suggested that Hitler was possibly in the grip of 'extremists' who were pushing him along the road to war. Kleist-Schmenzin denied this emphatically: 'The only extremist', he said, 'is Hitler himself.' He and his friends were willing to remove the regime, he concluded, but only if England made an unequivocal statement that an attack on Czechoslovakia would mean war. Only then would the bulk of the population understand the implications of Hitler's aggression.

The next day, **19 August**, Kleist-Schmenzin drove down into the Kent countryside to meet Winston Churchill, the veteran maverick Conservative politician whose warnings to his colleagues at Westminster about the growing threat posed by German rearmament and Hitler's aggressive foreign expansionism had largely fallen on deaf ears. Britain well remembered the all-too-recent recent horrors of the trenches, and was desperate to avoid another war with a resurgent Germany. Churchill drove his guest around his Chartwell estate, while his son Randolph took notes on their talk. The German people, like the British, asserted Kleist-Schmenzin, were peace loving and had no stomach for a second war. But the obedient Wehrmacht would only refuse Hitler's orders to march if they were certain that by attacking the Czechs they would bring down an attack from France and Britain. Kleist-Schmenzin begged his host to get that message through to Prime Minister Neville Chamberlain and Foreign Secretary Lord Halifax – neither of them friends of Churchill. The old warrior was pessimistic, but promised his German guest that he would pass his message on.

On **20 August 1938**, relaxing at Chequers, his official country residence among the Chiltern Hills in Buckinghamshire, Chamberlain digested three separate reports on Kleist-Schmenzin's visit from Churchill, Vansittart and Lord Lloyd, an imperialist friend of Churchill whom Kleist-Schmenzin had also lobbied. Chamberlain viewed none of the trio sympathetically, and their urgent reports made unwelcome reading. The premier, although unversed in foreign affairs, was convinced that he could establish a personal rapport with Hitler, and that by meeting man to man any differences could be ironed out. Although a non-combatant in the First World War, like many Englishmen, Chamberlain dreaded above all else a repeat of that mass slaughter. In a minute to his like-minded foreign secretary, Lord Halifax, Chamberlain dismissed Kleist-Schmenzin 'and his friends', comparing them to the eighteenth-century Jacobites who fruitlessly plotted and intrigued to return the Stuart dynasty to the English throne. 'I think we must discount a great deal of what he says,' Chamberlain concluded. Not for the last time, the anti-Hitler conspirators were on their own.

On **21 August 1938** Hitler officially accepted the resignation that Beck had proffered three days earlier. The Führer's relief was palpable, particularly when Beck accepted his suggestion that no public announcement be made. Beck's successor as Chief of Staff was General Franz Halder, who was at least in words as convinced an oppositionist as Beck himself, though clearly lacking Beck's moral backbone. 'Now you see what one can achieve with intellectual memoranda and elegant gestures of resignation,' the tactless Halder told his departing predecessor. 'The time for memoranda is past. We must adopt other methods.' Bitterly, Beck replied: 'Now everything depends on you.'

At first it looked as though Halder meant to stop Hitler's inexorable march towards war. Within a week of taking over from Beck, the new Chief of Staff summoned the leading conspirator, Oster, to his Berlin office on **27 August 1938**. Halder, in his blunt Bavarian way, asked Oster straight out how far preparations for a putsch had progressed, and requested the names of the civilians who were also involved in the conspiracy. Oster mentioned Goerdeler and Hjalmar Schacht, Hitler's former economics minister, who, disillusioned with the regime, had resigned the previous year and sought contact with the conservative opposition. Halder asked Oster to set up a meeting with Schacht. The same day, Kleist-Schmenzin reported back to Oster's chief, Admiral Canaris, on his mission to London. With his usual gloom, Kleist-Schmenzin told the Abwehr head that his trip had been a failure. The British, he said, wanted to avoid war at almost any cost and were ready to appease Hitler over Czechoslovakia to prevent a conflict. The same day, as ever keeping his options open, Canaris had another visitor: Karl Hermann Frank, the militant deputy leader of the Sudeten German party, who reported on a meeting he had held earlier that day with Hitler to receive his orders for increasing the pressure on the Prague government. The Nazi puppet – who would be hanged for his wartime atrocities against the Czechs – asked Canaris if Germany was ready to fight a world war on behalf of the Sudetenland. The wily admiral, of course, was non-committal.

So the dog days of August limped away, with the clock ticking towards Hitler's planned deadline of 27 September and the conspirators still irresolute: Erich Kordt had returned from London and informed Oster, Canaris and the head of the army, Brauchitsch, what his boss Ribbentrop and Hitler were prepared to risk: a war with all Europe united against Germany. On **3 September 1938** – a year to the day before Britain declared war on Germany, Hitler called Brauchitsch and his own military lackey, Keitel, to his mountain home, the Berghof, to finalise the plan for Operation 'Case Green', the codename for the coming attack on Czechoslovakia. In the meantime Oster had dispatched two more emissaries – the industrialist Hans Bohm-Tettelbach and Erich Kordt – to London to repeat the warnings that Hitler was hell bent on war, and that a firm British declaration 'that even a child could understand' as the forthright Oster put it – was necessary. Such an unequivocal statement from Britain would be answered by a military move against Hitler, Oster's messengers promised. Now on **4 September 1938** Oster set up the promised meeting between Halder, the new army Chief of Staff, and Schacht, Hitler's disillusioned economics supremo. The secret encounter took place in Schacht's Berlin apartment.

Halder, as usual, was blunt. In the event of Hitler's overthrow, he asked Schacht, would he be willing to take over the Reich's government as a caretaker chancellor? Schacht assured him that he would. Thus reassured, on the following day, **5 September 1938**, Halder called a veteran anti-

Dr Hans Bernd Gisevius giving evidence to the Nuremberg Tribunal in 1946.

Hitler conspirator to his own Berlin apartment. His guest, Hans Bernd Gisevius, was a young government lawyer who had left his post with the political police in disgust at the slaughter of the Röhm purge in 1934, and had since been both an inside witness to the atrocities of the regime and an impassioned opponent of the Nazis. Gisevius had kept his contacts with the police, and Halder wanted to know what stance this crucial pillar of state security would adopt in the event of an anti-Hitler putsch. Halder and Gisevius would both survive the war, and at this early stage, according to Gisevius's revealing memoirs, Halder was 'all fire and fury' against the regime, denouncing Hitler as a 'madman and criminal' whose bloodlust, as evidenced by the massacre on the Night of the Long Knives and the murders going on daily in the concentration camps, was quite possibly prompted by the Führer's sexual pathology.

Having damned Hitler, the two men got down to the nitty-gritty of how a putsch would proceed. The army, thought Halder, hated the SS and Gestapo so deeply that they would launch an attack on them without hesitation. On the other hand, Hitler himself still enjoyed wide popularity in the Wehrmacht as much as among the population at large. Unless he was dealt with, thought Halder, any putsch would be pointless. The army chief suggested several ways of getting rid of the dictator, although he thought any assassination should be disguised as a 'fatal accident'. For example, his train could be derailed, or his car could be strafed from the air in a wartime situation. Gisevius diplomatically declined to point out that Halder himself was in a prime position to eliminate Hitler personally, since he saw the Führer regularly and had his service pistol in a holster at his side every time. The meeting ended with Halder asking Gisevius to coordinate with Oster over the police's participation in the coming putsch.

On **7 September 1938**, Erich Kordt's diplomat brother Theo managed to meet Lord Halifax in person in London. Kordt repeated to the impassive and gentlemanly British foreign secretary the message that his brother and all previous German emissaries had brought: Hitler was determined to destroy Czechoslovakia by force and within the month. The only chance of stopping him was if the British government made him understand that any such attack would cause another European war. If he persisted with the aggression, said Kordt, quoting *Hamlet*, then his friends in Germany would 'take arms against a sea of troubles, and by opposing, end them'. Halifax listened politely, but said little.

A key figure in any successful coup would be the army general commanding the Wehrkreis Berlin, the army troops garrisoning the capital and its immediate environs. In September 1938 the man holding this crucial post was the infantry general who probably hated Hitler more than any other: Erwin von Witzleben. The general was a hawk-nosed old Prussian who yielded to no one in his hatred of the Nazis – when told of the Röhm Putsch he remarked that he wished he could have shot the SA leaders personally – although he strongly objected to the simultaneous murders of Generals Schleicher and Bredow. The disgraceful treatment of Fritsch had completed his disillusionment, and he was now ready to support or lead a putsch. At a meeting with Gisevius at his Berlin headquarters on **8 September 1938**, they went through the plans that Oster had drawn up: Witzleben's III Infantry Division, with the Potsdam Division commanded by Count Walter Brockdorff-Ahlefeldt acting as its spearhead, would seize and neutralise key points in the capital: the police and radio stations, telephone exchanges and major ministries. Outside Berlin, General Adam, commander of the Western Army Group was in on their plans, as was General Erich Hoepner, whose fast-moving 1st Light Division would have the crucial task of blocking the loyalist Waffen SS if they tried to move on the capital and stage a counter-coup.

**Nuremberg, 8 September 1938**: the annual Nazi rally or *Parteitag* took place as usual at Nuremberg in the first week of September. Conspirators on the fringes of the monster gathering were making discreet contacts. Halder was there, and so was his deputy General Karl-Heinrich von Stülpnagel, destined to play a crucial but ultimately tragic role in the events of 20 July 1944. Stülpnagel was able to get an assurance from

General Karl-Heinrich von Stülpnagel.

General Alfred Jodl, one of Hitler's military entourage, that the army would get at least two days' notice and probably five, before the invasion of Czechoslovakia was launched. Jodl did not know this, but it would give the conspirators a window of opportunity in which to execute their putsch. On the same day, Halder bumped into his old friend General Kurt Liebmann at the rally, and blurted out: 'There is only one way to stop the way things are going and that is the removal of Hitler by force.'

The next night at Nuremberg, on **9 September 1938**, Brauchitsch and Halder were called to Hitler's headquarters to formally present the military plans for the coming attack on the Czechs, 'Case Green'. They envisaged a pincer movement by the Second Army, attacking from the north, and the Fourteenth Army based in Austria, or the 'Ostmark' – as the Reich's new territory was now known – from the south. Hitler insisted on adding a third prong to the attacking force: the Tenth Army would be the *Schwerpunkt* ('Spearhead') of the attack from the west. The former corporal lectured his two senior military men until the small hours on strategy and tactics before sending them to their beds feeling, as Halder confided, that 'this man was leading Germany to its doom'.

On **10 September** at the police headquarters on Berlin's Alexanderplatz, with Oster's permission the ever-energetic Gisevius took the plunge and recruited Berlin's police president, Count Helldorf, to the conspiracy. This was a dangerous step. As we have seen from the Blomberg–Fritsch affair, Helldorf was a deeply ambiguous figure who liked to run with the conspiratorial hare and hunt with the Nazi hounds. In sounding him out, Gisevius was taking a huge risk: the police chief might well report or arrest him for treason. But he did not. Instead, he told Gisevius – who had known him for years – that he was willing to co-operate with the plot. Helldorf's deputy, Fritz-Dietlof von der Schulenberg, a friend of Claus von Stauffenberg, was already in the plot and acting as a communications channel between Oster and the Kordt brothers. Now that the two chiefs of the police were onside, the conspirators could go ahead with the military preparations for the putsch, safe in the knowledge that the only substantial government force in the capital would not lift a finger to oppose or hinder their troops on the day.

Planning for the putsch now moved into top gear. On the afternoon of **10 September**, Gisevius accompanied Generals Witzleben and Brockdorff-Ahlefeldt to meet Hjalmar Schacht at the ex-economic minister's country estate outside Berlin. At this meeting, they divided their labour for the coming coup. Gisevius would be responsible for the

Count Wolf Heinrich von Helldorf, Police President of Berlin and ambiguous plotter.

police, providing essential back-up – directing traffic and the like – to the troops of Brockdorff's 23rd Infantry Division, who would spearhead the putsch. Schacht himself would draw up a list of ministers for the emergency administration that would replace the Nazi government. The only issue that seriously divided the conspirators – and would prove a fatal handicap that would dog them to the end – was the vexed question about what to do with Hitler himself. They all knew that the Führer still enjoyed enormous popularity among the population at large. Himmler and Heydrich, by contrast, were feared and hated and any blow aimed at their sinister black-uniformed SS would be welcomed. Most of the plotters wanted the attack to be aimed at the regime's Praetorian Guard, while Hitler himself could be arrested and tried later when the public's eyes had been opened as to the true nature of the Nazi regime.

Only Gisevius, with a clear-eyed understanding of the Führer's demonic power, favoured the most radical solution of all: Hitler, he was sure, should be killed. Tyrannicide could be morally justified in Christian theology even by those whose religious principles forbade assassination. More practically, if Hitler was left alive – even in a jail cell – he would remain the focus of frenzied efforts by his supporters to attempt a rescue and restoration; only by eliminating the man, in Gisevius's ruthlessly realistic view, could the conspiracy be sure of success.

On **11 September 1938**, a chilly early autumn day, the commander of the coup, General Witzleben, celebrated the birth of his first grandson and used the family occasion to sound out his civilian cousin, Ursula von Witzleben, about the likely attitude of the most senior serving general, Gerd von Rundstedt towards a coup. Ursula had been raised in the Rundstedt household, and accurately replied that the elderly and stiff-necked Prussian could not be relied upon to rise against the state. Meanwhile, Gisevius and Brockdorff toured Berlin on a reconnaissance. Their driver was Elisabeth Gartner-Strunck, a wealthy friend of Oster who had been recruited by the dapper Abwehr man to the conspirators' ranks. The presence of a woman, reasoned Oster, would deflect any suspicious eyes of those who might wonder why a general and a police official were driving around Berlin peering at government buildings. Gisevius pointed out the key points that the men of Brockdorff's 23rd Division would be expected to secure: the government quarter around the Wilhelmstrasse including the Reich Chancellery, the SS headquarters in Prinz Albrechtstrasse and Goering's Luftwaffe Ministry in central Berlin. On the outskirts were the SS barracks at Lichterfelde – scene of mass executions during the Röhm Putsch – the radio relay station at Königs Wusterhausen and, north of the capital, the Sachsenhausen concentration camp where many of the regime's leading opponents were already incarcerated.

Halder returned from Nuremberg on **13 September** with Hitler's keynote speech to the party's serried ranks still ringing in his ears. To thunderous applause, Hitler had once again blatantly threatened the Czechs with war, even if Britain and France were ready to intervene. Fortunately, rasped Hitler menacingly, Germany was now strong enough to help the oppressed German people in the Sudetenland throw off their shackles, even at the cost of war. At a private meeting in his Berlin apartment with Oster, Schacht and Gisevius, Halder appeared as confident and committed to the coup as ever. He had ensured that he would have sufficient warning of the mobilisation for war, he said, and that would be the moment to launch the putsch. But, as they left the meeting, his confederates felt uneasy: if Hitler suddenly plunged into war, wouldn't the wavering Halder plead military necessity ahead of political considerations as an excuse to postpone the putsch after all?

All might yet have been well with the plotters' plans, had the guarantees of solid support from the Western Allies – for which they had, via their envoys, been vainly seeking – been forthcoming. Unfortunately, the policy of Neville Chamberlain's government in London, with Daladier's weak French administration – desperate for peace at almost any price – tailing obediently at its heels, was also tending towards defeatism and peace whatever the cost. Already on 7 September Geoffrey Dawson, the appeasing editor of *The Times* – in that era less a newspaper than the mouthpiece of the British establishment – had run an editorial suggesting that the Czechs preserve European peace by surrendering their German-speaking areas to Hitler.

**London, 14 September**: the day Hitler ordered his forces to mobilise for the attack on the Czechs, Chamberlain's cabinet rubber stamped the prime minister's proposal to hold a plebiscite in the Sudetenland to determine which parts wished to secede and join the Reich. Without so much as a word to his Czech allies, Chamberlain was prepared to dump them and dismember their state.

In order to preserve peace, Chamberlain told his astonished colleagues, he was proposing to go an extra mile more than he needed to. An air mile, in fact. The very next day the 69-year-old premier would, for the first time in his life, board a plane and fly to Germany to meet Hitler personally and plead for peace. It was as abject a surrender as Hitler could have wished for, and when he heard the news, the Führer admitted, it came as 'a bolt from the blue'. Without further ado, the British government agreed to this proposal too.

The news that Chamberlain was coming to see Hitler burst like a bombshell among the plotters. Halder and Witzleben heard it in the army headquarters in Berlin's Bendlerstrasse when they were discussing the logistics of the coming putsch. Canaris, round the corner in the Abwehr's headquarters, was given the news while he was having his supper. It quite spoiled his appetite and he retired, leaving his meal half eaten. Erich Kordt learned it in the Foreign Office and it left him flabbergasted: 'What, him . . . coming to see that man?' Their dismay is easily explicable: by approaching Hitler as if he was a supplicant on his knees, Chamberlain was lending credibility to the Nazi dictator's bullying and warmongering. At the same time he was cutting the ground from under the feet of the conspiracy. How could they claim to be acting against a recklessly aggressive policy that threatened to plunge the world into war for the second time in a generation, if the very powers they counted on to stop Hitler in his tracks were flinging themselves at his jackbooted feet? It was truly inexplicable. Gisevius, most realistic of all the conspirators, summed up their bewilderment, and their gloom: 'We bowed our heads in despair. To all appearances it was all up with our revolt.'

**The Berghof, 15 September 1938**: the first of Chamberlain's three meetings with Hitler was held. After his exhausting flight, the prime minister arrived at the Berghof, the Führer's mountain lair at Berchtesgaden. At this, their first meeting, he was shocked by Hitler's plebeian appearance – 'the commonest little dog,' he said later – but got straight down to man-to-man talks with only the Führer's interpreter, Dr Paul Otto Schmidt, present. Brushing aside Chamberlain's talk of a new Anglo-German understanding, Hitler said the priority was to resolve the Sudeten question without delay. Chamberlain surrendered all his cards at once: it made no difference to him, he told Hitler, if the Sudeten Germans dwelt within Czechoslovakia or joined their racial compatriots in the Reich. At a single stroke, and without consulting his cabinet colleagues, his French allies or, least of all the Czechs whose state he was proposing to demolish, Chamberlain had sold the pass. He departed, with the illusion intact that Hitler was a man of his word with whom he could do business.

Back in Berlin, Oster had found a hitman. What the conspirators lacked – now and all too often in the future – was an individual with a clear mind, courage and a ruthless capacity for action. One day both Henning von Tresckow and Claus von Stauffenberg would fill this role, but for now the man of action was a friend and former military colleague of Oster, Captain Friedrich Wilhelm Heinz. At first sight, Heinz was an unlikely figure to find among the ultra-civilised anti-Hitler conspirators. Like many members of his generation – Hitler, Goering and Röhm were other examples – Heinz's life had been moulded, and warped, by his terrifying experiences as a soldier in the trenches of the First World War while he was still a teenager. This frontline 'lost generation' had never successfully made the transition back to civilian life after the horrors of that cataclysm, and were permanently disoriented and ill-suited to a mundane civilian life.

Heinz had joined the paramilitary, freebooting Freikorps in the chaos of post-war Germany, choosing the most extreme and murderous unit of all: the *Ehrhardt* Freikorps, who had carried out the 1920 Kapp Putsch that had briefly overthrown the young Weimar republic, and who had subsequently been implicated in the assassination of leading left-wingers and republicans, including the Catholic leader and armistice

Friedrich Wilhelm Heinz, Freikorps fighter, anti-Nazi plotter, post-war spymaster.

signatory Matthias Erzberger, as well as the Jewish industrialist and Foreign Minister Walther Rathenau. Heinz had acquired a taste for such secret, underground work, becoming a propagandist for extreme right-wing organisations such as the nationalist veterans' paramilitary organisation the Stahlhelm and the Nazis themselves, becoming a party member in 1928. However, like so many other Freikorps veterans, he could not accept Hitler's dictatorial tendencies, and aligned himself with the left-wing Strasserite section of the party, for which 'offence' he was expelled in 1930. Along with Oster, Heinz had drifted into the Abwehr, where he was responsible for monitoring the German press, and where his friend had recruited him to the plotters' ranks.

Heinz's role was to lead a *Stosstrupp*, a commando of rough, tough soldiers like himself, into the Reich Chancellery and arrest Hitler. In recruiting this strong-arm group as the spearhead of the putsch, the former Freikorps man had cast a surprisingly wide net. Naturally, there were a score or so old comrades from the Freikorps and Stahlhelm milieux. Another dozen had come from fellow serving Wehrmacht soldiers, while there was also a sprinkling of students and even some socialist and trade union activists. In all Heinz had collected around fifty men – easily enough, he considered, to overpower the dictator's dozen or so SS bodyguards from the SS Leibstandarte *Adolf Hitler*. The only ties linking these disparate activists were a shared hatred for Hitler and a willingness to take decisive action against him.

On the evening of **20 September 1938** Oster invited the top conspirators to a final meeting at his apartment to meet Heinz and learn the fine details of the putsch. Present were Oster and Heinz, along with Witzleben; Gisevius; the plot's legal expert Hans von Dohnanyi; another Abwehr operative, Franz Maria Liedig; the military conspirator Lieutenant-Colonel Helmuth Groscurth and possibly Carl Goerdeler too. Having optimistically discussed the shape of a post-Nazi Germany, with most of those present favouring a restoration of the monarchy, the conspiracy's inner core moved on to discuss what would happen on '*der Tag*' – the day – planned for a week ahead, when their putsch would finally be launched. They agreed that the rushing of the Reichs Chancellery by Heinz's shock troopers was a sound strategy, but, as so often, the question of Hitler's fate was left dangling. Oster was well aware that senior members of the conspiracy – especially the more conservative and Christian amongst them – would not countenance the dictator's physical elimination, even though Oster himself, also a Christian, considered assassination essential for the plot's success. As it was, he successfully fudged the issue, promising his fellow plotters that Hitler would only be arrested and held to stand trial later.

Only after the conspirators had dispersed, having agreed to launch the putsch the moment Hitler issued the mobilisation order to move on Czechoslovakia at the end of the month, did Heinz, lingering behind, put his cards on the table. Hitler, he told Oster with a simple soldier's bluntness, had to die, since 'Hitler alive is stronger than all our divisions.' Oster, a soldier himself, agreed, but it must remain a secret between the two of them: a conspiracy within the conspiracy. The way to accomplish it was to shoot Hitler in the melee when the Chancellery was rushed, and blame the assassination on an accident of war. Besides, there would be plenty of time for hindsight discussion of an accomplished fact after the deed was done. Doing it, however, was the essential priority.

The conspirators were, however irrationally, counting on Chamberlain to stand firm at his coming second meeting with Hitler, designed to finalise the agreement of their informal Berghof meeting. At first it seemed that their confidence was justified. On **22 September 1938** Chamberlain was sped on his way by Lord Halifax, with Theo Kordt among the other onlookers at London's Heston Airport for his second flight to meet the Führer. He departed believing that he had peace in his pocket. He had persuaded the majority of his cabinet, the French and even a despairing Czech government to bow to Hitler's demands without a struggle: the Czechs must sacrifice the Sudetenland, and with it their mountainous natural defences against attack, for the sake of peace. Now, he thought, he was meeting the man he habitually called 'Herr Hitler' at the spa of Bad Godesberg on the Rhine to finalise a done deal. Chamberlain, however, was in for a shock. He sat down with the Führer in the plush Dreesen Hotel – where Hitler had been staying in 1934 on the night he flew south to settle final scores with Röhm and the SA – and, like an eager school swot reporting to a strict teacher on a difficult piece of homework successfully completed, he proudly confirmed that everyone had capitulated to Hitler's blackmail: both the British and French cabinets and even the Prague government were ready to cede the German Sudetenland once plebiscites there had confirmed the inhabitants' desire to unite with the Reich.

Then the blow fell. Harshly Hitler shook his head and replied: 'I'm sorry, Mr Chamberlain . . . the situation has changed. This solution no longer applies.' In mounting horror and indignation Chamberlain listened while Hitler upped the ante: his patience with the Czechs was over: without a plebiscite, without even maps to show which portions of their country were being torn from them, the Czechs, bag and baggage, must vacate the Sudetenland within four days. Shell-shocked, Chamberlain flew home the following day, bleating that Hitler had not supported his attempts to preserve peace. The conspirators, by contrast, were in high spirits. After being downcast when it looked as though Chamberlain would succumb without a squeak of protest, their rollercoaster had climbed back up now that Hitler's unreasonable demands would force even the supine Chamberlain to think twice.

'Thank God,' breathed Hans Oster when Erich Kordt brought news of the Bad Godesberg debacle. 'Finally we have clear proof that Hitler wants war, no matter what. Now there can be no going back.' He told Kordt to do what he could to lure Hitler back to Berlin – in order for the putsch to close its jaws around him, 'The bird must return to its cage.' It is noteworthy that, from the outset, the anti-Hitler plot had its supporters in the highest places. In this time of high international tension the Kordt brothers were dogging the steps of the foreign ministers of both Britain and Germany – Halifax and Ribbentrop. Friends in high places kept the group that was planning the putsch in Berlin abreast of events as they happened.

Hitler's hardline demands at Godesberg had buoyed the conspirators' resolve. They knew just by the grim looks of ordinary people in the streets that this time, in Gisevius's words, 'Hitler had gone too far . . . even Brauchitsch mumbled grim threats.' Oster confirmed to Erich Kordt at Godesberg that the army commander was 'ready to participate in a revolt'. But, despite all this fighting talk, the plotters still stayed their hand – waiting on a word from London. And that word, when it came, was deeply dispiriting.

Neville Chamberlain had been initially horrified by Hitler's sudden threat to occupy the Sudentenland instantly. But between leaving an intransigent Hitler to fly home in a mood of 'indignation' at his impossible demands, and meeting his cabinet on the morning of **24 September**, Chamberlain told his ministers, he had had a change of heart. The crucial moment in restoring his passion for peace at any cost had come when, returning from the Rhine, his plane had flown up another river, the Thames, and he had looked down to see the peaceful and vulnerable suburbs of London lying helplessly below. What if his plane had been a German bomber, Chamberlain wondered, or a fleet of bombers? The destruction would have been unimaginable, and not preventable, since Britain's Spitfire and Hurricane fighters had not yet come onstream. Had not his predecessor as premier, Stanley Baldwin, told MPs pessimistically that 'the bomber will always get through'? Faced with that terrifying scenario did not Hitler's demands suddenly seem not impossible bullying, but the tough bargaining position of a hard-headed but still reasonable statesman?

Chamberlain told his cabinet that Britain was in no position to wage a war, and had no realistic choice but to allow the Germans a free hand to occupy Czechoslovakia. Several cabinet members expressed their disquiet at this abject defeatism, although the majority still went along with Chamberlain's appeasement.

The next day, **25 September 1938**, the cabinet met three times in a crisis atmosphere. Prompted by his conscience, Chamberlain's hitherto closest ally in appeasement, the foreign secretary Lord Halifax, announced that after a sleepless night he had changed his mind. It would be dishonourable, said this upright aristocrat, for Britain to be dictated to by a man whose word could not be relied upon. Backed up by other cabinet ministers he insisted that an envoy, Horace Wilson, carry a letter to Hitler rejecting his outrageous Godesberg demands and warning that Britain and France would stand by the Czechs and go to war if Germany carried out its threat to occupy the Sudetenland immediately.

Czechoslovakia's ambassador, Jan Masaryk, son of the state's founder Tomas Masaryk, had told Chamberlain that Prague would not submit tamely to Hitler. 'The nation of St Wenceslas, Jan Hus and Tomas Masaryk will not be slaves.'

Spurred on by an indomitable Winston Churchill, and without consulting the prime minister, Halifax issued a press release on **26 September** re-asserting his new-found conviction that war was preferable to meek submission to Hitler's brute force: 'If, in spite of all efforts by the British Prime Minister, a German attack is made upon Czechoslovakia the immediate result must be that France will be bound to come to her assistance, and Great Britain and Russia will certainly stand by France.' The same day, a quaking Horace Wilson confronted an enraged Führer in Berlin, carrying a reluctant Chamberlain's letter announcing that the Czechs had refused his Bad Godesberg demands to give up one-quarter of their country.

Hitler almost burst a blood vessel at the news, and that night in the Berlin Sportspalast let the full force of his dammed-up frustration loose on an audience of 15,000 party bigwigs. Alternately sneering and ranting, he threatened the Czechs with fire and brimstone unless he was permitted to occupy the Sudetenland by 1 October – five days hence. Referring to the Czechoslovak president, Edvard Beneš, he concluded 'It is now up to Herr Beneš – peace or war!'

Europe was certainly preparing for war: in France reservists were called up; in London slit trenches were dug in the capital's parks; and in Germany itself army units were ordered up to the Czech frontiers in preparation for the coming invasion as Goebbels's propaganda campaign over the alleged Czech persecution of the suffering Sudeten Germans ratcheted up to a peak of hysteria. If this was all Hitler's bluff, it was a gigantically dangerous one. Claus von Stauffenberg's 1st Light Division, commanded by the future conspirator General Erich Hoepner, and bolstered by tanks and artillery, was one of the Wehrmacht units involved, moving from Hesse in central Germany, to the Jena area near the Czech border. By **27 September 1938,** along with six other divisions, they were poised to invade.

But, despite all Goebbels's careful propaganda preparations, the German population was far from enthusiastic about Hitler's war. The Führer had ordered Wehrmacht units to parade through central Berlin on 27 September to attempt to instil some martial ardour in the dour Berliners, but to no avail. Only 200 people gathered outside the Reichs

Chancellery to see the parade march by, and according to a civilian eye-witness, Ruth Andreas-Friederich, the grim-faced crowds stared stonily in silent disapproval as the parade passed by: 'They stand there with their tails between their legs . . . not a hand is raised anywhere. The tanks roll, the people keep silent, and the Führer, uncheered, vanishes from the balcony.' The American correspondent William Shirer, watching the same parade, recorded: 'Hitler looked grim, then angry, and soon went inside, leaving his troops to parade un-reviewed. What I've seen tonight almost rekindles a little faith in the German people. They are dead set against war.' A gleeful Gisevius commented: 'Never had soldiers been treated so badly in Berlin as they were on that day. In the workers' quarters clenched fists were raised against them; in the city centre people turned conspicuously away.' Even Hitler's interpreter Paul Otto Schmidt was startled by 'the completely apathetic and melancholy behaviour of the Berlin people'. In utter disgust, Hitler himself snarled to Goebbels: 'I cannot make war with such a people.'

The conspirators had not been idle. On the day that Hitler had seen for himself from the Reichs Chancellery balcony that his war fever had not infected his own people, Friedrich Wilhelm Heinz had assembled the raiding party whose task would be to break into the Chancellery and kill the dictator on the morning of the putsch. The raiders were hiding out at flats across central Berlin, conveniently close to the Wilhelmstrasse, which was the goal of their mission. Heinz gave his men their final marching orders. All they were waiting for was the signal to go.

In Britain, a reluctant Chamberlain mobilised the still-powerful British navy, and summoned parliamentarians back from their summer recess for an emergency session on **28 September.** The prime minister still favoured appeasing Hitler, but a growing swell of opinion in and outside his cabinet was pushing him towards drawing a line in the sand. However 'horrible, fantastic and incredible' it was, as Chamberlain had said in a radio broadcast, that the British people should be digging slit trenches and trying on gas masks because 'of a quarrel in a far-away country between a people of whom we know nothing', in the end, if Hitler's push became a shove, Britain would – albeit reluctantly – take up arms. This was the news the conspirators had been hoping and waiting for. At last, it seemed, appeasement had run out of road.

**Berlin, 28 September 1938**: the day dawned dull and grey. Silently, the men of Heinz's raiding party made their way through the streets and slipped into the army headquarters at the Bendlerstrasse (today

Stauffenbergstrasse). Heinz personally issued them with their weapons: short carbines and hand grenades, useful for close-quarter combat. Lips dry with nervous tension were licked as the men got used to their arms. As soon as the signal was received that Brockdorff's 23rd Division were on their way from nearby Potsdam, they would move. As they had been throughout the mounting crisis, the leaders of the conspiracy were keeping themselves abreast of the gathering storm, mainly through the work of the Kordt brothers, themselves close to the centre of the action in Berlin and London. Erich Kordt, at the side of Ribbentrop, who was urging Hitler to invade, was charged with ensuring that the great doors of the Chancellery would be open to admit Heinz's raiding party. He fully intended to play his part.

As Heinz's men assembled at the Bendlerstrasse, a few blocks away at the Abwehr headquarters, Oster was opening a copy of Hitler's reply to Chamberlain's letter informing the Führer that Britain and France would stand by the Czechs. Oster instantly alerted General Witzleben, who told the Chief of Staff, Halder. As he read Hitler's brusque rejection of Chamberlain's offer of further British mediation, 'tears of indignation' welled up behind Halder's pince-nez. Together, he and Witzleben decided that they could delay no longer.

They urged their immediate superior, the cautious army commander Brauchitsch, that the day for launching the putsch had at last arrived. Brauchitsch agreed in principle. He would support a coup, he said, as soon as he had visited the Chancellery and ascertained that Hitler was still bent on war.

But then, against all expectations, Hitler backed down. Almost simultaneously at the Reichs Chancellery he received two near-identical proposals from Chamberlain and Mussolini. Italy's Fascist dictator, with no wish to be dragged into war in Hitler's tank tracks, had responded positively to a last-minute plea from Chamberlain to get the Duce's German ally around a conference table. Both leaders now called for an immediate conference of the European powers to solve the crisis face to face. The only difference was that Chamberlain proposed Czech participation along with that of Britain, Germany, France and Italy. Mussolini would exclude the Czechs. Gratefully, Hitler accepted his Italian ally's idea. He was sure that he could get what he wanted without the bother of fighting a war, a conflict for which his generals – and his people – had shown such scant enthusiasm. And he was right.

Immediately, Hitler issued invitations to Chamberlain, Mussolini and the French premier Edouard Daladier to attend a conference in Munich the following day. At the same time, he ordered that the troops poised on the borders of the Sudetenland ready to invade Czechoslovakia should be stood down. Rather than face a messy campaign in which Britain, France and the not-inconsiderable thirty-four divisions of the Czech army would be ranged against him, he could, he reckoned, get his own way by the tried and tested formula of bullying and browbeating his potential adversaries over the conference table.

In London that afternoon, Chamberlain was just concluding a gloomy summing up of the crisis so far to MPs packed into a hushed and sombre House of Commons when a paper was passed to him. It was Hitler's invitation to the Munich conference. MPs on all sides stood and cheered, their voices hoarse with relief. Even the minority who felt that honour compelled Britain to fight did not actually *want* to fight. Desire for peace was overwhelming. Even Churchill shook Chamberlain's hand and wished him 'Godspeed' as he left the chamber for the Munich conference of **29 September**.

(Left to right) Chamberlain, Daladier, Hitler, Mussolini and Italy's Foreign Minister Count Ciano.

Chamberlain surrenders to Hitler.

Back in Berlin, news of the outcome of the Munich Conference took the wind out of the conspirators' sails and becalmed their putsch in a moment. The tension and dread that had been gathering towards an unbearable climax was punctured like a balloon by a pin. Drip by painful drip, the awful news leaked out: Chamberlain, with Daladier trailing in his wake, had given in to Hitler all along the line: the Sudetenland would be occupied – albeit to a slightly longer timetable than Hitler had originally required (**10 October** rather than **1 October**). Plebiscites would be held – albeit in areas already occupied by the Wehrmacht. The Czechs would not be permitted to dismantle any of the fortifications along their borders, and there would be no compensation for the land they were giving up. When the cheering that greeted Chamberlain's return to London had died away, the truth gradually began to sink in that Hitler had inflicted a total humiliation on the West.

Rather than the worthless piece of paper fluttering from Chamberlain's hand on his return to London, which he proclaimed as 'peace with honour', Munich represented, in Churchill's rather more realistic estimation, 'an unmitigated defeat – the first sip of a bitter cup that will be proffered to us year by year – unless by a supreme effort of moral health and martial vigour, we arise again and take our stand for freedom'.

As for the conspirators, Munich represented the shattering of all their hopes. Instead of their putsch being seen as a blow for sanity and moderation, Hitler would now be lauded by a people delirious with relief and starry-eyed with hero-worship as the divine, all-seeing, all-wise leader who could do no wrong.

To his leaden-eyed companions as the weary, depressed and defeated conspirators gathered in Oster's flat on the evening of 29 September, General Witzleben spoke a terrible truth:

> You see, gentlemen, for our poor deluded nation he [Hitler] is once more our dearly beloved Führer, unique, God-given, . . . and we, we are just a small heap of reactionary, malcontents . . . disgruntled officers and politicians who dared to scatter pebbles in the path of the greatest statesman of all time at the moment of his greatest triumph.

Any attempt at a putsch now, concluded Witzleben, would be seen by history, 'And not just German history, as nothing more than a refusal to serve the greatest German at a time when he was at his peak and the whole world recognized his greatness'.

A few days after Munich, the leaders of the conspiracy got together again at Witzleben's house to wrap up their aborted putsch. Gisevius, the only survivor of the gathering, described later how they tossed 'all our lovely plans and projects' into the general's fire. Afterwards they spent the rest of the melancholy evening ruminating 'Not on Hitler's triumph, but on Europe's calamity'.

# 5 Hitler's War

**Czech border**, **4 October 1938**: in accordance with the Munich agreement, Wehrmacht forces, including Claus von Stauffenberg's 1st Light Infantry Division, moved into the Sudetenland. The army shared the general sense of relief that the crisis had been resolved without war, the division's war diary remarking: 'The tension of the last few days is easing.' The German-populated towns, such as Mies, greeted the German occupiers with 'indescribable jubilation and a shower of flowers'. In stark contrast, places with a predominantly Czech population, such as Nurschan near Pilsen reacted with undisguised hostility. Stauffenberg himself, as the division's senior logistics officer, was concerned with organising the feeding of his own troops and that of the civilian population: the first real test of his organisational abilities outside the make-believe world of military manoeuvres. His ability earned him a special mention in his commander's report when the division withdrew to Germany on **16 October**. Meanwhile, on **21 October**, Hitler, angry at being deprived of his full prey, issued secret orders to the Wehrmacht to prepare for the occupation of the rump of Czechoslovakia the following spring. On returning to Berlin from Munich he had complained to Schacht: 'That fellow Chamberlain has spoiled my entry into Prague.' He would not be thwarted next time.

Countess Nina von Stauffenberg and her three young sons Berthold, Heimaren and Franz Ludwig, took up residence in Wuppertal, in **December 1938** to be close to her husband, whose divisional base was located in the un-lovely north-western city. The Stauffenbergs were near neighbours of the family of the division's adjutant, Captain Henning von Blomberg, son of the fallen war minister, and destined to die in North Africa in 1943, making way for Stauffenberg's near-fatal Tunisian assignment. For now, however, as the final months of European peace

Dr Joseph Goebbels at his desk in the Propaganda Ministry, where he organised the counter-coup on 20 July 1944.

ebbed away, the Stauffenberg children played happily with the young Blombergs.

**Germany, 9 November 1938**: a fateful date in German history. Squads of SA Brownshirts and crowds of ordinary Germans, egged on by a propaganda barrage created by Dr Goebbels, mounted a nationwide pogrom against Germany's remaining Jews. Dubbed the *Kristallnacht* ('night of broken glass') from the number of plate-glass windows in Jewish-owned stores smashed by the mobs, the mass violence saw scores of synagogues set ablaze in cities and towns across Germany. Tens of thousands of Jewish homes and businesses were wrecked, ninety-one Jews were murdered, hundreds more beaten and humiliated, and 30,000 carted off to concentration camps.

The pogrom was sparked off by the assassination in Paris of a junior German diplomat, Ernst vom Rath, by a young exiled German Jew, Herschel Grynszpan, who was enraged by the persecution of his family in Germany. It was a foretaste of the horrors of the Holocaust and revealed openly to the world – for those who had not already noticed – the criminal nature of the Nazi regime. Walking in the wintry woods near

A synagogue burns on *Kristallnacht*, 9 November 1938.

Wuppertal in **January 1939** Stauffenberg was asked by a friend, Rudolf Fahrner, what the army's attitude to the pogrom had been. Stauffenberg answered that disgust was so high that there had been talk of mounting a putsch. He added that Beck was the leader of military discontent and that his own commander, Hoepner, was also 'reliable'; but he cautioned against expecting any major move from the army as a whole. There was little point in expecting firmness, remarked Stauffenberg, referring to the Fritsch and Blomberg debacles, from those who had already had their backbones broken. But a time might come, concluded Stauffenberg, when the army would have to assume its responsibility as the saviour of the nation and the guarantor of Germany's honour.

On **15 March 1939**, Emil Hacha, the elderly lawyer who had succeeded Edvard Beneš as president of the rump Czechoslovak state after Munich, was summoned to the Berghof and presented with an ultimatum very similar to that which had been issued to Austria's chancellor, the hapless Kurt von Schuschnigg, on the eve of the *Anschluss* exactly a year before. Hacha was told that the full force of German military might, including a Luftwaffe air attack on Prague, would be unleashed unless he accepted that his truncated state – already shorn of large tracts of its territory to Hungary and Poland in the wake of Munich – accept German hegemony. The Czech-populated lands of Bohemia and Moravia would be incorporated into the Reich as a German 'protectorate' under military control; Slovakia would enjoy a nominal autonomy as a puppet state also under German 'protection'.

A horrified Hacha suffered a heart attack under Hitler's bullying onslaught, but after being revived with injections from the Führer's physician, he signed a document agreeing to the ultimatum, and German forces entered Prague the next day. Czechoslovakia had been wiped from the map of Europe.

On **21 March 1938** German forces also occupied the Lithuanian port of Memel. Ten days later, on **31 March**, Chamberlain issued a guarantee to Poland – which was clearly to be Hitler's next target – that Britain would come to that country's aid if it was menaced by outside aggression. France gave a similar guarantee. The stage was now set for the Second World War.

As the war clouds gathered in the spring of 1939, with Hitler issuing a directive on **3 April** that he intended to invade Poland, the logical end to Germany's aggressive foreign policy began to dawn on Stauffenberg. Visiting his friend Fahrner in Berlin in **May 1939**, Stauffenberg exclaimed, 'This lunatic will make war!' The following month, another friend, the classicist Karl Partsch, staying with Stauffenberg in Wuppertal, asked him if the time had come to form anti-Nazi cells within the army. Stauffenberg again poured cold water over any hope of expecting real resistance from the army. The officer corps, he said, was only interested in their promotion prospects.

Meanwhile, as the conspirators grasped the unpalatable fact that Hitler did not intend to stop with his Czech territories and was once again gearing Germany up for war, they began to re-tie the threads so brutally severed at Munich the previous autumn. In the summer of 1939, Halder met with Beck in Berlin; and von der Schulenberg and Gisevius travelled to Frankfurt, the location of Erwin von Witzleben's new command. Carl Goerdeler also called on Witzleben, who was proposing forming a new network of reliable conspirators' cells throughout the army. The garrulous Goerdeler told Witzleben of his latest plans for enlisting former trade unionist and socialist leaders in the ranks of the opposition – an idea that had already occurred to Stauffenberg, who had told Partsch at their May meeting that workers' organisations would be a much more reliable seedbed of resistance to Hitlerism than the army.

\* \* \*

**The Berghof, 22 August 1939**: before the plotters' plans could go any further, however, Hitler summoned his generals to the Berghof for another shock announcement. He was resolved, he said, to settle accounts with Poland. At that very moment, he revealed, Foreign Minister Ribbentrop was in Moscow negotiating a secret accord with the arch-enemy, Stalin's Russia, so they need fear no intervention from the east. His military audience sat in icy silence before him; Hitler waved aside any objections. The Western powers were worms – he had seen them at Munich – and would not intervene, despite their guarantees to Poland. He had Poland, he concluded, exactly where he wanted it – at his feet. The following day, the bombshell news of the Hitler–Stalin pact between the ideological polar opposites burst on the world. On **31 August** Hitler pressed the button for war, ordering the army to invade Poland the following day. Gisevius, meeting Canaris on a back staircase on the Bendlerblock, asked the Abwehr chief what he thought the outcome of the war would be. The little admiral replied with a two-word Latin tag: '*Finis Germanae*'.

Stauffenberg's 1st Light Division, of which he was by now quartermaster, had been moved up to Konstadt on the Polish frontier under its new commander, General Loeper. Stauffenberg was photographed on **1 September** with Loeper and other staff officers, dragging tensely on a cigarette, but looking suntanned and elegant in a forage cap and wearing white laundered shirtsleeves. Later that afternoon, they crossed the frontier, negotiated the rivers Prosna and Warthe. At a crossroads near the town of Wielun on **3 September** they heard the news that Britain and France had declared war. As the faces of his men dropped, Stauffenberg made a grim prediction: 'My friends, if we are to win this war it will depend on our capacity to hold out.' He forecast that the fighting would last for ten years. By **6 September** the division was storming the city of Radom against heavy Polish resistance. The fighting was fierce, Stauffenberg losing his coat and luggage when a staff car was captured by a stray Polish unit left behind by the German advance. He was instrumental in insisting on the court martial of a fellow officer who had had two Polish women shot out of hand for allegedly signalling to Polish artillery. But such upright and chivalrous behaviour was soon to become all too rare in the German officer corps.

On **10 September**, during a brief period of rest and repairs to their vehicles, Stauffenberg wrote home that they had 'won a great battle . . . It could turn into a second Tannenberg.' By the middle of the month, the

Stauffenberg (smoking) with fellow officers of the First Light Division at the Polish border on the day war began: 1 September 1939.

Polish campaign was effectively over and only mopping up remained. Stauffenberg found time to give his unflattering views of the Polish peasantry. Displaying a Teutonic arrogance confronting the hereditary enemy, he described them as 'an unbelievable rabble; very many Jews ... a people surely only comfortable under the knout. The thousands of prisoners-of-war will be good for our agriculture. In Germany they will surely be useful, industrious, willing and frugal.'

Stauffenberg had little idea that the bucolic agriculture-labouring future he envisaged for the Poles and Jews under benevolent German tutelage had little place in the genocidal plans that the Reich's leadership were already effecting. As the Wehrmacht advanced into Poland their tracks were closely followed by special SS *Einsatzgruppen* (task forces), squads of hardened killers trained and tasked for mass murder. Answering directly to the SS leader Himmler, their mission was to exterminate Poland's large Jewish population, as well as the aristocrats, priests and intellectuals who provided the nation's social, spiritual and political leadership. As the Wehrmacht became aware of the first round-ups and mass killings carried out by the *Einsatzgruppen*, complaints began to surface that the crimes were besmirching the honour of the German army. Several generals – Blaskowitz, Ulex and the future field marshal Georg von Kuechler – protested. One, Joachim Lemelsen, went so far as to arrest and court martial a member of Hitler's own bodyguard unit, the SS Leibstandarte *Adolf Hitler*, for massacring fifty Jews. All such protests were in vain: Hitler reprimanded Blaskowitz for his 'childish' attitude and commented that wars 'could not be won by Salvation Army methods'. When Blaskowitz persisted with his protest, complaining that 'Every soldier feels sickened and repulsed by the crimes committed in Poland by agents of the Reich,' he was summarily sacked. The activities of the SS and police auxiliary units in Poland were, as yet, but a foretaste of the wholesale atrocities that led ineluctably to the Holocaust itself, characterising Nazi actions in eastern Europe and the Soviet Union. But, as reports and rumours of what was happening just to the rear of the front lines began to circulate among the officer corps, though many continued to shut their eyes, no one could any longer pretend to be unaware that Hitler's rule meant a relapse into barbarism.

On **12 September 1939**, Hitler confided to his adjutant Rudolf Schmundt – destined to die as a result of injuries inflicted by Stauffen-berg's bomb on 20 July – that he planned to answer the Anglo-French declaration of war with an all-out assault on western Europe just as soon as the Polish campaign was wrapped up. On **15 September**, Stauffen-berg's division was pulled out of its rest area and thrown in to join the forces encircling Warsaw. 'The Poles,' Stauffenberg admitted admiringly, 'fighting with the courage of despair . . . got us into some nasty spots.' Two days later, on **17 September**, hearing that Stalin had carried out his part of his recently agreed accord with the hated Hitler by invading eastern Poland with seven armies, Stauffenberg's thoughts were with his fellow nobles in the Polish aristocracy:

> I do not have the impression that our friends the Bolsheviks are using kid gloves. This war is truly a scourge of God for the entire Polish upper class. They ran from us eastward. We are not letting anyone except ethnic Germans cross the Vistula westward. The Russians will probably make short work of them since . . . the real danger is only in

Adolf Hitler with Colonel Rudolf Schmundt and Rear Admiral Karl Jesko von Puttkamer at the Wolfschanze in 1941. Schmundt was destined to be killed by Stauffenberg's bomb, and Puttkamer to be injured.

the nationalistic Polish upper class who naturally feel superior to the Russians. Many of them will go to Siberia.

Once again, Stauffenberg was still under-estimating the savagery of twentieth-century totalitarianism. In fact, the fate that lay in store for the Polish officer corps at the hands of the Russians was far more terrible even than Siberia: 8,000 of them, along with more than 10,000 civilians arrested later, were murdered in March 1940 in the Katyn Forest on Stalin's orders, and buried in mass graves. The Germans trumpeted the massacre to a largely disbelieving world in 1943 after discovering the mass graves, which, in their eyes, went some way towards justifying their own acts of barbarous cruelty to Russian prisoners captured on the Eastern Front.

On **27 September 1939**, the day that Warsaw finally capitulated, Hitler summoned the commanders of his three armed forces, confided to them his plan to attack in the west, and ordered them to draw up operational details for the assault. To their horror, he insisted that the attack should be carried out as soon as possible, no later than mid-November. The

High Command – even pro-Hitler generals like Reichenau – voiced strong objections on both military and political grounds. The troops were exhausted after destroying Poland and needed time to rest, regroup and, not least, absorb the strategic and tactical lessons of the campaign. The winter, they protested, was never a good time to fight a war. Hitler turned a deaf ear to these objections, pointing out that the weather was the same for both sides. Besides, he said, the Allies would not expect an attack and surprise was always a winning factor in war.

In truth, Brauchitsch, Halder and the other generals were hoping that the war could be ended without the need for a further campaign. Although victorious, the Polish campaign had been far from bloodless: Stauffenberg's division had lost 300 men. They were well aware that an all-out attack on the West would cost even more lives – not to mention the danger that America would be drawn into the conflict if Hitler, as he envisaged, violated the neutrality of Holland and Belgium. They had assumed that by sitting out the winter along the Siegfried Line a window of opportunity could be created for diplomacy to end what they saw as an unnecessary war. Poland, the original *casus belli* that had brought Britain and France into the struggle, had been comprehensively crushed. The Western Allies had watched passively while this happened without lifting a finger to intervene. It was clear that they were at best half-hearted about continuing the conflict. So why not let sleeping dogs lie? Hitler's determination to press ahead with an early attack alarmed them; it upset all their calculations and opened the way to a wider war of unknown duration.

In the middle of October Stauffenberg's division returned to Germany, the campaign complete and Poland subjugated. On **18 October** it was re-designated the 6th Panzer Division to reflect the role of the tanks that had been added to its strength since the occupation of Czechoslovakia. Stauffenberg was flushed with victory and took a professional soldier's pride in his own part in the triumph. His success was reflected on **1 November** when he was promoted to the rank of captain and designated a permanent General Staff officer, entitled to wear the coveted broad scarlet stripe along the seams of his trousers. He would not agree with those of his fellow officers and even his own friends and relatives – such as Count Fritz-Dietlof von der Schulenberg and his uncle Nikolaus von Üxküll – who maintained that the war was criminal folly and that Hitler must be removed by force. Stauffenberg argued that it was impossible to act against him when the dictator was at such a peak of success.

Stauffenberg as General Staff officer of the 6th Tank Division, Hachenburg 1940.

Stauffenberg also pointed out that Britain and France had declared war against Germany, and that it was a German officer's duty to defend his homeland. His mind was anyway still on his professional military duties. He had issued on his own initiative a report on the lessons of the Polish campaign based on a questionnaire he had issued to all ranks. He pointed out that it had been the first example of *Blitzkrieg* in warfare, but that the army's training, logistics and structure only equipped it to fight an old-style slow-moving war. New warfare, he concluded, would require entirely new methods. He was not to know that it was exactly such methods that Hitler proposed to put into effect in the west within weeks.

The news that Hitler was planning to invade in the west galvanised the dormant conspiracy like a hungry fox entering a hen-coop. At the Abwehr Canaris and Oster held urgent discussions with the group of younger anti-Nazis whom Oster had deliberately recruited with a view to forming an activist nest of effective conspiracy: the lawyer Hans von Dohnanyi; Dohnanyi's cousin, the brilliant, young, balding and bespectacled theologian Dietrich Bonhoeffer; and his boyhood friend Justus Delbrück, along with the aristocratic historian Baron Karl-Ludwig von Guttenberg. Another nest of military conspirators, known as the Action Group Zossen, was based at the large eponymous military base south of Berlin. Further up the military chain of command, Brauchitsch and Halder were as horrified as their juniors. At the Foreign Office, diplomats Ernst von Weizsäcker, Erich Kordt and Hasso von Etzdorf wrote a memo arguing that a war in the west would ultimately mean the end of Germany.

Persuaded by such pressure, the Army Chief of Staff, Halder, encouraged his immediate superior, the more wavering army commander Brauchitsch to refuse outright to carry out Hitler's plans, and to lend his support to a new putsch if the Führer insisted on going ahead. Halder confided to one of the Abwehr conspirators – Helmuth Groscurth, who would later die of typhus in Russian captivity – that he himself always packed a pistol in his pocket when going to see 'Emil', as he derisively dubbed Hitler, but had so far lacked the courage to gun the dictator down.

Assassination was also on the mind of mild-mannered Erich Kordt, who on **1 November** during a meeting with Oster at Abwehr headquarters, answered Oster's complaint that 'no one could be found who will throw the bomb and liberate our generals from their scruples' by volunteering for the task himself if Oster would supply the necessary explosives. Oster promised to have a bomb ready by 11 November, the anniversary of the 1918 Armistice, the day on which Hitler had threatened to unleash another war on the West.

The conspirators' plans now began to move towards the same state of readiness that they had assumed the previous autumn when Munich had pulled the rug from under their putsch. Oster told the indefatigable Gisevius to dust down the old plans for a putsch and to re-activate the old gang of conspirators. Gisevius gleefully recorded in his diary: 'It's going ahead: Great activity. One discussion after another. Suddenly it's just as it was right before Munich in 1938. I rush back and forth between OKW [Army Headquarters], police headquarters, the Interior Ministry. Beck, Goerdeler, Schacht, Helldorf, Nebe and many others.'

**Berlin, 5 November 1939**: propped up by Halder, Brauchitsch met Hitler in the Reichs Chancellery. Plucking up all his scant reserves of courage, the army chief told the Führer that the attack could not possibly proceed as planned because the Polish campaign had exposed glaring flaws in the army: not merely the technical deficiencies of the kind highlighted by Stauffenberg's report, but also a fundamental flaw in morale, even instances of cowardice. Instantly, Hitler flew into one of his famous rages, storming at an ashen-faced Brauchitsch and demanding proof of his charges and whether such cowards had been shot. Then he abruptly left the room, leaving the hapless army chief standing helplessly.

As he and Brauchitsch drove back to Zossen – the base where Hitler had darkly hinted that a spirit of resistance to his plans lurked – a shaken Halder, fearing that someone had betrayed their putsch plans, gave orders that all documents relating to the coup should be destroyed. Thoroughly intimidated by Hitler's outburst of rage, both Brauchitsch and Halder now washed their hands of any plans for a putsch and resigned themselves to the coming war. They were not the only ones to suffer from cold feet.

On **8 November**, during a visit to the Western Front to sound out the army commanders Leeb, Bock and Rundstedt, the insouciant Oster produced from his pocket two proclamations written by Beck that were to be broadcast after the military takeover. Leeb's Chief of Staff, Colonel Vincenz Müller, insisted that he burn them in a large ashtray. As the conspirators' hopes were literally going up in smoke came shattering news that paralysed any further action in its tracks: a large bomb had exploded in the Munich beer cellar where Hitler had launched his abortive putsch in November 1923. Several people had been killed – but by some malign miracle, the Führer had survived.

# 6 Lone Wolf
## Georg Elser and the Bomb in the Beerhall

Like many of those who would come to resist Hitler, including Claus von Stauffenberg, Johann Georg Elser was a Swabian, a native of the sleepy, south-west corner of Germany that was a region of thrift, independence and sturdily liberal political traditions. Born in January 1903 into a family of lumberjacks, smallholders and millers, Elser shared the childhood burdens of his future intended victim, Hitler, having a loving mother yet suffering a violent, drunken father, Ludwig Elser. The eldest of five children from a Protestant family, Elser grew up a slight, wiry, thin-faced loner. Fun did not enter his world, and when he was not helping his mother care for his younger siblings, he was put to work early slaving for his father, whose almost nightly beatings produced a burning sense of injustice in the boy Georg, and a corresponding burning desire to right the wrongs of a profoundly unjust universe.

Elser graduated from his secondary school in 1917, and lost no time in distancing himself from his father's failing haulage business and taking up an apprenticeship in a foundry. But the hot, heavy work was uncongenial to the delicate boy, who always preferred his own company. He secured another apprenticeship, with a cabinet-maker, where he honed his skills at carpentry. A patient perfectionist by nature, young Elser was ideally suited to the long hours and delicate, laborious work demanded in working wood. But, although his woodworking skills became increasingly prized by a succession of employers, Elser's world was a profoundly isolated one. Lacking even ordinary social skills, he had no friends and few contacts of any kind outside his family and his shifting workplaces. Forming a relationship was a high hurdle for the tongue-tied loner, and, according to his Gestapo interrogators, he was still a virgin at twenty-five who did not even know how to masturbate.

Georg Elser.

Elser was one of the millions of victims of the Wall Street Crash of October 1929. Jobs – he had worked as a clock-maker, watchmaker and as an ordinary carpenter – dried up, and he was forced to return to his parental home in the village of Hermaringen. A late starter, only now did Elser begin to develop sexual and political interests. Making up for lost time, he formed several relationships in quick succession, the first with a woman named Brunhilde from Konstanze on the Bodensee, then – as he confessed to his Gestapo tormentors – with 'a certain Anna' and finally with 'Mathilde N', 'Hausfrau H' and 'Hilda N'. Despite an attempt to procure a Swiss abortion, Hilda bore Elser an unwanted son, Manfred, a child whom he was obliged to support financially, although Elser and Hilda did not live together; his payments were often either paid late or not at all. Elser, the embittered loner, would never make a contented family man, and after his father's business finally failed he left home for the last time and resumed his lonely existence as a wandering chisel for hire, while living in a succession of rented rooms.

Elser's revolt against the usual Swabian template of comfortable, conformist life extended to his politics. Although never a party member, he was briefly affiliated to the Communist Party's paramilitary arm, the

Red Front Fighting League, and he voted Communist at every election until the party was banned after the Nazis came to power in 1933. Although no Marxist, he regarded the KPD as the party of the working man, and believed that the pay and conditions of the working class had deteriorated sharply since Hitler had become chancellor. As an itinerant worker, he resented the increasing dragooning of the working class into state-run enterprises and, although not a religious man, he also resisted the implicit Nazi claim to replace the Christian religion with a sort of cod German paganism. Finally, Hitler's rearmament programme and his aggressive foreign policy had not escaped Elser's notice. He believed that the Führer was firmly set on a path to war and that he must be stopped. He was not afraid of demonstrating his hostility in public; once he ostentatiously turned his back, whistling and refusing to join the crowds giving the Hitler salute during a Nazi street parade. Such gestures could have dangerous consequences as the party tightened its grip on Germany, but Elser never lacked courage – or stubbornness. Then, in November 1938 in the wake of the Munich crisis that had brought the world to the brink of war, came the next logical step in his thought processes: if no one else was prepared to stop Hitler, then he, Georg Elser, the nobody from Hermaringen, would do the job.

On **8 November 1938**, Elser took a train for Munich. His self-imposed mission in the 'party capital' was to closely observe the annual Nazi commemoration of the failed 1923 Beerhall putsch, Hitler's premature attempt to seize power by naked force. The ceremonies celebrating this bloody fiasco every autumn had been elevated by the Nazis to the status of a quasi-religious cult. The increasingly portly party leaders squeezed with difficulty into their original Brownshirt uniforms and solemnly re-enacted their march through Munich's streets until they reached the Odeonplatz, the central square where a ragged volley from a police cordon had scattered the Nazis like autumn leaves, leaving fourteen of them dead (two more putschists were killed elsewhere). Hitler, Goering, Himmler, Hess and other Nazi leaders who had taken part in the putsch appeared publicly, regular as clockwork, each 9 November to rally the faithful, pay tribute at the tombs of their sixteen fallen comrades, and re-dedicate one of the party's founding myths.

This year, Georg Elser was also on hand to view the proceedings. On the evening of 8 November he wandered into the Bürgerbräukeller, the vast beerhall where Hitler had launched his putsch by hijacking a meeting addressed by Bavaria's conservative leaders. This event was marked each year by the Führer giving a speech to his 'Old Fighters' at the same location. After Hitler had finished this year's oration, Elser entered the beerhall and surveyed the scene with a practised eye as workmen began to take down the flags and bunting, and dirndl-clad waitresses lifted the heavy beer steins and swabbed down the long trestle tables. Here, Elser decided, was the ideal place to eliminate Hitler, either with a pistol – had not Hitler himself fired his handgun into the beerhall ceiling as the starting signal for his putsch? – or, more ambitiously, with a bomb.

The more Elser saw of the Bürgerbräukeller – and he visited it repeatedly over the next three days, making his modest stein last for hours as he eyed up the internal fittings and architecture – the more he liked what he saw. Virtually uniquely in the German calendar, he knew, twelve months in advance, exactly where Hitler would be standing a year hence. There was the speaker's lectern he always used, ideally positioned against a stout pillar. As Elser confessed to his Gestapo interrogators later:

> The idea slowly began to form in my mind that the best way to do it was by packing high explosive into the pillar behind the rostrum . . . some gadget would have to be found that would set the explosive off at the right moment. I picked the pillar because chunks of masonry from the explosion would hit the speaker and with a bit of luck the weakened roof might fall on him too.

Unbeknownst to Elser, he was not the only potential assassin at large in Munich that November with the Führer as his target. Swiss-born, French-speaking Maurice Bavaud was also a loner, but one with a very different background to the impoverished Elser. A pious Catholic, with a fervently moral standpoint, during the course of intensive discussions with his fellow students at a theological seminary in Brittany, Bavaud had become convinced that Hitler was the Antichrist and that it was his bounden duty to kill him. Learning German at his home in Neufchâtel in the summer holidays of 1938, Bavaud travelled to Germany and began a long series of fruitless attempts to gain access to Hitler. Procuring a pistol and ammunition in Berlin, Bavaud went to Hitler's mountain retreat at Berchtesgaden, where he practised his marksmanship in the woods and repeatedly tried to secure an interview with the Führer, even going to the lengths of forging fawning letters from French Fascist leaders in an attempt to smooth his path to Hitler's side.

Learning that his best chance of getting a clear shot at Hitler would be at the annual Beerhall putsch commemoration that November, Bavaud made his way to the Bavarian capital where he, like Elser, haunted the streets in the hope of getting a clear view of his target. He managed to get a grandstand seat in the front rank of spectators as the Nazi leaders' parade approached, but just as he was about to pull out his pistol and fire, a forest of right arms shot up in the Hitler salute, blocking the young Swiss's view completely. When the arms fell, Hitler had moved on, and Bavaud's last chance of killing the 'Antichrist' had vanished. He made one last frantic attempt to break through the security cordon protecting Hitler at Berchtesgaden, but when that failed, Bavaud's money ran out too, and he jumped on a train for Paris. Apprehended by a ticket inspector, his luggage was searched and his pistol discovered. Passed to the Gestapo, he was soon forced to reveal the details of his stalking of Hitler and he was sentenced to death by guillotine, a penalty that was eventually carried out on 14 May 1941, in Berlin's Plötzensee Prison – the same grim jail where the July plotters would also meet their agonising ends.

On receiving the Gestapo report of their investigation of Bavaud's abortive attempt on his life, Hitler remarked fatalistically that he was not surprised that 90 per cent of history's assassination attempts had been successful. If an assassin was fanatically prepared to sacrifice their own life in taking their target's life, said Hitler, then no security precautions on earth could stop them. The only effective way of lessening the chances of a successful assassination, the Führer opined, was by varying one's routine and changing plans at the last minute. Although Hitler reputedly had his cap lined with metal and reportedly even kept a parachute strapped beneath his seat whenever he flew, it was only just such a variation that would save his life yet again from a second stalker in Munich.

With the time slowly ticking down to his self-imposed deadline of November 1939, Georg Elser began to prepare his own time bomb. His first move was to steal a fuse and 250 grains of gunpowder from his current employer, who was, conveniently enough, a munitions manufacturer in the small town of Heidenheim. In **April 1939** he made a second visit to Munich to reconnoitre the location for his assassination attempt. Realising that he needed more sophisticated materials to fashion his bomb, he took a labourer's job at a quarry, the Steinbruck Georg V in the nearby town of Köningsbronn, where it was a comparatively easy task to steal explosives and a detonator from the carelessly guarded site store. Ever the lonely autodidact, Elser taught himself how to construct the bomb, toiling for long hours in his workshop and telling curious enquirers that he was inventing a new type of alarm clock. He learned how to handle explosives, and tested the result by letting off small charges in the fields around his home. After Hitler occupied the rump of Czechoslovakia in March 1939, Elser, more certain than ever that the Nazis were set on launching a new war on the world, returned to Munich to finesse his plans by taking measurements and making detailed sketches of the Bürgerbräukeller's interior. He even attempted – unsuccessfully – to get a job waiting tables at the beerhall. But, having failed in that, he resolved, undaunted, to gain access by more devious means.

At the beginning of **August 1939**, as the catalyst for the Second World War, Poland, began to bubble ominously, Elser gave up his job at the quarry and returned once more to Munich. He took with him his heavy tool chest; beside the usual tools of his trade – saws, hammers, chisels, files and planes – the wooden chest now contained, secreted in a hidden compartment, the illicit materials he had been working on over the previous nine months: including fifty kilograms of high-explosive sticks, detonators, wire, a battery and six clock movements with which he intended to fashion his infernal device. Like any good German, Elser reported his presence in Munich to the municipal police – then, as now, an obligatory requirement of all citizens – rented a room, and began work on his final preparations.

He followed an unvarying routine: every evening he would attend the Bürgerbräukeller, arriving around 9 p.m. A small, insignificant figure, Elser never attracted much attention at the best of times, but in the crowded, beery, raucous and smoke-filled atmosphere of the vast beerhall, sandwiched between bulky Bavarians bursting out of their lederhosen, the diminutive Swabian carpenter was almost lost to sight as he quietly sipped his beer, munched his sausage sandwich and waited for closing time. His nondescript presence became such a customary event, that the waitresses and bar staff got used to him and ceased to notice Elser altogether. He had, as he had hoped, become the invisible man: almost literally part of the beerhall's furniture.

Around 10 p.m., regular as clockwork, Elser would finish his modest meal, wipe his lips, and casually climb the stairs to a deserted cloakroom, carrying his toolbag like any home-going worker relieving himself of the night's intake of Bavarian beer. Here he would hide while the

Bürgerbräukeller staff closed its doors, cleaned up and went home. On the first night he waited silently in the darkness for another hour to check that there was no night watchman apart from the Bürgerbräukeller cats. Then he stole silently out and got to work. For the first three nights he used a fretsaw carefully to saw out a rectangular panel in the wooden cladding casing the brick pillar. Then he fitted tiny hinges to his homemade 'door' so it could easily be levered open, allowing him to attack the stonework beneath.

Working by the shaded light of a torch, pausing frequently to strain his ears for any disturbing visitors, he laboured for weeks, chipping out the mortar and prising the bricks from the pillar to create his bomb-holding cavity, night after endless night. Progress was agonisingly slow. Each rasp of his hand drill, each hammer blow, echoed monstrously loud in the eerie silence of the cavernous hall. He learned to time each blow of the hammer on the metal chisel's head to coincide with masking extraneous sounds, such as the passing of a tram, or the automatic flushing of the beerhall toilets. This made the work so slow and drawn out that Elser began to worry that his meagre and carefully hoarded funds would run out before the job was done. After his night's sawing and chipping, in the early hours he would meticulously collect every scrap of sawdust, every splinter of brickwork and every particle of dirt, so that no trace remained of his nocturnal labours. Above all he ensured that the door to the cavity he was hacking out fitted flush and snug with the rest of the wooden cladding. Invisible even to his eye, it would have to pass the minute inspection carried out by the Nazi security men on the eve of Hitler's speech.

Once he was satisfied that all trace of his presence had been removed, Elser would tiptoe back to his hiding place in the cloakroom and wait for the arrival of the beerhall's staff to open up and welcome the first of the day's customers – bleary-eyed early risers coming in for a fortifying slug of schnapps to ward off the chill of the early Munich winter. Cautiously, Elser would emerge from his hiding place, mingle briefly with the morning drinkers, then head back to his lodgings like the shift worker he was, for a much-needed daytime sleep.

He left the most intricate and dangerous part of his task to the last: priming the bomb itself. His aim was to be well clear of the beerhall by the time his months of back-breaking and dangerous toil climaxed in the huge explosion that he hoped would remove Hitler forever. Indeed, if his scheme worked out, he would not be in Munich at all – nor even in Germany. Elser's getaway plan called for him to be miles away, in the safety of Switzerland, by the time the bomb went off. Using the clock workings he had collected from his days as a watchmaker, he constructed a long-set timer that would run for up to 144 hours before activating a lever that in turn triggered an elaborate system of springs, weights and shuttles. The end result was a steel-tipped prong that would strike a live rifle cartridge embedded in the explosive. The meticulous Elser even added an identical second system in case the first one failed. The time bomb was enclosed in a wooden clock case that he had lined with cork to muffle the telltale ticking of the clock. For the final touch, he inserted a sheet of tinplate on the inside of his wooden door so that the cavity would not sound hollow if knocked by a nosy security snoop.

By the beginning of November, with perfect timing, all was ready. On **2 November 1939** Elser again visited the beerhall that had become his home from home and safely installed his bomb. Three nights later, on **5 November**, he set the timer to explode at exactly 9.20 p.m. on the evening of 8 November – right in the middle, as he hoped, of Hitler's speech. Finally, on **7 November**, after visiting his sister, and borrowing thirty marks from her to buy his train ticket to the Swiss frontier, he returned to the Bürgerbräukeller for the last time to make a final check that the timing device was still running. It was. Nothing, he calculated, could now prevent his device, so laboriously prepared and carefully concealed, from interrupting Hitler's annual address to the party faithful with what he hoped would be fatal consequences. After paying a farewell visit to his Munich lodgings, he bought a third-class ticket at Munich's Hauptbahnhof for the town of Konstanze on the border, a place he knew from his brief affair there with Brunhilde. As his train, dimly lit with the blue lamps of the blackout, gathered speed in the night, Elser allowed himself to relax. The Führer's fate was fixed.

Hitler flew into Munich airport on the afternoon of **8 November 1939**. For once, the dictator was distracted, with his mind not completely on the coming commemoration. His thoughts, rather, were on the war that he had launched just two months before. The day before his flight to Munich he had reluctantly rescinded his order for a surprise attack on France and the Low Countries to be launched on 12 November after receiving persistently unfavourable weather reports forecasting rain and fog for the foreseeable future. Determined to press the attack home, if at all possible, Hitler, in a foul and frustrated temper, had ordered a review of the weather situation on 9 November. That urgent business would call him back to Berlin rather earlier than usual – this year's elaborate parades and ceremonies would be curtailed, and the exigencies of wartime would be blamed.

He had seen the bad weather for himself during his flight south. So thick was the fog that his pilot, Hans Bauer, recommended that he return to the capital not by air, but in his armoured train 'Amerika'. That would mean a departure even earlier than anticipated. Hitler ordered that his address to the 'Old Fighters' in the beerhall should be brought forward by one hour – crucially, he would now begin speaking at 8 p.m. rather than at 9.

There was one piece of very personal business that Hitler attended to before duty called at the Bürgerbräukeller. He went to the hospital bedside of Unity Mitford, the half-demented English society girl who had fallen for him in a major way after stalking him at his favourite Munich restaurant, the Osteria Bavaria. With her china-doll blue eyes, blonde Aryan looks, her minor aristocratic connections and her evident dumb adoration, Unity appealed to Hitler, and he admitted her to his circle of hangers-on. In time, Unity introduced other members of her eccentric family to Hitler – including her sister Diana, who shared her sister's Fascist sympathies and eventually, in October 1936, married her lover, British Fascist leader Sir Oswald Mosley, in Berlin with Hitler and Goebbels as guests of honour. Mortified by the outbreak of war between her British homeland and her adopted Fatherland, Unity shot herself in the Munich park appropriately called The English Garden, on 3 September 1939 – the day Britain declared war on Germany. She botched the job and the bullet lodged in the back of her head.

Hitler placed his admirer – who really was a dumb blonde now, since the shot had rendered her speechless – in an expensive private clinic on Munich's Nussbaumstrasse and paid for her care under Professor Magnus, Germany's leading brain surgeon. But the bullet was too deeply lodged to remove and Unity lay for day after day, semi-comatose. Hitler stopped by, left a bouquet of flowers and gave orders for Unity to be sent back to England via neutral Switzerland as soon as she was fit enough to make the journey. Then he was driven to the Bürgerbräukeller where, in the back rooms where he had held Bavaria's ruling triumvirate hostage at the launch of the putsch in 1923, he made the final preparations for his speech.

He changed into a fresh uniform, with newly laundered silk underwear laid out by his valet Heinz Linge, gargled with glycerine and warm water to ease his throat, and began to psych himself up to meet his public.

Already he could hear the hubbub of the growing throng gathering in the main hall where Elser's bomb ticked on unheeded. Had Elser but known it, he need not have made the meticulous security arrangements to cover up his deadly handiwork, since the Nazis' own security in the hall was cursory to the point of negligence. After a spat between Munich's town police and the city council over responsibility for the historic hall's security in 1936, Hitler had given a judgment of Solomon that the party itself should look after security. This was a mistake: the sharp attention to danger of the ageing Old Fighters had atrophied and grown as blurred as their beer-sodden senses and as bloated as their swelling bellies. As a result, no search of the premises had been carried out before Hitler's address, and security on the night rested with a single guard, a former Munich police officer who had been drafted into the army, one Josef Gerum.

As usual, on this November night, the hall was packed. Three thousand beefy, beer-swilling Brownshirts were squeezed along the narrow benches in front of the trestle tables. As the band struck up the military tune, the 'Badenweiler Marsch', all eyes turned to a solitary figure who had marched into the room, bearing aloft the party's most sacred icon – the *Blut Fahne* or Blood Banner. This was the flag that had flown at the head of the Nazi marchers during the original putsch,

Hitler speaking at Bürgerbräukeller, 8 November 1939.

and had been stained with the blood of the party's fallen martyrs. This year and every year, the flag – used by Hitler to 'touch' every subsequent party flag with its sacred aura – was borne in by the whip-thin Old Fighter Josef Grimminger, an expressionless Hitler look-alike with the same toothbrush moustache, chosen for this signal honour because of his fanatical loyalty to the Führer.

Grimminger was closely followed by Hitler himself, processing slowly down the central aisle between the tables as the faithful rose to their feet and roared their '*Heil!*' from well-oiled throats. Hitler spoke for almost an hour, delivering an impassioned attack on England, claiming that as Britain had declared war back in September, it was they and not he – in particular the First Lord of the Admiralty, Winston Churchill – who were the warmongers. However, he was ready to fight such a war, he warned in an uncompromising message designed to stiffen the sinews of his people before the coming offensive in the west. Then, suddenly, almost abruptly, it was over. Just after 9 p.m., Hitler stopped speaking and left the hall, heading for his train – according to Party Secretary Martin Bormann's diary – at **9.07** precisely. Just eighteen minutes after the Führer had left the hall, at **9.20 p.m.**, right on schedule, Elser's bomb exploded.

Hitler's sudden departure had left the Brownshirts, despite their inebriated condition, somewhat deflated. Drunk on Bavarian beer and the stream of Hitler's impassioned words, they had cheered and roared their approval of his hard, slashing rhetoric, and when he abruptly left, there was a certain sense of letdown: Hamlet had departed and the drama was over. Quite quickly, in small groups and singly, the faithful trailed out and the hall began to empty. Within ten minutes, barely one hundred people remained: some were Nazis, disconsolately emptying the dregs of their beer, while others were musicians packing up their instruments and bar staff clearing up the detritus left behind after the rally.

Then Elser's bomb tore the night – and the hall – apart. What witnesses described as a blinding flash of violet light like a lightning strike streaked across the huge hall, accompanied by an ear-splitting blast. The device had all the devastating effect that Elser had hoped for, and more: it shattered the pillar in which it had been concealed, bringing the gallery it supported crashing down. The blast blew out doors and windows and smashed chairs, tables – and people – to fragments. Had Hitler still been standing on the rostrum he had just vacated he

An interior view of the Bürgerbräukeller showing the devastation caused by Elser's bomb. The explosion killed eight people and injured more than sixty others.

would have been instantly killed. As it was, three of his Old Fighters lay dead, while five more were dying, along with a waitress; sixty-three other people were injured – sixteen of them seriously. Shocked survivors, covered with dust and debris, their ears ringing, struggled out through a fog of smoke into the cold night air.

Half an hour before the blast, two German border guards in the lakeside frontier town of Konstanz were making their customary routine patrol along the tall barbed-wire fence separating Germany from Switzerland. Bored, they paused in a garden to listen to a live radio relay of Hitler's beerhall speech, when one of them noticed a movement in the bushes nearby. Unslinging their rifles, they arrested the diminutive Elser, who could give no satisfactory explanation for his presence. Taken to the Kreuzlinger Tor border post, he was ordered to empty his pockets. Their damning contents included a membership card from the banned Communist Red Front paramilitary wing, to which he had once briefly belonged. Along with this were other telltale pieces of evidence linking him with the enormity that was about to erupt at the Bürgerbräukeller. They included a postcard of the beerhall and instructions on manufacturing munitions.

At his confession to the German police, Elser sketching out from memory the preparation for his attempt on Hitler's life.

As if such clues were not enough for even the dimmest police official to start to entertain suspicions, Elser was also carrying a number of screws and pieces of metal, which he lamely maintained were necessary for his profession of clockmaker. One of his captors, an ex-soldier, was not to be so easily fooled: 'You cannot make a clock with those!' he exclaimed, 'They are for making detonators.'

So careless was Elser's conduct that night – he had made no effort to run away or escape – and so suspect were the clues he was carrying, that some historians long believed that he was a mere tool of some nefarious state conspiracy, concocted by the SS or Gestapo, who had manipulated or somehow induced Elser to make and plant his bomb. Was the whole plot, then, an inside job? Several factors make this unlikely – not least the appalling risk to the Führer and other leading Nazis if the bomb had malfunctioned and exploded prematurely. Instead, most historians now accept the simplest and most obvious truth: Elser was exactly what he said he was. He was a most unusual assassin, in that he worked alone and entirely without outside support, except for the small sum borrowed from his sister for his rail fare. He was, nevertheless, a very determined and ingenious assassin, and one whose bomb came nearer to killing Hitler than any other attempt – with the single exception of Stauffenberg's bomb.

The question then arises: why did Elser, this most meticulous and cautious of men, carry such obvious clues around with such wild abandon? Why, having got so far – and having succeeded in carrying out his scheme and come close to getting clean away with it – did he fall at this final, fatal hurdle when he was within sight of Switzerland and safety? The answers can only be conjecture: human psychology is so complex that a person who is infinitely painstaking in some areas can be careless to the point of negligence in others. The self-imposed strain that Elser had been under for months may have sapped his last reserves of calculation and made him throw caution to the winds. Having only known Konstanz in peacetime, he may have reckoned on the relatively lax border controls of pre-war days, forgetting that Germany was now at war and open to infiltration from its neutral neighbours, and that border controls were correspondingly stringent. He may well have deliberately carried the mementoes of his deadly deed as evidence to present to the Swiss authorities or opposition groups that he was presumably hoping to meet in Switzerland to show that he, Georg Elser, ex-nobody, was the lone bomber who had rid the world of Hitler. That he was a somebody now; that, after years of obscurity, he was a genuine hero.

At any rate, even before news of the bomb broke, the Konstanz Guards knew they had caught a suspicious character at the very least – a Communist, a liar, very possibly a terrorist. He was handed over to the tender mercies of the Gestapo.

The news of the bomb reached Hitler at Nuremberg, where his train was stopped and he was informed of the devastating attack by the local police chief. He rang Bavarian Gauleiter Adolf Wagner, who had taken charge of the investigation on the spot and demanded that the culprits be caught, and fast. Himmler was already on the case with his usual zeal. The entire surviving staff of the Bürgerbräukeller were arrested, and an enormous reward of 600,000 Reichsmarks was offered for the detention of those responsible. By the early hours of **9 November**, no fewer than 120 suspects – one of them Elser – were under arrest. Himmler fell in with his master's immediate assumption that the deadly English Secret Service were behind the bomb plot. The Nazi leaders, especially Hitler, Himmler and Heydrich, all had an exaggerated fear and respect for the wily machinations of SIS/MI6, and to an extent based their own covert operations on the supposed style of the British. (Heydrich even signed himself 'C' in green ink in imitation of his British counterpart.)

To Hitler and the SS overlord the beerhall bomb bore all the hallmarks of the treacherous foe, and they would spare no effort in finding links. As luck would have it, they had the ideal instruments immediately to hand. For some weeks one of Himmler's most trusted henchmen, the former lawyer Walther Schellenberg, had been holding talks in Holland with the chief of Britain's SIS station in the Netherlands, Major Richard Stevens, and Captain Sigismund Payne-Best, a long-time Dutch resident and veteran intelligence officer from the First World War. Payne-Best was the Dutch head of a secret section of MI6, the 'Z' section, which shadowed the 'official' secret service throughout Europe. Schellenberg had got in touch with the two British agents through a double-agent, Dr Fischer, who had claimed to represent a high-ranking clique of anti-Nazi German officers plotting to remove Hitler from power.

A series of meetings took place in the autumn of 1939 at which Schellenberg represented himself as one 'Captain Schaemmel', a liasion man for the anti-Hitler clique in the Wehrmacht. Schellenberg was, in fact, a major in the SS and Reinhard Heydrich's chief of counter-intelligence in the SS's security service, the Sicherheitdienst (SD). In London, Prime Minister Neville Chamberlain had been kept personally informed of these 'negotiations' and had authorised full British support for a military putsch against Hitler that would end the war and lead to a new British–German alliance against Stalin's Russia. It was a typical intelligence game of double bluff, in which Schellenberg was playing the long game, presumably hoping to extract evidence of Britain's wartime intentions and its post-war plans, while at the same time compromising Britain diplomatically, undermining its stated war aims and finding out as much as he could about the country's legendary intelligence services.

Following his narrow escape, Hitler, jumping to the conclusion that the long arm of Britain's secret service had been behind Elser's bomb, ordered that Schellenberg's game be brought to an abrupt and typically violent conclusion. At the next scheduled meeting – which had already been arranged for 9 November – the two Britons were to be seized, and, in blatant violation of the Netherlands' neutrality, abducted across the border and interrogated in depth and at the SD's leisure in Germany.

Another of Heydrich's most trusted men was placed in charge of the kidnap. But Alfred Naujocks was an altogether more thuggish character than the intellectual Schellenberg. He was the man who had been entrusted with the job of staging the 'Gleiwitz incident' – the mocked-up attack on a German radio station on the Polish–German frontier that had been one of Hitler's excuses for attacking Poland in August 1939, thus triggering the Second World War. In this coup, Naujocks had left the corpses of murdered concentration camp inmates, dressed in Polish uniforms, strewn outside the radio station in a flimsy effort to suggest that Poland had attacked Germany. Now, 'the man who started the war' was to be entrusted with staging another 'incident' on another border.

Alfred Naujocks: 'the man who started the Second World War'.

As soon as Stevens and Payne-Best, along with their Dutch military minder, Major Dirk Klop, arrived at the small town of Venlo, very close to the Dutch border with Germany, Naujocks's plan was activated. Two high-speed Mercedes limousines, filled with a dozen burly SS men, were driven through the frontier and, after a brief gun battle that ended with Major Klop being shot dead, the two startled Britons were seized and rushed back into Germany. The whole thing was over in a couple of minutes. Astonishingly, the inexperienced Stevens was found to be carrying – uncoded – a list of SIS's agents throughout Europe.

The 'intensive interrogations' that the pair were about to undergo were hardly necessary: Himmler and Heydrich already had a virtually complete picture of the structure of British Intelligence on the European continent. What they did not have – and never would possess – was indisputable evidence connecting British intelligence with Georg Elser and his bomb. Despite being subjected to the most gruesome tortures that the Gestapo could devise, including a beating personally administered

(Left) Café Backus on the Dutch–German Frontier near Venlo, where the SS team shot Major Klop dead and arrested Stevens and Payne-Best. (Right) Major Dirk Klop.

by Himmler himself, and despite successfully building a complete replica of the bomb that he had designed at his captors' invitation, Elser never furnished evidence of the grand conspiracy that Hitler insisted lay behind the attempt on his life. This was not because Elser did not want to – like any torture victim, he would have said or done anything to end his torment – but because he could not. No such evidence ever existed.

This did not, of course, prevent Goebbels's propaganda machine from going into overdrive in a frenzied denunciation of the hidden hand of British intelligence that, it trumpeted, lay behind the outrage at the Bürgerbräukeller. The convenient capture of the two SIS men at Venlo, and the death of Major Klop provided more grist to Goebbels's mill: not only had two top agents of MI6/SIS been caught red-handed at their nefarious tricks, but the presence of the ill-fated Major Klop at their side was evidence that the Dutch were hand-in-glove with the British and that the neutrality of the Netherlands was a sham. Thus was another excuse provided for the coming attack on the West.

Elser's bomb and the Venlo Incident, as the double abduction soon became known, had two long-term consequences, both equally malign, for the true conspirators in the Wehrmacht who, in contrast to Schellenberg's sham, really were determined to put an end to Hitler's regime. The first consequence was that it terminally prejudiced Whitehall – and Winston Churchill in particular – against holding any talks, secret or otherwise, with any Germans, no matter how anti-Nazi they were. This cordon sanitaire isolated the resistance and almost guaranteed its ultimate failure.

The first photographs released to the German press by the Gestapo, showing Georg Elser, Major R. H. Stevens and Captain S. Payne-Best. The linking of the three men implied that Stevens and Best had been involved in the Bürgerbräukeller attempt on Hitler's life.

The second malign consequence for the conspirators who wanted to eliminate him was that Hitler's security was dramatically tightened. The icily efficient Reinhard Heydrich decreed that the protection of the Führer's life came before all other tasks, and took it upon himself to install a raft of reforms making the assassin's job all but impossible: no one was allowed to carry a weapon in Hitler's presence; a new beefed-up security detail would be on hand at all times and would be authorised to carry out spot checks and searches even on the most high ranking of visitors. No mail, parcels or even innocuous bouquets of flowers would any longer be presented to Hitler personally, or would be handled by him until they had been thoroughly examined by white-gloved SS guards.

Hitler himself was inclined to credit the power he called Providence for his lucky escape. He claimed, with increasing conviction, that he had left the Bürgerbräukeller early, not for the prosaic reason that he had a train to catch, but because an inner voice had been urging him to get out of the building as fast as he could. The fact that he had obeyed the voice and had thus saved his own life he interpreted as confirmation that he was Germany's chosen man of destiny, divinely ordained to lead the Fatherland to undreamed-of heights of greatness. From now on all doubts were removed, all questions or cautions treated as akin to treason.

Guided and protected by Providence, Adolf Hitler prepared to lead Germany into the abyss.

# 7 The Devil's Luck
## Henning von Tresckow and the Army's Plots against Hitler

The outbreak of war in September 1939 and the swift success of Hitler's lightning campaign against Poland had left the conspirators somewhat deflated. One of the more determined among them, however, Baron General Kurt von Hammerstein-Equord, from an old Prussian aristocratic family, attempted to remove Hitler on the very day that war was declared on Germany by Britain – **3 September**. He hoped to lure Hitler to Cologne, headquarters of his Army Group A watching the Rhine in the west, on the pretence of inviting him to make an inspection tour, during the course of which Hammerstein planned to arrest him. Understandably, however, Hitler's eyes were firmly on Poland at that moment, and Hammerstein's invitation was declined.

Hitler was always unlikely to enjoy having Hammerstein as his host. The general had long been an outspoken opponent of Nazism – he referred to the party as 'a gang of criminals' and 'filthy pigs' – even before their seizure of power, when he had been one of the army's top commanders. He had gone so far as to extract an assurance from President Hindenburg that he would never appoint 'the Bohemian corporal', as the old soldier referred to the Nazi leader, as chancellor. When that promise was broken within days, Hammerstein had openly warned Hitler that he would be removed if he acted illegally. Instead, Hitler moved first, firing Hammerstein in January 1934 for his 'negative attitude' towards Nazism. Hammerstein had been reluctantly recalled to duty when war loomed, and, although he died of cancer in 1943 before the military conspiracy had reached its fulfilment, his two sons Kunrat and Ludwig took part; miraculously, they were among the few who managed to escape the Nazis' vengeance.

Colonel Henning von Tresckow (centre right) with officers including Ewald Heinrich Kleist-Schmenzin, Georg Schulze-Büttger, Fabian von Schlabrendorff (far right).

The winter of 1939/40 was the period of the 'phoney war', or the 'bore war', when Britain and France – at a loss now that their *casus belli*, Poland, had been comprehensively conquered – tinkered with half-hearted war plans and wondered what to do next. Conspiratorial activity among high-ranking Germans was near its nadir. Instead, diplomacy had its day. A young Foreign Office official, Adam von Trott zu Solz, Oxford educated and a keen Anglophile, sounded out opinion in the United States during a winter journey. At the same time, Josef Muller, a Bavarian Catholic lawyer, at the request of Oster visited the Vatican to gauge tentatively, through Britain's ambassador to the Holy See, the attitude of the British towards a putative change of regime. In the wake of the Venlo Incident his feeler was smartly rebuffed, as were all future approaches to London from the conspirators. Whitehall had had its fingers burned at Venlo and would not extend the hand of peace again.

In stark contrast to the feeble war effort of the Western Allies, and the depressive paralysis that was gripping the conspirators, Hitler was steaming ahead towards completing his military mastery of Europe. His plans to attack in the autumn having been repeatedly shelved, he spent the winter in building up the Wehrmacht's military machine. Bitterly frustrated by the inability of the opposition to break the spell that Hitler had seemingly cast over the German people, Hans Oster resolved, after

Adam von Trott zu Solz at his wedding to Clarita Tiefenbacher in the summer of 1940.

much inner anguish, to take his own opposition a devastating step further: into actual treason against his country.

This was a decisive watershed, and one that Oster felt he could only take alone. The military opposition to Hitler, he had learned by the bitter experience of its repeated failure in 1938/39, was fatally hamstrung by its own defects. The iron Prussian tradition of obedience to authority and a superior's orders was virtually bred into the bones of the would-be opposition. They therefore found the role of conspirators, whose whole *raison d'être* was deception, disobedience and defiance, impossible to fulfil. This inability to transform themselves into determined, successful plotters led to paralysis, lethargy, indifference – and ultimately to moral cowardice. Oster, however, decided to break the mould. He was well aware that he was committing treason, and that in revealing details of Hitler's future military plans – to which, as deputy head of the Abwehr he was now a party – he was in fact endangering the lives of his fellow German servicemen. Oster, however, had calculated that he was serving a greater good.

As a Christian, he had decided that the Nazis represented a conscious return to barbarism. Indeed, he had instructed the young Abwehr lawyer Hans von Dohnanyi to start compiling a file of evidence of Nazi atrocities in Poland for a future trial of war criminals. For this reason, he considered that doing all that he could to frustrate Hitler's plans would prevent a greater catastrophe for Germany. In preventing further Nazi conquests, not only would more lives ultimately be saved, but the ends of good would be served, rather than those of evil. On the very day that he communicated his first batch of military secrets to his close friend Colonel Bert Sas, the Dutch military attaché in Berlin, Oster, overcome with the intensity of the pressure he was feeling, blurted out to his driver: 'I have just committed high treason, and if I am discovered, I shall be hanged.' He added: 'It is far easier to take a pistol and kill someone; far easier to charge into a hail of machine-gun fire when you believe in the cause, than to do what I have done.'

Tragically, all Oster's risk taking was in vain. Like the boy who cried 'Wolf!' too often, when Sas repeatedly relayed his German friend's warnings that a German invasion of the neutral Netherlands was imminent to the Dutch High Command in The Hague, and when each date passed with no invasion forthcoming (the invasion was scheduled and then postponed a total of nearly thirty times between November and May), Sas's superiors lost what little faith they had in the reliability of his informant and merely filed his reports away.

Desperately, Oster upped the ante: he took another foreign diplomat representing a country threatened by Hitler's aggression into his confidence. This time the Norwegian ambassador was the recipient of his warnings. Once again, Oster was risking all for nothing. His warning that Hitler had decided to strike first at the Scandinavian nations of Denmark and Norway was ignored by the envoy as an obvious piece of German misinformation, and he did not even bother to forward the information to Oslo. Then, on **9 April 1940,** Hitler at last struck.

The simultaneous German invasion of Denmark and Norway – 'Fall Weserübung' (Operation Western Exercise) – was a textbook *Blitzkrieg* operation. In Denmark, it literally was all over by breakfast. For the loss of a couple of planes and an armoured car, an entire country was almost bloodlessly occupied. In Norway it was a different story. Although the combined naval and air invasion went off as planned, the Germans ran into fierce opposition, from the Norwegians themselves and belatedly from the British and French. Germany lost three cruisers and a number of smaller naval vessels, and British troops occupied the port of Narvik in the far north of the country, defending it against the 3rd Mountain division commanded by General Eduard Dietl. The result was a month-long slugging match that only ended when the British finally evacuated the port.

The fiasco of the Norway campaign caused a political crisis in Britain, resulting in the futile Chamberlain at last being dragged kicking and screaming out of 10 Downing Street, and the more determined and bellicose Winston Churchill succeeding to the premiership in his place. But, even as Churchill at last occupied the position he had coveted all his political life, the supreme crisis of Britain's war was beginning.

One month after the prelude of Fall Weserübung, on **10 May**, Hitler, based in his western forward headquarters – the Felsennest in the Eiffel hills close to the Belgian border – launched the main act: 'Fall Gelb' (Operation Yellow), his invasion of the Netherlands, Belgium, Luxembourg and France. The crucial component of the attack was the strike into France, *Sichelschnitt* (sickle cut), which had been devised by General Erich von Manstein, a taciturn, hook-nosed Prussian, and a tactical genius. Manstein envisaged, in contrast to the Schlieffen Plan – the great, wheeling movement to the south-west that had brought the Germans almost to the gates of Paris in 1914 – a reprise in reverse. His thrust, spearheaded by armour and parachutists, would move through the wooded Ardennes and aim west, bypassing the chain of French fixed fortifications, the Maginot Line, then slash north to trap the northern French armies and the British Expeditionary Force with their backs to the Channel ports of Boulogne, Calais and Dunkirk. Hitler liked the daring audacity of the scheme and approved it. Oster's contacts, typically, ignored it.

Surprise was almost total, and the advance went exactly – indeed, even better – than planned. The crooked-winged Stuka dive-bombers, with their screaming sirens, striking ahead of the advancing columns on the ground, hit Brussels, Lyons, Orleans and Strasbourg, their bombs terrifyingly tumbling from the sky. On **11 May** the key Belgian stronghold of Fort Eben Emael, believed to be impregnable, fell to an airborne glider surprise attack. On **12 May** General Kleist's 6th Panzer Division, with Claus von Stauffenberg serving on its staff and with the vanguard commanded by another young Swabian, Erwin Rommel, successfully cleared the Ardennes – an area lightly defended by the French as it was thought to be impassable to armour – and moved towards the River Meuse. On **13 May**, already fearing encirclement,

Erwin Rommel with Hitler on the occasion of his promotion to Field Marshal, Berlin, September 1942.

the French pulled back from Belgium, into which they had tentatively advanced, leaving their Dutch and Belgian allies naked and exposed. The same day the Germans reached the Meuse.

The surprise crossing of the Meuse, and the collapse of the French forces defending the river's western bank was the decisive moment of the campaign. A combination of artillery and low-level aircraft strikes cleared the way for German engineers to paddle across the river in dinghies on **14/15 May**, near Montherme. They secured a bridgehead and built a pontoon bridge for Heinz Guderian's armour to cross and fan out across the countryside. The same day the Dutch, depressed by a German air raid that had reduced the centre of the port of Rotterdam to ashes, surrendered. The French premier, Paul Reynaud, though slightly premature, was not wrong when he phoned Britain's new prime minister, Churchill, wearily on **16 May** to confess, in a broken and panicky voice: 'We are beaten . . . the war is lost.'

Once over the Meuse, reaching the next rivers was child's play. Though some isolated French units stood and fought, elsewhere mass panic and headlong retreat were the order of the day, as fleeing soldiers, discarding their weapons, joined the endless columns of refugees that already clogged the roads, pushing or dragging their belongings on prams and carts. Amid these chaotic scenes, Guderian's tanks advanced an extraordinary fifty-five miles to reach the River Oise on **17 May**, the same day that the Belgian capital, Brussels, fell to the Army Group of General Rundstedt, who had captured the great port of Antwerp the previous day.

On **18 May**, as the Germans reached the River Somme and its cargo of memories from the 'war to end wars' only two decades earlier, Stauffenberg found time to write to his wife from his command post on the Oise. The French army had collapsed, he said, its defeated and captured columns streaming east into German captivity, without guards, so low had its morale sunk. The victor lamented the fall of 'a great nation, not only militarily, but above all psychologically'. The British had yet to be seen, he wrote, but they would need to look sharp to guard their own lines of retreat via the Channel ports, for that was where the German advance was headed: the coast. Meanwhile, he himself was well and happy, and this being France, there was plenty of captured wine to drink. Indeed, a comrade on the campaign, Major Topf, gave a pen portrait of Stauffenberg at this time – giving orders in his usual relaxed yet multi-tasking style, one hand in his pocket, the other holding a wine glass.

On **19 May**, in the biggest mistake since the Trojans brought the wooden horse within the walls of their city, a desperate Premier Reynaud brought the aged Marshal Philippe Pétain into his government as vice-premier, while another First World War hero, Maxime Weygand, replaced Maurice Gamelin as French Commander-in-Chief. Pétain, old and gloomier even than he had been in the First World War, was a defeatist bent on hoarding French lives like the thrifty peasant he was. Weygand was little better. Both were vain, Anglophobe and prepared to make terms with the old German enemy. On **20 May**, as the cities of Amiens and Abbeville fell, the Germans reached the coast near St Valery, cutting the French army in two and threatening the encircled British Expeditionary Force with annihilation.

Over the course of the next week, as the desperate British defence of their perimeter around Dunkirk hardened, the twin Channel ports of Boulogne and Calais fell. On **24 May** Hitler acceded to Rundstedt's cautious plea for a 'pause' in the headlong advance to give the Panzers and their crews time to rest and regroup. Hitler had memories of the waterlogged Flanders plain from the First World War and was easily persuaded that the tanks might bog down. Although the advance was resumed after forty-eight hours, it gave the beleaguered British in Dunkirk a vital reprieve, and a breathing space in which to organise Operation Dynamo – the successful evacuation of most of the BEF, and much of the French army besides, from the port.

On **27 May**, the day that Belgium's King Leopold surrendered, Stauffenberg wrote his second letter home. After saying that England now faced a 'battle of annihilation', he reported that much to his chagrin he was being transferred away from the fighting front to the organisational branch of the General Staff, becoming, in his words 'a bureaucrat' rather than a frontline soldier. In fact, the posting was a recognition of his superb administrative skills – his ability at unravelling tangles and organising transport and supplies – which had again been amply demonstrated during the French campaign. As another mark of the high regard in which he was held, on **31 May** he was decorated with the Wehrmacht's highest honour – the Iron Cross, First Class.

After a despairing Reynaud resigned France's premiership during his government's pell-mell flight to the south-west, first to Tours and then to Bordeaux – power passed into the palsied hands of Pétain, who immediately sought an armistice. Paris itself fell without a fight on **14 June**, and on **21 June** in the nearby Forest of Compiègne, the French suffered the supreme humiliation of having to sign an armistice in the very same railway carriage where their Marshal Foch had dictated terms to a beaten Germany in November 1918. For Hitler, who attended the ceremony, revenge was very sweet.

Once again, however, a half-hearted military plot aimed at Hitler by officers on the staff of the newly promoted Field Marshal Erwin von Witzleben, Commander-in-Chief of Army Group D in the west, misfired in a pattern that was to become all too familiar over the next four years. Two officers on Witzleben's staff, Major Alexander von Voss and Captain Ulrich Schwerin von Schwanenfeld, volunteered to kill the Führer, if he could be lured to the field marshal's headquarters on a visit. This was to be accomplished either by tossing a grenade at him or having a sniper shoot him during the German victory parade along Paris's Champs-Elysées. However, the parade was repeatedly postponed and then, on the inauspicious date of **20 July**, definitively cancelled. Now and hereafter, Hitler would exhibit an uncanny tendency to appear to be aware of impending danger, and take steps to avoid it. Even so, however, it seems unlikely that the German army conspirators could have mustered the will to kill their victorious Führer at the very moment of his greatest triumph. For the conspirators, the fall of France represented *Null Stunde* – zero hour.

The first hint that Hitler was thinking, not as was almost universally expected, of the invasion and subjugation of England, but of an attack on his ostensible – if temporary – ally, Stalin's Russia, came as early as **21 July** when, fresh from humiliating France, he ordered the Army High Command, the OHL, to begin thinking about renewing operations in the east, possibly as early as that autumn. In August, this vague scheme had hardened into a definite operational plan – codenamed 'Otto' – for a two-pronged thrust aimed at Moscow and the Ukrainian capital Kiev. As the Luftwaffe joined battle with the RAF in the blue summer skies over south-east England in the struggle that became known as the Battle of Britain, the Führer's mind was on other fronts.

Hitler's obsessive drive to attack Russia was prompted by both ideological motives – his need to 'settle accounts' with Communism, and to extirpate 'Jewish' Marxism – and by Nazi racial doctrine. The Slavs, as their name implied, were an inferior stock, destined to serve the Teutonic *Herrenvolk* as a race of downtrodden serfs. According to Nazism's twisted theories, once the Bolshevik regime had been smashed and its leaders – along with the large Jewish population of Russia and eastern Europe – exterminated, the Russian masses would be turned into a race of deliberately uneducated peasant helots, serving their German masters peacefully on the farmsteads that would dot the endless Russian steppes.

When it finally dawned on Germany's military command what Hitler was planning, they were less than enthralled. The prospect of opening an entirely new campaign – and against an enemy as vast as Russia – leaving Britain and her empire still unsubdued in their rear, raised the unwelcome prospect of a reprise of the First World War when Germany had fought a long and ultimately fatal war on two fronts. The officers in charge of marshalling and husbanding Germany's resources grew fearful that their Fatherland was in danger of becoming fatally over-stretched.

Stauffenberg, from his new eyrie in the General Staff, which moved in rapid succession from Bad Godesberg on the Rhine to Chemay in Belgium, then to Fontainebleau outside Paris, was at first supremely confident that Germany could take on and beat any opponent it chose. He even found words of praise for Hitler as 'a son of war'.

It is striking that the anti-Hitler conspiracy always had a central figure directing, badgering and above all inspiring resistance when spirits were low and the prospects of success scant. What is equally noticeable is that this commanding figure changed. In the beginning, up to the outbreak of war, Hans Oster was the inspiring figure, the centre of the spider's web. At the end, the undisputed leader was Stauffenberg. But now, as the war entered its middle stage, the mantle passed from Oster to Colonel Henning von Tresckow, a balding, outspoken and courageous officer with twinkling, clear sardonic eyes. Like most of the other conspirators Tresckow came from a family steeped in Prussian military tradition. His record in the First World War was impressive: a teenage soldier, he won the Iron Cross – the first of three awards of the same medal – as a seventeen-year-old lieutenant. Tresckow married Erika von Falkenhayn, only daughter of Erich von Falkenhayn, the Kaiser's former war minister

Colonel Henning von Tresckow, the indefatigible conspirator.

and as Commander-in-Chief of Germany's armies the mastermind of the ultimately disastrous Verdun offensive.

Like several other future conspirators, Tresckow was initially dazzled by the Nazis as the radical but non-Communist force needed to invigorate Germany. Tresckow's clear eyes began to be opened to the true nature of the Nazi regime by the lawless atrocities of the Röhm purge in 1934. The Fritsch–Blomberg affair and Hitler's reckless gamble with war in the Czechoslovak crisis of 1938 shocked him deeply, and the seal was set on his disillusion by the activities of what he called the Nazi 'murder squads' let loose on the Polish population and the country's Jews in 1939. Tresckow did not baulk at the logic of where his hardening opposition was taking him. 'Hitler', he told friends, 'is a whirling Dervish. He must be shot down.'

Nonetheless, the rigid codes of the Prussian officer class died hard. Throughout 1940 Tresckow, to all outward appearances, remained the obedient, consummately professional soldier. He even ensured that Manstein's war-winning *Sichelschnitt* plan for the thrust into France reached Hitler's attention via his friendship with his old regimental comrade Rudolf Schmundt, now the permanent Wehrmacht adjutant at Hitler's headquarters, who made sure that Manstein's daring scheme was submitted to the Führer after other senior, more conventionally minded soldiers had sought to suppress it. Hitler instantly seized on the plan and ensured its implementation.

As a staff officer, Tresckow saw clearly the consequences of an attack on Russia; such a war could only end in defeat for the aggressor, 'as surely as the Amen in church'. He was even more disturbed by the series of secret directives issued by Hitler to his army commanders in the run-up to Operation Barbarossa, as the invasion of Russia had now been baptised with an extra third prong added to the attack, aimed at the northern city of Leningrad. Irritated by the complaints he had received from Wehrmacht officers about atrocities and massacres already committed in Poland, Hitler called a meeting of 250 senior commanders in his Berlin Chancellery on **30 March 1941** to explain to them his conception of the new type of warfare that the attack on Russia would entail.

It would, said the Führer, be a war of annihilation – not a civilised, gentlemanly game between soldiers as the war in the west had been (though that too had been marked by massacres of Allied prisoners and civilians by the SS), but a ruthless struggle to the death between two incompatible ideologies, and two competing races. In this savage warfare, he ranted, no quarter would be asked – or given. He concluded his two-and-a-half-hour address by issuing one of his most notorious orders: the so called 'Commissar Order', under which the Communist Party officials posted at the side of every senior Soviet commander would be liquidated if captured. Such men were criminals, he declared, and harshness towards them would be 'kindness to the future'. As Hitler left, the hall of the Chancellery was in stunned silence, but a hubbub of voices broke out once he was gone. No one in the room was in any doubt that what they were being ordered to do was mass murder and against all accepted laws of war. But equally, no one present was prepared to make more than a token protest. Henning von Tresckow was.

In **May 1941**, as the final touches were put to the plans for Barbarossa – Hitler had already annexed or occupied the Balkan countries of Romania, Bulgaria, Yugoslavia and finally Greece to guard the vital southern flank of the coming attack – instructions were issued that *Einsatzgruppen* execution squads, formed by Himmler's SS and special police auxiliaries, were to be given carte blanche to move behind the advancing armies carrying out 'ruthless and energetic action against Bolshevik agitators, guerrillas, saboteurs, and Jews, and the total elimination of all active or passive resistance'. For Tresckow, this was the final straw: his beloved Wehrmacht with its high traditions of honour was being befouled by the criminality of the Nazis and something would have to be done about it.

Fortuitously, in preparation for Barbarossa, Colonel Tresckow was given a promotion that would position him literally at the centre of the coming offensive, and thus ideally placed to convert his command into a nest of conspiracy. He was posted to Posen in Poland and given the job of operations chief, the senior staff officer in Army Group Centre, the central prong of Hitler's three-pronged attack on Russia, whose ultimate goal was the taking of Moscow itself. By happy coincidence, Army Group Centre was headed by Field Marshal Fedor von Bock – Tresckow's uncle. Bock was tall, thin, humourless, granite faced and able rather than brilliant. No Nazi, he was nonetheless possessed of the narrow view of the German soldier's role so typical of his caste, and while physically brave, entirely lacked his nephew's moral courage.

On **10 June**, the day that his headquarters received official written notification of the Commissar Order, Tresckow hastened to Bock's villa clutching a copy of the order, which he flourished at the officer accompanying him, a fellow critic of the Nazi order named Major Rudolf Christoph von Gersdorff. 'You realise what this means?' demanded an outraged Tresckow. 'This will still have an effect in hundreds of years,

Field Marshal Fedor
von Bock.

and it will not only be Hitler who is blamed, but rather you, me, your wife and my wife, your children and my children, that woman crossing the street, and that boy kicking a ball. Think about it.' Tresckow was right in predicting the guilt that would fall on generations of Germans who had no responsibility or hand in Hitler's crimes. But for now he and a few close comrades like Gersdorff were lone voices in the wilderness.

When Gersdorff showed the orders to his chief, Bock too expressed outrage. 'Horrible!' he agreed. But he declined Gersdorff's suggestion that he and his two fellow commanders, Rundstedt, head of Army Group South, and Leeb, chief of the northern group, should fly together to Hitler's headquarters and demand that the offending order be withdrawn. Instead he dispatched Gersdorff to the headquarters of the High Command, where he was told that though the Wehrmacht's supreme command shared Army Group Centre's distaste for the orders, Hitler was not to be denied. Brauchitsch refused point blank even to raise the subject any longer after a tirade during which the Führer had flung an inkwell at his Wehrmacht commander.

Gersdorff returned empty handed to report on the failure of his mission. Bock received the news philosophically. 'Let it be noted, gentlemen,' he told Tresckow and his other staff officers, 'that Field Marshal Bock protested.' That was to be the extent of Bock's participation in the resistance. His nephew, however, was made of sterner stuff. Tresckow began to gather around him as his staff officers like-minded men who would put the moral duty of ridding Germany of Hitler ahead of their

Major Rudolf Christoph von Gersdorff (above, right) with Henning von Tresckow. These photographs, from the collection of Gersdorff's daughter, have never been published before.

Major Fabian von
Schlabrendorff.

professional job as soldiers. Besides Gersdorff, these men included Fabian von Schlabrendorff, a young lawyer who had joined the army as a reserve lieutenant and became Tresckow's aide-de-camp (his wife was Tresckow's cousin); Count Carl-Hans Hardenberg; Berndt von Kleist, the scion of one of Prussia's most distinguished military dynasties; Count Heinrich Lehndorff; Lieutenant-Colonel Georg Schulze-Buttger; Lieutenant-Colonel Alexander von Voss, the man whom Witzleben had selected for the abortive assassination of Hitler in Paris a year before; Lieutenant Eberhard von Breitenbuch and the Catholic brothers Georg and Philipp von Boeslager. These men formed the kernel of the conspiracy that would repeatedly try to remove Hitler by killing him over the next three years.

It would not be easy. On **22 June 1941**, to the amazement of a watching world, Hitler launched his legions on a Russia that had remained in blithe denial about the attack despite repeated warnings from the Comintern's worldwide network of spies, including the German-based 'Red Orchestra', and even the evidence of their own border troops who heard and saw evidence of the massive military build-up. As the invasion force swept into the wide open spaces of Russia, Tresckow's headquarters followed the advancing armies into Belorussia, where they relocated at Borisov. Also following the Wehrmacht's advance came the sinister *Einsatzgruppen*, Himmler's merciless squads, who set about their gruesome task of exterminating Jews, Communists and any civilians who got in their way with fiendish efficiency. Seeing the *Einsatzgruppen* at work only hardened the resolve of Tresckow and his team to remove those responsible for such satanic actions.

Their first chance came in early August. After repeatedly – as was his habit – announcing and then suddenly cancelling his visit to Borisov, Hitler finally appeared on **4 August**. Tresckow's tentative plan was to provide a car for the Führer to drive the few miles between his airstrip and the headquarters and then arrest him. However, as so often before, luck, coupled with Hitler's uncanny sixth sense for danger and the stringent security system introduced by Heydrich after the beerhall bomb, contrived to foil the plan. Hitler flew in on schedule, but declined the offer of a staff car and instead travelled the short distance in a convoy of SS vehicles.

He hurried into a meeting with Bock and General Heinz Guderian, whose 2nd Panzer Group, along with the Waffen SS *Das Reich* division and Heer *Grossdeutschland* division, formed the spearhead of Army Group Centre. Hitler impatiently urged his generals to continue their drive towards Moscow. The initial phase of Barbarossa had been a triumph, in which huge numbers of Russian troops had been encircled and had surrendered. This proved, claimed Hitler, the accuracy of his prophecy that once the door to the Soviet Union had been 'kicked in', 'the whole rotten edifice will come crashing down.' He reminded them that he had been proved right on every previous occasion when they had advised caution, retrenchment or retreat: the occupation of the Rhineland; the annexation of Austria; the confrontation with Czechoslovakia; the invasion of Poland and the attack in the west. All had initially been opposed by his generals, and all had been triumphant successes. So, he forecast, it would be again in Russia. As Hitler swept out, Tresckow exchanged a few brief words with him: the Führer confided what his ultimate plan would be when Bock's armies reached the Russian capital. Moscow must not be captured, but surrounded, said the dictator. Any attempt by its population to escape would be beaten back by force. The city would then, he commanded, be flooded, turned into a gigantic lake and its surviving population, civilian and military, drowned. Tresckow was left feeling that he had talked with Satan himself, who had unveiled a picture of hell. His resolve to remove Hitler hardened anew.

After the initial euphoria of the midsummer when the German *Blitzkrieg* bore all before it and vast amounts of Russian soldiers and *matériel* – including two and a half million prisoners and eighteen thousand tanks – fell into Wehrmacht hands, the pace of the German advance slowed markedly as autumn neared. German plans were not helped by strategic confusion at the highest levels. As a direct result of his August visit to Army Group Centre, Hitler denuded Bock's victorious command of resources. Instead of concentrating on capturing Moscow, Hitler put the main weight of the offensive to the south, heading through the Ukraine towards the Don, Stalingrad and the vital Caucasian oilfields. He was also eyeing the north, where he was magnetically drawn towards Leningrad, birthplace of the Bolshevik Revolution, and the Baltic Sea. He ordered the transfer of Bock's 3rd Panzer Group to Army Group North, and the 2nd Panzer Group along with the 2nd Army to take Kiev in the south. Kiev fell on **19 September**. A highly disgruntled Bock was shorn of 80 per cent of his armour, and three infantry corps, plus many

(Top) General Heinz Guderian.

(Middle) General Erich Hoepner.

(Bottom) Ulrich von Hassell.

of his aircraft, forcing him to halt his advance and to go onto the defensive.

Taking advantage, the Russians counter-attacked on Bock's front, forcing Hitler to undo the orders he had just issued and doubling the confusion. On **1 October** Bock finally launched Operation Typhoon, the long-awaited offensive against Moscow. Progress at first was swift. The Panzers of Generals Guderian, Kluge, Hoepner and Hoth broke through Red Army lines and enveloped Soviet troops in a series of pockets, pushing almost one hundred miles towards the Soviet capital. But a week later, ominously, the first snows of the winter fell. Snow alternated with lashing rain, turning unpaved roads into rivers of mud, and slowing the advance to four or five miles a day. Goaded beyond endurance by what he called Hitler's 'bloody amateurism', Brauchitsch suffered a heart attack and effectively gave up the fight to resist the Führer's interference, setting a fatal precedent for his successors, who allowed free rein to the Nazi dictator's fantasies that he was a military genius – with disastrous results.

Meanwhile, Tresckow kept in touch with the conspirators in Germany via Fabian von Schlabrendorff, who made frequent trips to brief Beck, Oster, Goerdeler and two diplomats, Ernst von Weizsäcker and Ulrich von Hassell. Weizsäcker and Hassell already saw that the military campaign in the east, contrary to current appearances, could only end in catastrophe and were exploring the possibility of a compromise peace through unofficial secret contact with Allied diplomats. Tresckow himself was near despair, prophetically lamenting: 'I wish I could show the German people a film called "Germany at the End of the War". Perhaps then they would realise, with horror, what we're heading for.'

What Hitler thought he was heading for was Moscow. But – for the first time in his spectacular career – the prize was to be denied him. On **30 October 1941**, with thousands of his vehicles stuck fast in mud and slush, and with the Luftwaffe blind and grounded by the appalling weather, Bock halted his offensive still some seventy miles shy of his goal. His plan was to wait for temperatures to plummet and for the ground to freeze hard so that the tracks of his armour could find some purchase. The weather obliged, and on **15 November** Bock resumed the offensive.

The sub-zero temperatures brought their own problems: the lubricants in tanks and mobile guns froze and 30 per cent of Bock's vehicles were immobilised. The Russian winter, which had ended the ambitions of so many invading armies over the centuries, was sharpening its teeth to devour a new prey. Amidst dreadful conditions, Bock's forward units managed to push into Moscow's outermost suburbs, six miles from the capital's centre. But the Russians held firm, refusing to evacuate the city and employing the human resources of the vast totalitarian state – civilian and military, women as well as men – to dig tank traps, trenches and erect barriers of rubble. This was the closest that the Wehrmacht would ever get to the enemy capital.

On **5 December**, the Russian General Zhukov, eventual conqueror of Berlin, struck back at Bock. Using soldiers transferred from Siberia who emerged like ghosts through the snow in their white, well-padded uniforms, the Red Army relentlessly pushed the Germans back. Hitler, in the first of countless similar decrees, ordered that no ground must be given up and every man must die where he stood. Thousands of them did, but their lives were spent in vain. The tide had turned and, despite many setbacks, fortune, however wanly at first, began to smile on the Allies and frown on the Nazis. Two days later, on **7 December**, the day that President Roosevelt declared would live in infamy, the Japanese made their devastating strike on the US fleet at Pearl Harbor; when Hitler, unprovoked, declared war on Washington in support of his Axis ally, the die was well and truly cast.

With the teeth of the ravenous Russian winter biting through their skimpy summer uniforms, the Wehrmacht's soldiers were already feeling their Führer's folly and their High Command's overweening arrogant lack of foresight in failing to provide them with adequate seasonal clothing. On **19 December** Hitler, furious at being thwarted, sacked Brauchitsch for the failure to take Moscow and also acceded to Bock's request to be relieved of his command. With this double dismissal of two scapegoats, the Führer assumed personal command of the Wehrmacht. For the conspirators, the enemy now stood in plain view.

* * *

The anti-Hitler plotters would have a further year of frustration in 1942. They acted with the increasing realisation that even if their plans to eliminate Hitler bore fruit, it would probably not be possible to reach an acceptable accord with the Allies. With the massive might of the United States and the Soviet Union thrown into the scales on the Allied side, there could be only one outcome to the war, however long it was delayed. Once the Allies agreed in Washington on **1 January 1942** not to make a separate peace with Germany, a precursor to their demand that Germany should surrender unconditionally, then the kind of peace that most of the more conservative and nationalist-minded conspirators wanted – one that would leave German borders intact and might even retain some of Hitler's pre-war gains – became increasingly hard to imagine. More and more the impetus to remove the Nazis would spring not from the hope of achieving salvation for Germany, but from the sheer moral necessity to revolt, however hopelessly, against an immoral, un-Christian and progressively more barbaric tyranny.

These were the motives that impelled Claus von Stauffenberg into the ranks of the resistance. Although he arrived relatively late in the day despite his distaste for the regime's policies, he compensated for being a latecomer by bringing to the task his enormous energy, organisational skill and an unrivalled driving will to action. Stauffenberg's position before 1942, as he had told his brother Berthold – who was in touch with Helmuth von Moltke's Kreisau Circle – back in September, was that the war must be won before the military returned to deal with the Nazis, or the 'Brown plague', as he dubbed the movement. Now it began to dawn on him that a successful or even a compromise conclusion to the war could not be hoped for. That January he had a conversation with Lieutenant Julius Speer, who expressed astonishment at seeing a large portrait of Hitler behind Stauffenberg's desk. 'It is so that visitors can see how mad he is,' replied the young major in his usual teasing style, before adding: 'There is only one solution. It is to kill him.'

Bock's replacement at the head of Army Group Centre was Günther 'Hans' von Kluge, one of his own army commanders. Known as 'Clever [Kluge] Hans' in a punning tribute to his name and technical brilliance, Kluge was woefully short on moral courage, and tended to agree with the last person who spoke with him. Tresckow tried to make sure that this last person was always him. Schlabrendorff teasingly dubbed Tresckow 'the watchmaker' because Kluge had to be wound up each day until his resolution had reached the pitch that Tresckow had inculcated in him the night before. Among Tresckow's minor achievements was to persuade his chief to receive Carl Goerdeler at his headquarters. Indiscreet as ever, the leading civilian conspirator chattily confided his ambitious plans to overthrow the regime to the field marshal, which thoroughly scared Kluge off. Like so many top commanders, he retreated behind the oath of loyalty he had sworn to Hitler as an excuse for failing to move against him.

One of Tresckow's most trusted lieutenants, Major Rudolf Christoph von Gersdorff, was tasked with assembling and testing the explosives that Trescow had settled on as the best way of disposing of the Führer. Gersdorff, who had access to the material as an explosives officer, eventually assembled a collection of dozens of different combustibles, along with the timer fuses that would set the bombs off. After testing the explosives along the banks of the River Dnieper, Tresckow and Schlabrendorff selected an extremely adaptable British-made plastic explosive of the type that had been dropped all over Europe by the RAF to equip the burgeoning resistance movements in countries occupied by the Nazis. The conspirators decided that the explosive was ideal for their purpose; it was extremely powerful, yet easy to conceal since its fuse functioned silently without a telltale hiss. With the consistency of tough plasticine, a bomb the size of a book could rip a room apart, killing everyone in it. Odourless and relatively light, it could be easily concealed in any convenient receptacle such as a bottle, or a briefcase.

The timer fuse, too, was deadly in its simplicity. It consisted of a wire that held down the firing pin of the detonator. When squeezed, a small phial of acid broke and silently ate away at the wire, which, depending on its thickness, could be timed for five to ten minutes, half an hour, or two hours. When the time was up, the wire dissolved, the firing pin was released, the detonator was struck and the bomb exploded. The only problem revealed by the tests was that extreme cold – such as the temperatures experienced in a Russian winter – tended to slow down the corrosive action of the acid and thus delay the explosion.

The next problem was the extremely practical one of how to bring together Hitler and the explosive that would kill him. Then, on **27 May 1942**, this problem suddenly became much harder. In Prague, a car carrying the dreaded Reinhard Heydrich to the airport en route to a meeting with Hitler was ambushed by a pair of British-trained Czechoslovak agents, Kubiš and Gabčik. Ironically, the SD overlord, who had been carrying out his extra task of running the rump Czech state with his customary ruthless efficiency, was arrogantly careless when it came to looking after himself, despite having tightened the security cordon around Hitler. Apart from his driver, Klein, Heydrich was alone in an open-topped car and completely unescorted. As the car slowed to take a hairpin bend, the attackers struck. One attempted to fire the simple but notoriously unreliable British-made Sten sub-machine gun, and when that jammed – as it was wont to do – his companion hurled a powerful grenade. The bomb bounced off the car, but exploded next to its rear wheel, spraying Heydrich with tiny fragments, including dirty horsehair from the car seat. These lodged deep inside his spleen, sparking off fatal septicaemia. Mourned by very few, Heydrich died on **4 June**.

Though publicly praising and honouring Heydrich as 'the man with the iron heart' and the ideal Nazi at a lavish funeral in Berlin, privately Hitler was enraged by the stupid carelessness that he saw as being directly responsible for Heydrich's assassination. Not only did the Nazis unleash a torrent of bloody vengeance, which cost the lives of hundreds of innocent Czechs, but Hitler's paranoia and fears for his own life became more acute. Never, he vowed, would he let Heydrich's fate overtake him.

\* \* \*

Reinhard Heydrich:
'the man with the
iron heart'.

At the same time as Heydrich's richly merited death, Stauffenberg learned the full truth of what was happening behind the lines on the Eastern Front. A Foreign Office diplomat involved in administering the parts of Russia occupied by the Wehrmacht, Hans von Bittenfeld, informed him that the rounding-up and mass murder of Jews was now official policy. (Heydrich himself had chaired the infamous Wannsee Conference in January that had given the green light for the implementation of the 'final solution'.) Upon hearing from Bittenfeld how SS men had rounded up the Jewish population of a Ukrainian town, made them dig their own graves in a field and then shot them, Stauffenberg remarked that Hitler must be removed, and it was the duty of the senior commanders to act against him.

He repeated the remark to several different acquaintances that summer, and when as a loyal Catholic he began to quote the medieval theologian St Thomas Aquinas's justification for tyrannicide, it became plain that his clear-sighted mind was turning towards the necessity of removing the 'dirty criminal' physically. Alongside his Catholic faith, Stauffenberg was given to quoting one of his spiritual mentor Stefan George's poems, 'The Antichrist', with reference to Hitler:

> The High Priest of Vermin extends his domain;
> No pleasure eludes him, no treasure or gain.
> And down with the dregs of rebellion!
>
> You cheer, mesmerised by demonic sheen,
> Exhaust what remains of the honey of dawn,
> And only then sense the debacle.
>
> You then stretch your tongues to the now arid trough
> Mill witless as kine through a pasture aflame
> While fearfully brazens the trumpet.

It was becoming clear to him that in the absence of the willingness of his superiors to strike, the task of removing 'the High Priest of Vermin' might fall upon him, Claus von Stauffenberg.

Militarily, the focus of fighting on the Eastern Front that summer had shifted to the south where Hitler, thirsty for the oil of the Caucasus to fuel an army that now stretched from the Arctic Circle to the North African desert, and from the River Don to the Atlantic, ordered his Army Group South under Field Marshal List to take the Baku oilfields.

On **1 September** 1942 the spearhead of the advance, Paulus's 6th Army, entered the city of Stalingrad on the Don. Stauffenberg, who had visited Paulus earlier that year, was only one of many officers fearful that Hitler had over-extended his army's reach, laying it open to a Soviet counter-attack. In addition, Stauffenberg had seen for himself the anarchic disorder that the Führer's obsessive interference and micro-management had injected into the army's orderly command structures, reducing a once well-oiled machine to chaos.

Another element in Stauffenberg's discontent was Hitler's stubborn refusal, based on Nazi racial ideology, to enlist the subject peoples of the Soviet Union to fight on Germany's side. Stauffenberg, like many officers, was painfully aware that Germany's finite resources were already strained to the limit and that they needed all the material and manpower help that they could get. When the Wehrmacht first burst into the Soviet Union they were surprised – and delighted – to find themselves widely greeted as liberators from Stalin's arbitrary and brutal rule, which, especially to the downtrodden inhabitants of the Ukraine, is how they must have appeared. If, at that point, the Ukrainians and the thousands of Russian soldiers who surrendered without a fight had been put into German uniforms, given guns, turned eastwards and told to boot out the Bolsheviks, the eventual outcome of the war might have been very different. To the bewildered fury of Stauffenberg, one of whose many duties was to investigate the possibility of raising and equipping just such volunteer units, Hitler appeared not just indifferent, but positively hostile to the whole idea. To him all Slavs were *untermenschen* worthy only to be treated as dirt. It did not take long for the initial enthusiasm of Stalin's subjects for their new German masters to dissolve into bitter resentment and finally raging fury. The same emotion was beginning to rise in Stauffenberg's own breast.

On **24 September** Hitler's clashes with his commanders came to a head, and wise old Halder, his Chief of Staff, was sacked for issuing one too many warnings that disaster was waiting on the Eastern Front. At a meeting of staff officers held the following day Stauffenberg, unable to contain his anger, sprang to his feet shouting, 'Hitler is responsible. No fundamental change is possible until he is removed. I am ready to do it!' A Rubicon had been crossed.

Another link in the closely connected but far-flung chain of conspiracy that was steadily being forged within the army was fixed when General Friedrich Olbricht was appointed technical chief of the Reserve Army

Stauffenberg with Mertz von Quirnheim at the 'Werwolf' headquarters in Vinnitsa, Ukraine, summer of 1942.

based in the Bendlerstrasse in Berlin. Olbricht, a quietly efficient, mild-mannered, bespectacled officer, was a long-standing opponent of the regime who had never been seduced by Hitler's promises, even in the Nazis' glory days. Now he was a dedicated opponent, who had concluded as early as 1940 that Hitler would have to be removed by force, and who, quietly but smoothly, started planning for the putsch that would supplant the Nazi Party. Lacking Stauffenberg's glamorous charisma, Olbricht effectively became the conspiracy's backroom boy and Chief of Staff.

The spreading discontent with Hitler's inept conduct of the war, and the Wehrmacht's growing disgust with the crimes committed behind the lines, was not confined to the tight group around Tresckow at Army Group Centre and Olbricht's Reserve Army staff in Berlin. As **1943** opened, with Paulus's 6th Army facing encirclement in the ruins of Stalingrad, General Hubert Lanz, the tough-minded commander of a special force of troops trained for mountain warfare, was operating in the Ukraine and had been ordered by Hitler to hold the city of Kharkov at all costs against the advancing Red Army. The odds against Lanz were formidable. He had just three divisions against three complete

General Friedrich Olbricht (centre), chief of the Army General Office in Berlin's Army High Command.

Soviet armies. Lanz's Chief of Staff – who would later perform the same function under Rommel in Normandy – was a bespectacled Swabian and a sworn anti-Nazi, Major-General Hans Speidel. Speidel slyly pointed out to Lanz that obeying Hitler's orders was impossible and tantamount to suicide. Because the troops that the Führer was preparing to sacrifice included the men of the elite Heer *Grossdeutschland* Panzer division, Speidel appealed to Lanz's judgement as a soldier: where was the sense in treating such troops as expendable cannon fodder? Speidel, aided and abetted by one of Lanz's corps commanders, the delicately named Colonel Hyazinth von Strachwitz, worked on their chief and eventually prevailed on him to act.

The plan they conceived called for Hitler to be arrested during a visit he was due to make to the headquarters of Army Group B at

Major-General Hans Speidel (left) with Rommel.

Poltava. Strachwitz guaranteed that his men would overpower Hitler's security detail – even hardened Waffen SS troops as they were – if they resisted the arrest. But the plan was unwittingly scuppered by Lanz when he disobeyed Hitler's direct order and abandoned Kharkov to its fate on **15 February 1943**. A furious Führer, enraged that his orders had been disregarded, cancelled his visit to Lanz and flew instead to the headquarters of the general's superior, Field Marshal Manstein at Zaporozhye, to demand that the insubordinate subordinate should be summarily sacked. Lanz was relieved of his command and assigned to the Balkans where, ironically, he ordered a massacre of civilians on the Greek island of Cephalonia.

Tresckow was himself furious that a golden opportunity to do away with the dictator had been passed up. Angrily he upbraided the conspirators for not having had the courage to act: 'We have been waiting for this chance for months!' he raged. 'Waiting for it; longing for the day when we can kill this scoundrel who is destroying our Germany! The day never comes! Each time, it's no use! Each time, something goes wrong! And you here in Zaporozhye who see things the way we do, you let the opportunity slip!'

Tresckow was himself determined not to make the same mistake. With an increasingly paranoid Hitler proving ever more reluctant to visit the Eastern Front, he evolved a two-phase plan for both the assassination and the subsequent putsch to seize the state from the Nazis.

In the Bendlerstrasse Olbricht was quietly fitting the pieces of the putsch together. He had assigned to Colonel Fritz Jäger the crucial job of seizing the key strongpoints in Berlin itself with two armoured units. Colonel Alexander von Pfuhlstein was tasked with neutralising the Nazi Party's military and paramilitary cadres – the SS and the SA – who would undoubtedly oppose the coup. Two other officers, Captain Ludwig Gehre and Friedrich Wilhelm Heinz, whom we last encountered preparing to storm the Reichs Chancellery during Oster's abortive 1938 conspiracy, were assigned the ticklish job of dealing with – in other words, killing – those Nazi leaders in the capital who would organise resistance to the putsch.

Another figure from 1938, Hans Bernd Gisevius, was also in the Bendlerblock, assisting Olbricht. It was agreed that the titular leaders of a post-putsch regime would be Carl Goerdeler as chancellor, with the retired general, Ludwig Beck, as war minister and Field Marshal Witzleben, who had been eased out of active service after a painful operation for piles, to be the conspirators' army Commander-in-Chief.

But all these ambitious schemes depended on one awkward but necessary pre-condition: killing Hitler.

Tresckow's plans for accomplishing this were now well advanced technically. His explosives had been tested and re-tested and found to work perfectly dozens of times, and now he only awaited the brief window of opportunity that would be provided if Hitler decided to visit the Eastern Front. At last, on **13 March**, he did so. Tresckow and Schlabrendorff had thought of what seemed to them a perfect plan for killing the Führer. Tresckow had suggested moulding the British-made plastic explosive into a cleverly designed parcel that when wrapped would resemble the distinctive square-shaped bottles of the brandy liquor Cointreau. Schlabrendorff prepared the bomb so that the fuse could be activated from outside without unwrapping it, then, on the eve of Hitler's arrival, he locked the deadly parcel safely away in his room.

On the morning of **13 March**, Kluge, accompanied by Tresckow, drove to Smolensk airport to meet the Führer's flight. To Tresckow's dismay, Hitler's large entourage – including an SS security detail as well as his personal physician, the pill-prescribing quack Dr Theo Morell, and his vegetarian cook – arrived in two identical aircraft, putting the first spanner in the spokes of their plan to smuggle the bomb aboard the dictator's plane: what if they put it on the wrong one? Tresckow and Schlabrendorff briefly considered bombing Hitler's conference with Kluge and the other generals – as Stauffenberg would do in July 1944. But they rejected the plan on the grounds that too many of those needed in a post-Hitler Germany would also die. Similarly, they rejected any idea of bombing Hitler while he was consuming lunch: too many other diners, including their friends and comrades, would perish with him.

Schlabrendorff watched in horrified fascination as Hitler wolfed his lunch. He found it:

> . . . a most revolting spectacle. His left hand was placed firmly on his thigh; with his right hand he shoved his food, which consisted of various vegetables, into his mouth. He did this without lifting his right arm, which he kept flat on the table throughout the entire meal; instead he brought his mouth down to his food. He also drank a number of non-alcoholic beverages which had been lined up beside his plate.

During the meal Tresckow approached Colonel Heinz Brandt, one of Hitler's aides, and casually requested a favour. He asked him to carry a

Hitler at Army Group Centre in Smolensk on 13 March 1943. Hans Günther von Smart introduces Hitler to (from left to right) Hans Georg Reinhardt, Walter Model, Gotthard Heinrici, Walther Weiss and Hans Krebs.

small present, two bottles of brandy, as a gift to General Helmut Stieff – an officer attached to the General Staff at Hitler's headquarters at Rastenburg who was disliked by Hitler, who called him 'the poison dwarf' on account of his dimunitive stature. Tresckow added by way of explanation that the gift was a forfeit for a wager he had lost against Stieff.

Schlabrendorff had already put preliminary preparations for the putsch in Berlin in motion by phoning Captain Gehre in Berlin, giving him the codeword 'Flash'. This meant that Hitler was about to be assassinated and that the plotters in the capital should get ready to launch the seizure of power in the city.

After lunch, Schlabrendorff fetched the parcel bomb from his quarters and drove to the airport in the same convoy as Hitler, Kluge and Tresckow. As Hitler took his farewells, Schlabrendorff looked hard at Tresckow and received an imperceptible but unmistakable glance in return: he should go ahead and plant the bomb.

Using a key, Schlabrendorff pressed down hard on the parcel bomb to activate the fuse – in half an hour the deadly device would explode, blowing Hitler's aircraft and all aboard it into fragments somewhere above Belorussia. Schlabrendorff handed the bomb to Brandt, who climbed into the plane Hitler had already boarded. Escorted by fighters, the two planes carrying Hitler and his entourage took off and flew north-west towards East Prussia and Rastenburg. Schlabrendorff and Tresckow watched them go, fervently hoping and believing that they would never reach their destination.

Tresckow and Schlabrendorff drove back to their headquarters and Schlabrendorff again phoned Captain Gehre in Berlin, giving him the second codeword signalling that the assassination attempt had actually been triggered. Despite all Hitler's security precautions – which included special fixtures dividing his plane into separate cabins, with Hitler's compartment being fitted with armoured plates and even a personal parachute for the Führer tucked under his seat – the two conspirators were certain that the high-powered explosive would rip Hitler's aircraft apart, plunging him to a fiery end over the city of Minsk. They sat, in a state of mounting tension, next to a telephone as the minutes ticked agonisingly by. Then, after two hours came the disastrous news: Hitler's plane had landed safely (at the same airstrip at Rastenburg destined to be used by Stauffenberg before and after his assassination attempt on 20 July 1944). Hitler was alive and for some inexplicable reason the bomb had not gone off.

The two conspirators looked at each other with horror. Not only had the assassination miscarried but fatal evidence – in the square shape of their bomb – was now in the possession of Colonel Brandt, and might explode or be opened at any time – exposing their plot and laying them open to the Nazis' terrible vengeance. Schlabrendorff's first priority was to call Gehre in Berlin and get him to stand down the putsch plans. Next, after a hasty and anxious review of their options, Tresckow called Brandt at Rastenburg on some spurious pretext. During their conversation, Tresckow casually asked Brandt whether he had already given the Cointreau bottles to General Stieff. Brandt answered that he had not yet had a chance to do so. In that case, said Tresckow, he should hang on to the parcel – there had been a mix-up and the wrong package had been handed over. Schlabrendorff would be flying to Rastenburg the very next day and would bring with him the correct gift of Cointreau.

Sure enough, Schlabrendorff flew to Rastenburg on **14 March**, carrying with him a seemingly identical package to the deadly parcel he had handed to Brandt the day before. This time, however, the parcel contained two genuine bottles of Cointreau. (Their easy availability makes it clear just how well General Staff officers lived behind the lines on the Eastern Front; and the liquor's French origins gives a glimpse into how thoroughly the German army had plundered conquered France.) As he handed the parcel over to the hapless Brandt, Schlabrendorff experienced another moment of sickening fear: Hitler's aide, naturally unaware of the parcel's deadly contents, playfully pretended to snatch the package back as he handed it over. Maintaining an outward calm that he was far from feeling inwardly, Schlabrendorff took the bomb to the nearby railway junction of Korschen and boarded a train for Berlin.

Once inside the train, Schlabrendorff locked himself into his reserved compartment and began, with extreme care and raw fear, to slit open the deadly parcel with a razor blade. Gingerly removing the wrapping paper, he slowly eased out the fuse and inspected it carefully. Everything appeared to have worked as expected: the phial had been broken, the acid had eaten through the wire holding down the firing pin, the pin had been released – but the detonator had not gone off. Schlabrendorff concluded that the explosive was a 'dud' that had somehow slipped past the British inspector of explosives. Just as likely, however, given the fact that the explosive was known to malfunction in extremely low temperatures, is that the compartment of Hitler's planes that Brandt had been travelling in at high altitude had been too cold for the explosive to detonate.

Whatever the cause, Hitler had again enjoyed his customary devil's luck, and the conspirators were back to square one.

Downcast though Tresckow and Schlabrendorff were by the inexplicable failure of their carefully prepared attempt, fate was about to present them with another golden opportunity to eliminate Hitler. Tresckow was informed that the dictator had decided to attend the annual Heroes Memorial Day ceremony in Berlin on **21 March** – the anniversary of the opening of Ludendorff's great series of spring offensives on the Western Front in 1918 – and make a short address. He then proposed to visit an exhibition of captured Soviet weaponry and equipment in an adjoining hall of the glass-topped Zeughaus on Berlin's main boulevard: the tree-lined Unter den Linden. The reason that Tresckow was made privy to this highly restricted secret information – Hitler's staff, on pain of death, were sworn to silence on his future movements – was that most of the kit on display had been captured by Kluge's Army Group Centre, and the exhibition had indeed been mounted by the group's intelligence department. Hitler therefore issued a personal invitation for Kluge himself to attend the show.

Tresckow instantly grasped the opportunity that this presented to recoup the disaster of the abortive 'Cointreau' bomb. Hastily, he summoned Rudolf Christoph von Gersdorff. As one of the organisers of the exhibition, Gersdorff had a perfect excuse to attend the Führer's function and, in Tresckow's estimation, had the cool nerves and iron convictions necessary to carry out what would – although he did not spell this out specifically to his young colleague – in effect, be a suicide bombing; the world's first experience of this now grimly familiar phenomenon. He put the matter plainly enough to Gersdorff as they walked the banks of the great Dnieper river. 'Isn't it terrible?' he asked rhetorically. 'Here we are, two officers of the German General Staff, discussing how best to murder our Commander-in-Chief.'

But the deed, said Tresckow, had to be done: 'This is our only chance. Hitler must be cut down like a rabid dog.' Would Gersdorff, he asked, be prepared to do the job? The would-be assassin hesitated only briefly before accepting the novel assignment. Hastily, the preparations were made for the ad hoc attempt. Having secured permission from a reluctant and suspicious Brigadier-General Rudolf Schmundt for Gersdorff to show Hitler round the exhibition, Tresckow gave his young friend his orders. Gersdorff would fly to Berlin the next day, quickly reconnoitre the Zeughaus – appropriately Berlin's old armoury – and decide on the best method of planting the bomb. If he could sneak it past the dictator's increasingly stringent and watchful SS security men, then well and good; if not . . .

Once again, Schlabrendorff would be the bomb carrier. He would arrive in Berlin by train the next evening, carrying with him the same explosive that he had retrieved from Colonel Brandt with such difficulty and hand it to Gersdorff, who would fit the bomb with the only timer wire available – one that gave only ten minutes before detonating. Meanwhile, Tresckow used his powerful persuasive arts to prevail on Kluge not to attend the Zeughaus ceremony. Tresckow had developed a grudging affection for his weak-willed chief, and did not wish to see him lose his life alongside his Führer.

Gersdorff's discreet reconnaissance of the Zeughaus was not encouraging. Security was already in place at the old hall, and there was absolutely no chance, as he had desperately hoped, of planting the bomb – Georg Elser-style – beneath the platform from which Hitler would make his address. The pfennig at last dropped. If the dictator was to die, there was only one way of accomplishing it: Gersdorff himself would have to get close enough to Hitler to trigger his bomb and blow himself up along with the Führer. He would have to sacrifice his own life to rid humanity of this scourge.

Understandably, Gersdorff spent a sleepless night. Bleary-eyed but wide-awake, he entered the Zeughaus and watched while most of the Nazi leaders filed in with Hitler to the strains of the gloom-laden first movement of the Seventh Symphony of Hitler's favourite composer, his fellow Austrian Anton Bruckner. Goering, ludicrously resplendent in one of his gaudy uniforms, snow-white, set off by red leather jackboots and make-up; the sinister figure of Himmler in his contrasting black SS uniform; Keitel, Hitler's lickspittle army Chief of Staff; and Karl Dönitz, the lupine Nazi loyalist who had succeeded Raeder as head of the navy and would, one day, succeed Hitler himself. If his bomb went off, Gersdorff realised, the whole Nazi leadership would be wiped out along with their boss.

At 1 p.m., an hour later than scheduled, the ceremony began. Hitler mounted the dais and delivered a speech appropriate to the solemn occasion: mourning and honouring the dead, yet spitting defiance at his many enemies. As the room erupted in the obligatory applause Gersdorff, his uniform pocket heavy with explosive, manoeuvred himself close to the Führer's party ready to assume his role of guide around the exhibition. Expecting the visit to last a good hour, he anticipated that he would have plenty of time for the bomb to explode, decapitating the Nazi warlords who were leading Germany into the abyss. Gersdorff surreptitiously reached into his jacket pocket and activated the fuse. Hitler now had ten minutes left to live.

Gersdorff greeted his Führer with suitable, heel-clicking respect and began the tour. He attempted to interest Hitler in the various exhibits, explaining their function and the circumstance of their capture, but realised at once that the Führer was not listening. Seemingly distracted and lost in his own thoughts, Hitler raced past the exhibits in record time. Desperately, conscious of the acid eating through the fuse in his pocket, Gersdorff started a lengthy explanation of one particular item: an eagle standard of Napoleon's Grande Armée recovered from the bottom of the River Berezina at Borisov when Army Group Centre had had its headquarters there. It was, perhaps, not the most tactful of icons to show Hitler, who could not help being reminded of the fatal hubris of his predecessor – the last warlord to dare to invade Russia's vast hinterland – but even this did not detain the dictator. With barely a glance, he 'ran' (as Gersdorff recalled later) out of a convenient side door onto the Unter den Linden, and vanished with his entourage. The exhibition tour that had been supposed to last for thirty minutes had in fact taken only two.

Gersdorff was left bereft. There was only one thing to do. Hastily he adjourned to the nearest toilet and ripped the deadly fuse out of the bomb. Then, doubtless shaking with nervous strain, he adjourned to a nearby club to restore his composure with a stiff drink. He could not understand Hitler's bizarre behaviour. It was almost as if he had experienced a sixth sense warning of the danger threatening him. Ironically, having hurried out of the exhibition so precipitously, he spied a Russian tank outside, climbed on board and spent several minutes examining it. By that time, though, Gersdorff's official duties were over. At his club, he ran into an old acquaintance who remarked that he 'could have killed Adolf today'. The man bragged that he had seen Hitler in his open car driving in slow solemnity down the Unter den Linden towards the Zeughaus. It would have been the work of a moment, the braggart boasted, to have lobbed a grenade across the pavement and into the car, like the bomb that had done for Heydrich. Hastily, without divulging his own hair-raising experience, Gersdorff agreed that it was indeed an opportunity lost.

# 8 Enter Stauffenberg
## The Head, Heart and Hand of the Conspiracy

It was the utter disaster that had overtaken the German Sixth Army at Stalingrad at the end of **1942** that finally convinced Claus von Stauffenberg that Hitler must be done away with. Having observed both the vacillating timidity of top commanders in the face of Hitler's interference in military matters and his sheer bungling incompetence, Stauffenberg was clear where the blame for the defining catastrophe of the war in the east must lie: squarely on the Führer's own stooping shoulders. He himself had visited the Sixth Army's headquarters in May 1942, and subsequently wrote a letter of appreciation to its commander, General Friedrich von Paulus, which hinted at his growing disillusion when he remarked:

> How refreshing it is to get away from this atmosphere [at Staff Headquarters] to surroundings where men give of their best without a second thought, and give their lives too, without a murmur of complaint, while the leaders and those who should set an example quarrel and quibble about their own prestige, or haven't the courage to speak their minds on questions which affects the lives of thousands of their fellow men.

Quite how literally true this was, Stauffenberg was about to discover. Halder, after all his hesitations about actually removing Hitler, had himself been dismissed as Chief of Staff at the end of September 1942 for repeatedly warning the Führer that by pressing on into Stalingrad in the face of steadily stiffening Soviet resistance, the Sixth Army was advancing into a dangerous *Sackgasse* – a cul-de-sac. The city that bore his great rival dictator's name seemed to mesmerise Hitler, and he refused

The destruction of
Stalingrad, 1942.

to countenance any let-up in the advance, although Halder pointed
out that Paulus's men were up against seemingly inexhaustible Soviet
numbers – a superiority in men (1.5 million against about 300,000)
and in *matériel* (Soviet tank production now totalled 1,200 a month).
In addition, Kleist's tanks, which had carried all before them on the
rolling steppes of the Ukraine, were next to useless in the savage street
fighting that the struggle for Stalingrad had become. For voicing such
inconvenient truths, Halder had been summarily sacked.

Courageously, Stauffenberg visited the fallen general at his Berlin
home in October, despite the fact that Halder was virtually under house
arrest, with all his movements monitored by the Gestapo. Stauffenberg
told the deposed Chief of Staff that the atmosphere at Staff Headquarters
was now deeply depressing. In the wake of Halder's fall, no one was
prepared to raise his head above the parapet and speak out of turn. Any
ideas that went against Hitler's policy of stubbornly sticking to every
inch of conquered ground was frowned upon. Even the former free

exchange of ideas in informal discussions had vanished, Stauffenberg reported; it had been replaced by a depressing mood of silence and fear in which nemesis approached without anyone lifting a finger to stop it.

Halder's successor as Chief of Staff, Kurt Zeitzler, was a relatively unknown officer who had been selected by Hitler as he had been impressed by Zeitzler's optimistic reports in his previous posts. The Führer also imagined that this pastor's son would prove more pliable than the stiff-necked Prussian aristocrats who still composed the bulk of the officer corps. He was disappointed. Zeitzler concurred with the disgraced Halder's view that the Stalingrad pocket that the Sixth Army had been pushed into was a dangerous trap: a sack waiting for its open end to be nipped off and tied. He recommended an immediate withdrawal from the Volga to the Don River. Hitler flew into one of his increasingly frequent temper tantrums, screaming that he would not be moved from the Volga – the Sixth Army would stand or fall at Stalingrad.

On **9 November 1942**, while Hitler was in Munich for the annual commemoration of the Beerhall Putsch, so rudely interrupted by Elser's bomb three years before, the Red Army sprang the jaws of the trap it had prepared. Attacking simultaneously north and south of Stalingrad, within days the Soviets had pinched off the Stalingrad pocket and the Sixth Army was encircled and cut off. By **23 November** Paulus's men were trapped like cornered rats in the shattered ruins of the city they had strived so hard to capture. Stalingrad had become a *Kessel* – a cauldron – in which the flower of the army would shrivel. On **2 February 1943**, despite having been promoted to field marshal by Hitler because no German field marshal had ever capitulated before, Paulus emerged from his bunker and surrendered the freezing, starving, battered and bewildered remnants of his Sixth Army to the Russians. 90,000 men limped into Soviet prisoner-of-war camps from which only around 5,000 eventually emerged. 250,000 remained in and around Stalingrad as frozen corpses. Stauffenberg's worst fears had been realised and the fortunes of war had swung irrevocably against his beloved Germany.

At last, this loyal and patriotic German soldier, with his courageous refusal to indulge in wishful thinking, was ready to take the first step down the radical path of conspiracy that others – Oster, Tresckow, Gisevius, Beck, Goerdeler and Witzleben – had trodden before him. In 1933 he had hoped, like most other Germans, that the Nazis would give a desperate and demoralised nation a new sense of discipline and purpose. In 1934 he had, like many others in the army, seen the Night of the Long Knives purge as a long overdue, if excessive, settling of accounts with the brawling thugs of the SA. In 1938, he had applauded Hitler's tough diplomacy that had annexed Austria and the Sudetenland to the Reich without a war. In 1939 and 1940 he had taken professional pride in the rapid *Blitzkrieg* conquests of Poland, Norway, Denmark, the Low Countries, and finally France. Even at the beginning of 1942, when Hitler assumed direct personal command of the army, Stauffenberg had been optimistic that this would simplify the chain of command and sweep away the confusion and muddle that his clear mind abhorred.

Now, though, his dismay and disillusionment were complete. The straw that broke the camel's back, he told a military colleague, Werner Reerink, on 14 January, on the eve of the final surrender at Stalingrad, had been a conference in November at which the army chiefs believed that they were on the verge of persuading Hitler to order Stalingrad's evacuation while there was still time. Even Goebbels, said Stauffenberg, had been persuaded of the wisdom of this course. Then, at the decisive moment, Goering had lumbered in and, in his habitual boastful style, assured Hitler that the Luftwaffe alone could keep the Sixth Army supplied by air indefinitely even if it were cut off. Stauffenberg saw this as more than vainglorious boasting; it was a betrayal of the army, he said bitterly, and had effectively condemned 300,000 men to a lingering death. Such criminal irresponsibility could no longer be borne. Word of Stauffenberg's conversion to the conspirators' cause and of his involvement in their ranks soon spread among the select few. In late January 1943, General Olbricht told his aide Hans Bernd Gisevius: 'Stauffenberg has now seen the light and [is] participating.'

But before he could take further action, Stauffenberg was plucked from the war in the east and the sterility of an atmosphere where Hitler's word was the only law, to another theatre where Germany was also facing a devastating defeat: North Africa. Long gone were the days when Erwin Rommel's Afrika Korps had carried the tide of German conquest almost to the banks of the Suez Canal and the gates of Cairo. British Commonwealth forces advancing from Egypt through Libya in the east, and newly arrived Anglo-Americans who had landed in Algeria at the end of 1942, had moved towards the Germans in Tunisia. The situation was critical and Zeitzler had personally chosen Stauffenberg, who had been made up to lieutenant-colonel on **1 January 1943**, to be senior staff officer (operations) to the 10th Panzer Army as one of the most able staff officers available. After the war, Zeitzler explained that he wanted to give Stauffenberg more experience of command on an active front, so as to prepare him for the future command of a corps or army. Delighted as he was by the move to a 'clean' war between soldiers rather than the moral quagmire that the war in the east was becoming, Stauffenberg was about to get more action than even he had bargained for.

On **2 February**, the day that Paulus surrendered at Stalingrad, Stauffenberg and his wife had lunch with another army couple, Colonel and Frau Burker, at the fashionable Berlin restaurant, Kempinskis. Dining with them was Frau Beate Bremme, a friend of the Stauffenbergs from their pre-war days in Wuppertal. Frau Burker was the daughter of Field Marshal Blomberg, the war minister disgraced and dismissed in the Blomberg–Fritsch scandal of 1938: her two brothers, Henning and Axel, had both been killed in North Africa and the Middle East, and Stauffenberg could have been under no illusions as to the toughness of the assignment ahead of him. Burker had himself been summoned home from North Africa by Hitler after the deaths of his Blomberg brothers-in-law, and during the lunch briefed Stauffenberg about the job. The conversation then turned to the situation at Stalingrad, and Stauffenberg left no one within earshot in ignorance of his own views.

Stauffenberg writes to Blomberg post-Stalingrad.

After the war, Frau Bremme recalled: 'They talked loudly and very critically, Stauffenberg more than Burker . . . the waiter came along and insisted that they talk more softly, but they took not the slightest notice and in fact talked even louder.'

A few days before, Stauffenberg had been equally indiscreet in urging Field Marshal Manstein to take action against Hitler while there was still an army and nation left to save. The war, he insisted, could no longer be won by military means and a diplomatic solution must be sought. So insistent did Stauffenberg become in his urgings that a nervous Manstein threatened to have him arrested. Stauffenberg was contemptuous about the field marshal's quivering pusillanimity. He told his friend Dietz von Thungen, 'These guys have their pants full of shit and their skulls full of straw. They don't want to do anything.'

After a week's embarkation leave with his family, Stauffenberg arrived in Tunis, flying via Naples, on **11 February 1943**. His first duty was to visit his badly wounded predecessor, Major Wilhelm Burklin, in hospital. Recalling the visit later, Burklin remarked that he had particularly warned his successor to beware of strafing by low-flying enemy aircraft. Stauffenberg arrived at his divisional forward post on **14 February**, in the very midst of battle. The previous day Rommel, who had received reinforcements and was confident of success with his battle-hardened African veterans against the green and ill-trained Americans, had launched 'Operation Spring Breeze' – a series of offensives in different directions designed to disrupt the Allied vice that was tightening around Tunisia, turned by the British moving up from the south, and the Americans advancing out of the west.

Despite his inexperience of desert warfare, Stauffenberg was in his element, working fourteen-hour days and demonstrating his customary ability to multi-task: doing several jobs simultaneously and chafing, charming and persuading others to do his bidding. His divisional commander, Brigadier Baron Friedrich von Broich, was new to the job too, having been appointed at the same time as Stauffenberg. Broich was a simple soldier, described later in a report by his British captors as 'a jolly ex-cavalry man [with] a twinkle in his eye . . . not particularly intelligent but always most amusing and charming'. Broich, like Stauffenberg had 'a horror of Nazism' and his letters home to his wife were so anti-Hitler that she warned him to be more discreet for fear of the Gestapo. When told of Stauffenberg's 20 July bomb by his British captors, Broich described his former deputy as 'an excellent man . . . one of the cleverest,

Stauffenberg (right) talking to General Baron von Broich in North Africa, Kasseringe Station, 20 February 1943.

exceedingly well-educated, [and] a brilliantly clever fellow'. Broich's only regret was that the bomb Stauffenberg had used had apparently been too small to kill Hitler.

Even while they had been together fighting the battle of Sidi Bou Zid – in which the old sweats of the Afrika Korps savaged the greenhorn Americans, killing 1,200 and destroying over 100 tanks – Stauffenberg, with his customary frankness-to-the-point-of-madness made no secret of his detestation of Hitler and the Nazi regime, remarking in the hearing of lower ranks that 'That guy [Hitler] ought to be shot.' He and Broich would sit late into the night in their mobile command post – a captured British battle bus – over a bottle of heavy Tunisian red wine setting the world to rights and deploring Hitler's wrongs. The Nazis, they agreed, would have to be removed by force.

Operation Spring Breeze developed into a series of fiercely fought actions for control of the strategic Kasserine and Faid Passes over the Atlas Mountains in central Tunisia. At first the experienced Germans carried all before them, picking off the inferior American M3 tanks with their giant new Tiger tanks, which packed an 88-mm cannon, and putting the GIs to rout. Stauffenberg, easy, relaxed, yet efficient and always willing to speak his mind, proved both capable and popular with all ranks. For his part, he enjoyed a return of the carefree spirit of 1940, appreciating the uncomplicated joys of soldiering amid like-minded comrades.

As March turned to April, however, the effects of the Allied command of the Mediterranean became increasingly felt as supplies began to dwindle and dry up and the German offensive stalled. Rommel fell sick and was evacuated from the Africa where he had made his name, and the USAAF and RAF roared across the clear desert skies, virtually unimpeded by any intervention from the Luftwaffe. As the Americans licked their wounds and regrouped, learning the lessons of their defeat as they did so, the experienced British Commonwealth Eighth Army moved up to attack the Germans entrenched behind the Mareth Line. As in the east, the dice of war began to roll against Germany.

Early on the morning of **7 April 1943**, Claus von Stauffenberg's career as a fighting soldier came to a sudden and brutal end, and his brief life as an active conspirator – destined to end equally violently – began. He was on duty in a narrow defile near a range of hills known as Sebkhet en Noual, supervising a tactical withdrawal eastwards towards the Tunisian coast. He was uneasy and uncharacteristically tense. Before taking leave of him that morning, Broich had issued the customary warning to beware of low-flying enemy aircraft. Stauffenberg told a Lieutenant Reile, who saw him standing in his Horch jeep – a distinctive figure as he strove to direct the traffic through the dangerous defile – 'We shall be lucky if we get out of this. As usual we disengaged twenty-four hours too late.' Reile left him, keeping one eye on the ground, and the other on the threatening sky.

Suddenly, out of the clear morning skies, the enemy struck. Flight after flight of American fighter-bombers roared in, strafing and shooting up the vehicles in Stauffenberg's column. Ammunition trucks exploded, lorries overturned or ran off the road; vehicles juddered to a halt as the enemy aircraft thundered in. Desperately, directing his jeep up and down the line of stricken traffic, Stauffenberg strove to save what he could from the carnage. Then a plane picked him out and screamed in to attack with all guns blazing. Instinctively, Stauffenberg hurled himself from the jeep, his hands hiding his handsome face as he hit the desert dust and stones. But the bullets killed a lieutenant sitting at the back of the jeep and found Stauffenberg too.

As the raid ended, Stauffenberg lay in helpless agony. His left eye was a mass of blood and jelly. Both his hands were in a similar state, and his head, back, arms and legs were riddled with shrapnel splinters. A passing medical officer, Second Lieutenant Dr Hans Keysser, dressed Stauffenberg's wounds. Apparently from nowhere, an ambulance appeared, and Stauffenberg was gently lifted in. It took him to No. 200 Field Hospital at Sfax on Tunisia's eastern coast, where his desperate condition was stabilised. From there he was taken north to a hospital outside Tunis near ancient Carthage: a pain-wracked journey. Here the remains of his left eye were removed, his right hand was amputated and all but three fingers cut from his left as well. After a fortnight he was well enough to be evacuated by sea to the Italian port city of Livorno, where he was put on a hospital train for Munich.

Here, strings were pulled to get him admitted to the First General Military Hospital in Lazarettstrasse, where Germany's greatest surgeons, Ferdinand Sauerbruch and Max Lebsche, operated. In the weeks that followed, further surgery was carried out to remove splinters of steel and rock from his scalp and middle ear. These were excruciatingly painful, not least because Stauffenberg steadfastly refused to dull the pain with opiates such as morphia: his fortitude during this agonising ordeal astonished his doctors, as did his swift powers of recuperation from his ghastly injuries.

Within weeks, Stauffenberg, sporting an eye-patch, was on his feet and insisting on learning to write and dress himself with his left hand, skilfully using his teeth and his remaining three fingers. A steady stream of visitors, both family and brother officers, were equally impressed by his vitality and courage. They included Zeitzler, the Chief of Staff himself, who brought him his Wound Badge in gold and a case of wine. Soon, Stauffenberg's keen interest in current events returned. He asked about the White Rose, a small group of Munich University students who had openly scattered leaflets calling for the end of the regime, and had recently been beheaded for their pains. To his maternal uncle Nikolaus von Üxküll, or 'Uncle Nux', whom he knew to be a fierce opponent of Hitler, he remarked, 'If the generals won't do anything, then it's up to us colonels to take action.' He added that he did not think his survival a matter of mere chance. His life, he believed, had been spared for a purpose. It is said that amidst the bouts of high fever that he suffered as his post-operative infections came and went, he muttered in delirium: 'We must save Germany.'

On **3 July**, Stauffenberg was well enough to leave hospital and join Nina and his children in Bamberg, where a new townhouse was being

Stauffenberg's letter to his friend Willy Burklin. The letter, sent from the Munich military hospital, shows that Stauffenberg had difficulty writing with the three remaining fingers on his left hand.

Stauffenberg with his son Heimeran, daughter Valerie, niece Elisabeth, nephew Alfred and son Franz Ludwig in Lautlingen, summer 1943.

prepared for them in the home of his parents-in-law. On **5 July** the family arrived at their summer country house in the Swabian Alps. Lautlingen, with its happy memories of Stauffenberg's own childhood, was the ideal place for Stauffenberg to complete his convalescence and consider his future options in the bosom of his family. He told enquirers that he was eager to get back to the front, refusing to make any concessions to his serious disabilities: he was now one-eyed, and however dextrous (which he was, so much so that he joked that he did not know what he had done with all ten fingers when he had had the full set) he only had three fingers left on one hand. But his future had already been decided.

In May General Olbricht, head of the General Army Office in Berlin's Bendlerstrasse, had already decided that Stauffenberg – maimed though he was – was the perfect man to be his Chief of Staff. Olbricht had known Stauffenberg during his previous staff work in the organisation branch, and had been hugely impressed by the young officer's calmness, efficiency and his air of natural authority. Beyond such professional considerations, though, there was something else. Olbricht had also observed that Stauffenberg was a man of principle, a Christian and an idealist, and as such was unlikely to be impressed by the Nazis' behaviour in power, nor with Hitler's increasingly insane conduct of the war. Olbricht was ready to recruit Stauffenberg to the conspiracy. He did not yet know that his recruit was already ripe and willing.

\* \* \*

Two days before Stauffenberg had been wounded, on **5 April 1943** the circle of conspirators gathered around Oster in the Abwehr had suffered a fatal blow that led to the unravelling of their plans and the beginning of the decline of the Abwehr itself under the leadership of Admiral Wilhelm Canaris. Just before 10 a.m. two officials from the legal branch of the Gestapo, Manfred Roeder – the remorseless judge who was responsible for breaking up the Red Orchestra spy ring – and Franz Sonderegger, arrived at the Abwehr offices in the Tirpitzufer, armed with a warrant from the president of the high-powered Reichskriegsgericht to search the offices and arrest anyone whom they suspected of financial corruption, currency fraud – or treason.

They saw Canaris, and demanded access to Hans von Dohnanyi's office, who, they told the admiral, was guilty of numerous currency violations and possibly of even more serious crimes. Dohnanyi had been

Hans von Dohnanyi.

Dietrich Bonhoeffer.

under Gestapo observation for some time, and Canaris had vainly warned both him and Oster to destroy any incriminating documents, and, above all, not to keep them on the premises. Intent on planning their anti-Nazi plots, and on gathering evidence about persecutions by the Nazis and other crimes of the regime, the two men had blithely ignored their chief's warnings and were about to suffer the consequences.

Told that Dohnanyi was about to be arrested, Oster defiantly demanded: 'Then please arrest me too, for he has done nothing that I don't know about.' He, Canaris and the two Gestapo men then trooped into Dohnanyi's office next door, where the lawyer was formally arrested and the keys of his safe demanded. The contents of this proved damning, and Oster and Dohnanyi drew attention to the most incriminating documents by their flustered and inept attempts to destroy three papers that specifically linked the Abwehr to military plans to overthrow the regime, to contacts with Christian Churches in enemy countries and, not least, to administrative plans for governing a post-Nazi Germany. This was rank treason.

Oster's famous boldness had finally overstepped the line – unforgivable in a professional intelligence officer – separating courage from foolhardy carelessness, and he and his associates would now pay the price. It was a heavy one: Dohnanyi was duly detained, initially on a holding charge of illegal currency transactions. More Abwehr conspirators were swept into the Gestapo's net, including the young Protestant theologian Dietrich Bonhoeffer and the Catholic lawyer Josef 'Joe Ox' Muller. These were the men who had, through their contacts in the worldwide Protestant Churches and the Vatican respectively, attempted to acquaint the Allies with the activities of the resistance and enlist their support. Their efforts had been in vain: only a few weeks before, in **January 1943**, at the Casablanca conference, US President Franklin D. Roosevelt and British Prime Minister Winston Churchill had issued a demand that Germany must surrender unconditionally: the conspirators' last hope of a negotiated end to the war had finally been dashed.

Oster was sent home under house arrest, forbidden to wear his military uniform, and officially placed on a list of suspects. Desperately trying to distance himself from the disaster, Canaris officially dismissed his deputy from the Abwehr on **15 April**. Oster was being hung out to dry and was left in a kind of limbo, shunned by those still active in the conspiracy because he was now constantly under Gestapo surveillance. Canaris's caution – or cowardice, depending on one's view of the little admiral – availed him little. He too was a marked man, tainted in the Gestapo's eyes by his ambiguous nod-and-a-wink attitude to Oster's treason. The debacle now unfolding, in Gisevius's words, was 'the direst stroke of fate that could possibly have befallen the resistance movement'. The diplomat Ulrich von Hassell, another resistant, commented crisply that: 'The Canaris outfit has utterly compromised itself and utterly failed to live up to expectations. Unless the good guys are as wise as serpents and as gentle as doves, nothing will be achieved.' It was now up to Stauffenberg.

**July 1943** was a month of military and political disaster for Germany. It saw, at the mighty tank battle of Kursk, the greatest reverse for German arms after Stalingrad: a German attempt to emulate the Soviet success at Stalingrad turned into a disastrous rout. The Germans tried to nip off the Soviet salient around Kursk, with a pincer attack from the north under Kluge and from the south under Manstein involving a total of 900,000 men. The Red Army, forewarned, withdrew most of its men from the salient, replacing them with entrenched defences. Despite being spearheaded by Waffen SS Panzer divisions equipped with their new Tiger tanks, the Germans were unable to make significant headway, and were then hit by a massive Russian counter-attack of more than two million men, which succeeded in taking the cities of Kharkov and Orel and put the Germans on the defensive on the Eastern Front – as it turned out, permanently.

Meanwhile, having rounded up the remaining Axis forces in Tunisia, the Anglo-Americans successfully invaded Sicily, and occupied the island, a first step towards the invasion of the Italian mainland. A majority of Mussolini's colleagues on the Fascist Grand Council in Rome voted against him, and he was arrested on the king's orders after leaving the meeting. Though Hitler loyally ordered the rescue of his mentor-turned-protégé in a daring glider-borne commando raid on Mussolini's mountain-top prison a few weeks later, it was clear that the Duce's downfall was another fatal body-blow to the Axis from which it could not hope to recover.

On **10 August**, at the Berlin home of General Olbricht, Stauffenberg was introduced to the man who had preceded him as the mainstay of the anti-Hitler conspiracy: Henning von Tresckow. Temporarily removed from the Eastern Front thanks to a transfer to the Reserve Army in Berlin, Tresckow has lost none of his zeal for plotting against Hitler, and had recently recruited General Stieff – the unwitting recipient of Schlabrendorff's brandy-bottle bomb – to the ranks of the conspiracy. Stieff was an important recruit: along with General Fellgiebel, the signals expert attached to Hitler's headquarters as head of communications, Stieff was the highest-ranking conspirator in Hitler's immediate entourage. An administrative genius, Stieff had been appointed head

(Left) General Hellmuth Stieff. (Right) Hitler at the presentation of new field uniforms, with Stieff in the middle, early summer 1944.

of the organisational section of Hitler's headquarters staff despite the dictator's dislike of him, a disdain that Stieff returned with interest. Asked by Tresckow if he would kill Hitler in person at one of their many meetings, Stieff had at first accepted, then – amidst much vacillation – declined the deadly honour. Stauffenberg would have no such doubts.

Tresckow instantly recognised, on meeting the maimed young colonel, that Stauffenberg was a man after his own heart. Though physically now only half a man, his undimmed energy, enthusiasm and sheer radiant charisma put other tired and dispirited members of the conspiracy to shame. In the wake of the failures of that spring – the misfired bomb plots and the collapse of Oster's Abwehr network – Stauffenberg's presence came like a breath of fresh mountain air to revitalise the conspiracy. Even before he took up his post with the Reserve Army on **1 October** he set to work.

His official job was to revise and update Olbricht's officially approved plan, codenamed 'Operation Valkyrie', designed to counter any possible uprising staged by the armies of foreign workers who were now toiling inside the Reich. These workers consisted both of volunteers from countries such as France, and slave labourers from Russia, Poland and other conquered countries in the east, who had been drafted in to make good the enormous shortfalls in manpower caused by Hitler's insatiable demands for German cannon fodder to throw into the Eastern Front. Thanks to the Nazis' demented refusal to allow women to take up factory work, labour was woefully short and the war industries of the Reich were more and more dependent on these discontented foreign hordes, who now totalled more than a million.

Obviously the potential for disturbances from these unwilling workers was a real one, and Hitler had personally approved the plan that Olbricht had drawn up for dealing with it. Under it, diffuse groups of reliable military or paramilitary men – trainees, frontline soldiers on leave, guards at prisoner-of-war camps, anti-aircraft defence units and similar assorted groups – would be brought together as emergency fighting units to face down any revolt by the foreign workforce. Now, under cover of Olbricht's original 'Valkyrie I' plan, Tresckow and Stauffenberg developed a secret second plan, 'Valkyrie II', under which officers privy to the conspiracy would take charge of these emergency reserves in the wake of a successful assassination of Hitler, and use them, not to suppress a non-existent foreign workers' revolt, but to seize key points throughout the Reich and crush opposition from loyal Nazis – primarily the SS and what was left of the SA. That done, they would establish order so that the new government – headed by Beck, Witzleben and Goerdeler – could smoothly assume power.

Together, in sublime confidence Tresckow and Stauffenberg even drew up the proclamation – marvellous in its ambiguity as to the actual cause of the Führer's demise – that would be issued and broadcast in the wake of a successful assassination: 'The Führer Adolf Hitler is dead! A treacherous group of party leaders has attempted to exploit the situation by attacking our embattled soldiers from the rear in order to seize power for themselves. [Therefore] the [new] Reich government has declared martial law in order to maintain law and order!'

Bold and simple though the Valkyrie plan was, it had several glaring flaws that, in the event, were to prove fatal. First, it depended on the successful assassination of Hitler, an event that, as previous bitter experience had proved, was a consummation that, however devoutly to be wished, was infuriatingly difficult to achieve. Second, the whole gigantic edifice of the putsch would be built upon a lie. The plotters' proclamation skated skilfully over the central contradiction at the core of their plan: it pretended that the putsch emanated from the Nazis themselves: 'a treacherous group of party leaders', rather than the anti-Hitler conspirators. Therefore those troops called out to suppress the revolt, who would mostly be loyal to the regime, would, unbeknownst to them, be acting against their own side. How they would react when they realised the deception that had been practised on them was a question that the conspirators did not address. Third, Olbricht and Stauffenberg were the number two and three men in the command hierarchy of the Reserve Army. The number one – the Reserve Army commander who would be responsible, after Hitler himself had agreed to it, for issuing the signal to set Valkyrie in motion – was General Friedrich Fromm.

Fromm was a towering, bullet-headed general of artillery who, after an undistinguished career, had been placed in charge of what was then the backwater of the Reserve Army soon after the conclusion of the Polish campaign. Hitler reputedly trusted Fromm, calling him 'The strong man in the homeland'. But Fromm's strong, oak-like appearance was deceptive. In reality he was a flabby flip-flopper who made even Field Marshal Kluge look like a stone wall of consistency. In fact Fromm made a virtue of his tendency to haver, boasting that he always came out on the winning side in any situation. He was indeed to do so again on 20 July, but only at the cost of his own life.

Though not the most perceptive of men, even Fromm was well aware of what his Chief of Staff Olbricht and Stauffenberg were planning, but

Colonel-General
Friedrich Fromm.

he steadfastly refused all pleas and blandishments to join the conspiracy. The most he would do was to imply that he would join them if Hitler died and they looked like the winners.

Meanwhile, they were on their own. Undeterred by their failure to win Fromm over, Tresckow, Olbricht and Stauffenberg proceeded with drawing up their plans. Warned by the fate that had overtaken the Oster group, they took more care of security than had the Abwehr plotters, entrusting the written documentation to Tresckow's wife Erika and a trusted secretary in the War Ministry, Margarete von Oven. Both women were careful to wear gloves when handling the papers to prevent them leaving telltale fingerprints for the Gestapo to discover. By **November 1943** all the plans were literally signed and sealed, Field Marshal Witzleben, designated Commander-in-Chief of the post-Hitler regime, had put his hand to the proclamation of martial law.

Tresckow was now unexpectedly ordered back to the Eastern Front. He attempted to secure a post on the staff of Manstein, the commander of Army Group South, hoping to exercise the same persuasive talents he had used on Kluge to influence the militarily talented but morally timid field marshal to join the conspiracy. Manstein, doubtless guessing Tresckow's intention, refused him a staff job and assigned him command of an infantry regiment instead. Along with Olbricht, Stauffenberg was left in Berlin to see Valkyrie through. Now that he was committed to the project Stauffenberg was indefatigable. He was clear that a post-Nazi regime must be drawn from the widest possible spectrum of society, from socialists and trade unionists on the left, to ultra-conservative nationalists on the right. To that end he insisted on meeting representatives of both wings of the conspiracy: men such as Carl Goerdeler, who still entertained the illusion that Hitler could somehow be persuaded to change his ways; and Julius Leber, a former Social Democratic Reichstag deputy, who had survived a spell in a concentration camp in the regime's early days, and maintained a principled opposition to the Nazis. After meeting both men Stauffenberg, unimpressed by the garrulous Goerdeler, recommended that Leber serve as vice-Chancellor representing the left in the post-putsch regime.

The search now started in earnest for an assassin to accomplish the essential first step of eliminating Hitler – and, if possible, the other leading Nazis too. Deciding against the hesitant General Stieff, whom he described as 'nervy as a racing jockey', Stauffenberg turned his attention to more junior officers, in line with his dictum that if the field marshals and the generals so dismally lacked the moral courage to match the physical bravery they had showed as soldiers, it was up to the colonels, majors, captains and even lieutenants to do what had to be done. Through his friend, the lawyer Count Fritz-Dietlof von der Schulenberg, whose job in the Army Reserve gave him access to all army units, Stauffenberg was introduced to a young captain, 24-year-old Baron Axel von dem Bussche-Streithorst.

Von dem Bussche became an impassioned opponent of Nazism exactly a year before, on 5 October 1942, when he had witnessed one of the innumerable atrocities on the Eastern Front: the massacre of the Dubno Jewish ghetto. Dubno was a small town in eastern Poland that had been annexed by Stalin under his 1939 pact with Hitler. Like many East European towns, it had a large Jewish community, who made up around half of its 15,000 inhabitants. Jews had lived in Dubno since the Middle Ages, but when the town was overrun by the invading Germans in 1941, the Jews were rounded up and herded into a ghetto, a riverside compound fenced in with wood and wire, where for a time the fit toiled

Captain Axel von
dem Bussche-
Streithorst.

as slave labourers for their new Nazi masters, while the unfit died of hunger and disease in their hundreds.

In the summer of 1942 orders came down for the Dubno ghetto to be liquidated. Daily, scores of Jews were driven out in trucks to a hill outside the town where they were compelled to dig their own graves before being stripped and shot. The cold-blooded executions were carried out by Ukrainian militiamen – a rag-bag assortment of Ukrainian nationalists, fanatical anti-Semites and criminal thugs – supervised by the SS. By October, despite the slaughter, there were still around 5,000 Jews left alive in Dubno, and a further order arrived to speed up the killings. A hardened group of SS killers, the *Einsatzgruppe C*, were given the task of finishing the grisly job, with the Ukrainian militia acting as their willing auxiliaries.

The scene of the slaughter was an old airfield on the outskirts of town. The remaining Jews were beaten into trucks with truncheons and whips, driven to the airfield and ordered to strip. Their clothes were sorted, with Teutonic efficiency, into separate piles: shoes, clothes and underwear. Shivering naked in family groups, the Jews awaited their fate. One witness, who was later to stun the Nuremberg Tribunal with his evidence, was a German civilian building contractor who happened to be working in the area, Hermann Graebe. He saw families taking tearful last farewells. Some wept, some tried to comfort uncomprehending children; all awaited the inevitable quietly, with dignity and courage.

Behind a wall of earth, three rectangular pits had been dug – thirty metres long and three deep. On the lip of each pit stood a score of SS killers armed with rifles. One by one, groups of twenty Jews were counted off and marched to the edge of the pit, where the bodies of their predecessors already lay, some twitching or still writhing in their death agony. The newcomers were forced to descend into the pits and lie on top of the corpses. Then another series of shots rang out. Graebe saw terrible scenes: a grandmother hugging a child too young to understand, who was cooing with delight; a father pointing to the heavens and explaining to a fearful older child that this was their destination; a painfully thin, apparently paralysed old woman being carried to her death by two others. A young woman who passed him, pointed to herself and said simply: 'Twenty-three years old'.

The massacre at Dubno was nothing unusual for the SS. The number of victims of the *Einsatzgruppen* totalled more than a million even before the systemised death factories of Auschwitz-Birkenau, Treblinka, Majdanek, Sobibor, Chelmno and the other camps were up and running. It is remembered today for Graebe's chilling account, which led him to become a 'righteous Gentile' by protecting the Jewish labourers working on his building projects, and for the effect it had on a second witness: Axel von dem Bussche.

Von dem Bussche was not, like Graebe, a civilian who just happened to find himself in Dubno, but a tough professional soldier serving in the 9th Infantry Regiment, who had been through all three of Hitler's early campaigns: Poland, the fall of France, and the invasion of the Soviet Union. He had sustained three serious wounds, and was convalescing with his regiment in the rear area around Dubno from the latest injury, a gunshot wound in the chest, when he found himself an involuntary witness to the ruthless slaughter at the airfield.

Ordered to assist the SS in their bloody work, von dem Bussche's commanding officer refused, but stood by helplessly as the massacre unfolded before his horrified eyes. Like other military conspirators, von dem Bussche was a committed Christian schooled in the chivalric, gentlemanly traditions of Prussian soldiering. He begged his commanding officer to stop the massacre, by force if necessary, and when he realised that it was the SS who had the superior firepower, thought wildly of stripping off his Wehrmacht uniform – which suddenly felt like a stain upon his skin – and joining the doomed Jews in their trenches of death. He did not, but the horrific scenes he had witnessed imprinted themselves indelibly on his mind. After Dubno, he thought, there were only three options open to him: death in battle, desertion or joining the resistance. Despite his wounds, death in battle had so far obstinately eluded him; as a Prussian aristocrat, deserting to the Red Army did not appeal – so he opted for the resistance.

He had no hesitation, therefore, in accepting the proposition that Stauffenberg put to him in the autumn of 1943. The plan was for von dem Bussche, who would be introduced to the Führer by Stieff, to model a new uniform – a heavy greatcoat, designed to withstand the rigours of a Russian winter – before Hitler. Then, during the show, he would embrace the Führer for a vital few seconds and simultaneously detonate a bomb, equipped with a four-and-a-half second fuse from a German stick grenade, in the greatcoat pocket. Tall, blond and blue-eyed, von dem Bussche was an ideal 'Aryan' specimen and would be more than suitable as a male model. He made the journey to Hitler's eastern headquarters, the gloomy Wolfschanze at Rastenburg deep in the forests of East Prussia in late **November 1943**, ready for his unaccustomed dual role as clothes-horse and suicide bomber.

Once again, however, Hitler's fabled sixth sense seemed to warn him of the impending danger. Time and time again the inspection was scheduled – and then postponed. The tension became almost unbearable: 'The sunny late autumn days amidst the forests and lakes are imbued with the heightened intensity a soldier feels before an attack,' von dem Bussche wrote. Then the tension broke: the consignment of the precious new greatcoats, stored in an army goods train, were destroyed during one of the increasingly heavy and frequent Allied air raids on Berlin. Replacements would not be available before January. Disconsolately, von dem Bussche returned to the Eastern Front, expecting to be recalled as soon as the new consignment was ready. But fate intervened; in December, he was severely wounded yet again, this time losing his leg. He spent the rest of the war in hospital and played no further part in the conspiracy. He was, however, left with an embarrassing – and potentially damning – reminder of his near-miss: the bomb itself. The explosive was kept in a suitcase and moved round with von dem Bussche from hospital to hospital. Not until the autumn of 1944, long after Stauffenberg's attack, was he able to dispose of it when a like-minded fellow officer threw it into a lake for him.

*   *   *

On **23 December 1943** Stauffenberg made the first visit in his new job to what would soon become a familiar location: the Wolfschanze. While waiting in Hitler's antechamber, it suddenly occurred to him that, despite his injuries, he too could perform the assassin's task and blow himself up along with the dictator. He subsequently put the plan to both Beck and Olbricht, who objected that the sacrifice of such a brilliant mind and winning personality would be a waste. Germany needed Stauffenberg alive. The search for another viable assassin continued.

Germany's straits as the year ended were dire indeed; already defeated in the south at Stalingrad and in the centre at Kursk, now the northern front crumbled as well, with the lifting of the terrible 900-day siege of Leningrad, which had reduced the population of Russia's second city to eating dogs, cats, and each other.

In Italy, the Allies had landed successfully at Salerno and Anzio, and although desperate fighting lay ahead, the war was only going in one direction – northwards. Meanwhile the nerve-shredding nightly raids of the RAF's Bomber Command on the embattled Fatherland were joined by the daily attacks of the USAAF. Germany's cities were being ground to rubble between the upper and nether millstones.

Von der Schulenberg now produced a new candidate for the assassin's role. In **January 1944** he introduced Stauffenberg to another young officer who was equally committed to the conspirators' cause. Ewald Heinrich Kleist-Schmenzin, an infantry lieutenant, was the son and namesake of Ewald von Kleist-Schmenzin, the conservative lawyer who had travelled twice to London in 1938 as Beck's emissary, vainly seeking support ahead of Oster's coup. Stauffenberg quietly asked whether Ewald Heinrich would be prepared to sacrifice his own life to kill Hitler while modelling the new greatcoat. Understandably, the young man asked for time to think it over. He went straight to consult his father, who did not hesitate. 'You have to do it,' he told young Ewald. 'Anyone who falters at such a moment will never feel at one with himself again.' Once again, however, the elusive greatcoat presentation failed to materialise.

Growing desperate, Stauffenberg asked his own adjutant, Werner von Haeften, assigned to him since November, whether he would be prepared to do the deed. At first Haeften agreed, but changed his mind after consulting his older brother, Hans-Bernd von Haeften, who – although a member of the conspiracy – as a committed Christian, had strong ethical objections to assassination. Haeften withdrew, although later he was to be at Stauffenberg's side throughout the events of 20 July.

The last choice for the role of assassin, before Stauffenberg finally concluded that he would have to do the job himself, was another protégé of Tresckow: a cavalry captain named Eberhard von Breitenbuch. Originally recruited to the staff of Army Group Centre by Tresckow, Breitenbuch had stayed on after the departure of Tresckow and Kluge – who had been seriously hurt in a car crash – in the autumn of 1943 to become aide-de-camp to the new commander, Field Marshal Ernst Busch, an over-promoted Hitler yes-man. Like von dem Bussche, Breitenbuch had been converted to the conspirators' cause by brutal atrocities he had witnessed on the Eastern Front.

At the beginning of **March 1944** Breitenbuch was given the opportunity to strike a blow for the cause. He had been chosen, he told Tresckow, to accompany Busch on a briefing mission at Hitler's Bavarian mountain retreat, the Berghof near Berchtesgaden. He would be willing, he said, to attempt an assassination while he was there. Eschewing Tresckow's offer of explosives, Breitenbuch said he preferred to rely on his trusty Browning pistol, to accomplish what Tresckow reminded him might be 'a unique chance to end with his own hands the war, with all its horrors'.

On the morning of **11 March** Busch and Breitenbuch flew in to Salzburg airport and drove up the winding mountain roads to the heavily guarded Berghof. A clear indication of the heightened security surrounding Hitler was a new requirement for all visitors to remove their caps, uniform belts and sidearms before being allowed to meet the Führer. Breitenbuch – who had already taken the precaution of removing his watch and wedding ring and sending them to his wife together with a farewell letter – kept his pistol with its safety-catch off in his trouser pocket. As they awaited Hitler, Reichsmarschall Goering kept the company entertained in his vulgar style with a stream of coarse jokes. Breitenbuch felt too keyed up to join with the sycophantic laughter of the others: 'My heart was beating in my throat,' he wrote later, 'as it was clear to me that within half an hour, I would be dead.' Most of the Nazi top brass arrived for the briefing conference: as well as Goering, Goebbels and Hitler's two top military aides, Generals Keitel and Jodl, were there. Just as Breitenbuch was wondering whether there would be time to loose off more shots and decapitate the entire Reich leadership, the doors to the Berghof's great hall swung open and an SS officer indicated that the Führer was at last ready to receive them.

As the group streamed obediently in, the SS man informed Busch that his aide was of too lowly a rank to participate and would not be required. Busch argued vainly that he was needed, but the doorkeeper was adamant: Breitenbuch, along with another adjutant, was barred. They went outside to kick their heels on the wide terrace of Hitler's home with its magnificent views across the mountains. As they relaxed, Breitenbuch's companion noticed that he was not well – he was distracted and, despite the keen March mountain air, was sweating profusely. Anxiously he asked if Breitenbuch was sick, and whether he needed to be taken to hospital in Berchtesgaden. Breitenbuch shook his head; he would be fine in a moment, he said. In fact, Breitenbuch's nerves had been shattered by his abortive few minutes as an assassin-in-waiting. When asked if he would be prepared to undertake the role again he shook his head: 'You only do something like that once,' he said.

Meanwhile, the security vice was tightening around the outer edges of the conspirators' circles. In the tight totalitarian state that was Nazi Germany, informers were rife, and as the suffering caused by the war increased, the swelling numbers of those opposed to the Nazis were inclined to grow careless, just at the time when the security organs of the state were stepping up their repression. The groups opposed to Hitler – apart from those in the army planning his actual assassination – ranged from Communist cells galvanised by the invasion of the Soviet Union, such as the Red Orchestra, who carried out acts of espionage and sabotage, to middle- and upper-class liberal discussion groups such as the Solf and Kreisau Circles, whose membership overlapped, and who largely confined themselves to drawing up high-minded plans for the constitution and policy of a post-Nazi Germany.

The year 1942 saw an all-out state assault on left-wing groups at a time when the Wehrmacht was engaged in its life-or-death struggle with the Soviet Union. In **February 1942** Berlin's largest Communist underground organisation, based on a network of secret cells in key factories – including armaments works – was broken up and its leaders arrested. These Communist militants, including Robert Uhrig, a KPD veteran since 1920, and Josef 'Beppo' Romer, were arrested. Romer was an unlikely Communist, since he was had been an army officer in the First World War and subsequently joined a Bavarian Freikorps called the Bund Oberland, which, along with the Nazi Party itself, was the main component of Hitler's 1923 Beerhall Putsch. Romer, however, like several other Freikorps veterans, was bitterly anti-Nazi and rapidly moved leftwards, finally joining the Communist Party. Both he and Uhrig served spells in concentration camps after the Nazi seizure of power, and, following their release, continued to work covertly for the cause, printing an underground newspaper and doing what they could to sabotage and spy on Hitler's drive to rearm Germany. Penetrated by the Gestapo, their network was smashed, with two hundred people arrested and more than fifty-five sentenced to death. The same spring a similar underground group, the Revolutionary Socialists, was broken up in Bavaria and Austria. Finally, in **August 1942**, it was the turn of the famous Red Orchestra.

The *Rote Kapelle*, as the Gestapo christened it, was actually a conflation of two separate organisations. The original Red Orchestra was set up in 1938 in Belgium by Leopold Trepper, an Austrian-born Jewish professional Communist, and a trained spymaster of Soviet military intelligence, the GRU. Based in Belgium, Trepper had recruited an international team of agents, largely in Western Europe, whose main job was to report on Nazi Germany and its expansionist military plans. The Red Orchestra contacted a broad-based organisation of left-leaning German anti-Nazis that, although Communist in sympathy, did not wish to subordinate themselves as totally to Stalin's control as Trepper's outfit did. Nonetheless, Trepper supplied this resistance network – whose leading lights were the Marxist economist Arvid Harnack, and his American-born wife Mildred, and an Air Ministry official named Harro Schulze-Boysen, with his wife Libertas – with radio sets so that they could report on Hitler's preparations to invade the Soviet Union. These sets gave the network its Red Orchestra nickname, as the Gestapo likened them to 'musical boxes' and their operators to musicians, but they also brought about its downfall when Army Intelligence picked up their signals. On **7 September 1942**, the Gestapo swooped. The Harnacks and the Schulze-Boysens, together with scores of their associates, who had attempted to alert the outside world to atrocities on the Eastern Front and to Hitler's aggressive plans, were arrested, tried and executed. All told, some 143 members of the organisation – ranging in age from 16 to 82, and including artists, writers, theatre people as well as civil servants, died. Unusually for an anti-Nazi resistance movement, some 40 per cent of the German Red Orchestra's members were women.

On a macabre note, they were the first political prisoners to be slowly hanged from nooses suspended from meat hooks. Previously, judicial executions had been carried out by guillotine, but Hitler sadistically decreed that the agonising slow strangulation, which could take twenty minutes before death ensued, should be the method employed in future. Trepper's parent Red Orchestra did not long survive either. Betrayed

Arvid and Mildred Harnack of the Red Orchestra.

by Johann Wenzel, a Belgian arrested by the Abwehr, who turned double-agent, the Soviet spy-ring was rounded up in the autumn of 1942. Trepper himself, who was detained while sitting in the dentist's chair, managed to survive the war to write his memoirs. Despite a post-war spell in Moscow's notorious Lubyanka prison, he remained an unrepentant Communist until his dying day.

In **January 1944,** the Gestapo finally neutralised what was left of the civilian resistance. The fuse had been lit beneath the bomb that Himmler at last detonated that January on **10 September 1943** at an apparently innocuous tea party held in Heidelberg. Here members of the Solf Circle, a civilian opposition group, discussed plans for a post-Hitler Germany. Unfortunately, one of their number, a Swiss doctor named Rieske, was also a Gestapo informer who carefully noted the names of all those present, and the subversive subjects under discussion. He duly reported to his Gestapo controllers who placed the Circle under surveillance so that more fish could be lured into the net. Tipped off by a sympathiser in the Air Ministry that the Solf Circle had been 'burned', Helmuth von Moltke, the English-Prussian aristocrat whose country home at Kreisau lent its name to the discussion group that he frequently convened, tried to tip off the Solf Circle's leader, Otto Kiep. He was too late: on **12 January 1944** the leading members of the Circle, including Kiep, were arrested, ironically, while taking tea, an apt symbol of their amateurishness. A week later, the Gestapo came for Moltke himself. Finally, on **11 February**, the spider at the very centre of the web, Admiral Canaris, was sacked and taken for a leisurely Gestapo investigation to the medieval castle of Lauenstein in Saxony.

The Abwehr itself was absorbed into the fully Nazified SS/Gestapo/ SD security apparatus, becoming a mere department within Heydrich's old empire, which had been run since his death by the unholy triumvirate of the scar-faced Austrian Ernst Kaltenbrunner; the young lawyer who had masterminded the Venlo Incident, Walther Schellenberg; and the former Weimar police chief who had become the boss of the state's political police, Heinrich 'Gestapo' Müller. With the collapse of Oster and Dohnanyi's Abwehr network, and the rounding up of most of the civilian conspirators, the military plotters were now very much alone.

On **6 June 1944,** D-Day, Anglo-American forces stormed ashore in Normandy, opening the long-awaited second front against Hitler's Germany. The news brought Stauffenberg close to despair; now that defeat was not just highly likely, but absolutely inevitable, the last remaining strategic cards were being snatched from the plotters' hands. There was now no chance whatsoever that the Allies would agree to a negotiated peace, the war would be fought to the bitter end and millions more lives would be lost. A putsch against the Nazis – even in the unlikely event of it succeeding – would be a futile gesture at best, since any post-Hitler government would be faced with the equally unpalatable options of unconditional surrender or fighting a hopeless war to its inevitable conclusion. Using a fellow aristocrat and army officer, Count Heinrich Lehndorff, as his liaison, Stauffenberg sent a despairing message to Tresckow, who was back at his old post as Chief of Staff of the Second Army in the southern sector of Army Group Centre.

Stauffenberg asked if there was any point in continuing with attempts to assassinate Hitler now that the war was irretrievably lost and Germany faced certain conquest. Tresckow's reply came immediately. It was at once uncompromising and prophetic: 'The assassination must be attempted, come what may. Even if it fails, we must take action in Berlin [to launch a coup]. For the practical purpose no longer matters; all that counts now is that the German resistance movement must take the plunge before the eyes of the world and of history. Compared to that, nothing else matters.'

# 9 Valkyrie
## 20 July 1944

Even if Stauffenberg – like Christ himself – had his moment of fear and doubt before the Calvary that awaited him, his hesitation was only momentary. Having heard and accepted Tresckow's stiffening message, he redoubled his efforts, and devoted his formidable energies to melding the disparate threads of the conspiracy finally into a workable plan. As ever, his major strength lay in his ability to multi-task, and he devoted almost as much time and thought to the political side of the plot as he did to its military aspects.

Though far from a leftist himself, Stauffenberg was adamant that any post-Hitler regime must be broadly based, extending from conservatives and nationalists on the right to Social Democrats and possibly even Communists on the left. He was very critical of the Reichswehr leaders under the Weimar Republic who, in opposing Bolshevism, had also set their faces against the moderate Socialists of the SPD, who represented a large proportion of the German electorate. In their rejection of the Social Democrats, Stauffenberg felt, the army commanders had opened the door to Hitler. Indeed, Stauffenberg respected many Social Democrats as being among the most principled and unwavering opponents of Hitler from the 1920s when many Germans – including himself – had been prepared to give the movement the benefit of the doubt.

Julius Leber.

One Social Democrat in particular who attracted Stauffenberg's admiration and interest was Julius Leber, the former Reichstag deputy and the SPD's spokesman on defence, who was (unusually for a party tinged by pacifism) a First World War army officer. Also unexpected in a nominally Marxist party Leber, like Stauffenberg, was a fervent Catholic. Introduced to Leber by Fritz-Dietlof von der Schulenberg – the main middle man of the resistance, who had also put him in touch with von dem Bussche and Ewald von Kleist-Schmenzin – Stauffenberg soon marked him down as a likely future Chancellor of a post-war Germany, even though the ultra-conservative Goerdeler was the conspirators' official choice for the post.

Ever since he had begun work at the Reserve Army in the Bendlerstrasse, Stauffenberg had been living in the leafy, wealthy Berlin suburb of Wannsee, ironically the scene of Heydrich's notorious conference in 1942 which had given the green light for launching the Holocaust. Stauffenberg shared a large house at No. 8 Tristranstrasse with his brother Berthold and his uncle, Nikolaus von Üxküll – both seasoned members of the conspiracy. The house became the scene of hectic late-night meetings between the Stauffenbergs and surviving civilian conspirators, including Leber and his SPD and trade union colleagues Wilhelm Leuschner and Jakob Kaiser, Goerdeler, Yorck von Wartenburg and the theologian Eugen Gerstenmeier.

One of the main talking points was the political orientation of a future government. Stauffenberg, conscious of the need for popular, working-class support, urged Leber to take up the position of Chancellor. Leber, equally conscious of the disastrous post-1918 history, declined, saying he did not want a future Hitler to brand him a 'November criminal' who had presided over another government that had stabbed Germany's soldiers in the back. Another point of angry discussion was the attitude of the conspirators towards Germany's once-mighty Communist Party. Stauffenberg, as a Catholic aristocrat who had been involved in raising and equipping the anti-Communist 'Vlasov Army', composed of Soviet prisoners of war prepared to turn their coats and fight with the Germans against Stalin, naturally did not want to replace a dictatorship of the extreme right with one of the far left. He was scornful of Field Marshal Paulus and other senior officers captured by the Russians who had formed a so-called 'Committee of Free German Officers' under Soviet auspices, remarking: 'I am betraying my government; they are betraying their country.' Nonetheless, Stauffenberg did not wholly rule out German Communists playing some part in Germany's future politics, and he even grasped at the straw that a Germany rid of Hitler could make a separate peace with Stalin's Russia, after the repeated rebuffs the conspirators had suffered at the hands of the Western Allies.

\* \* \*

On **21 June 1944** leading conspirators met at Yorck von Wartenburg's home to thrash out the Communist issue, which had sharply divided them, with some plotters fiercely opposed to Communist participation in a future government while others – including Leber and Stauffenberg – argued for opening talks at least to explore what attitude the Communists would take towards a putsch. Despite violent opposition, the meeting reluctantly agreed to allow Leber to carry on with exploratory contacts with the Communist underground after he revealed that he had been invited the very next day to meet two Communist functionaries – Anton Saefkow and Franz Jacob – with whom he had shared a plank bed in a concentration camp in the early days of the Nazi regime.

On **22 June** Leber, accompanied by Adolf Reichwein, a Socialist educationalist and former Kreisau Circle member, duly met Saefkow and Jacob in the Berlin flat of a Communist-sympathising doctor. Ominously, a third man was present: a stranger who, against all security rules, addressed Leber by his real name. Leber was instantly aware that the Communists had been infiltrated by the Gestapo, and that he was now a marked man. Although he did not turn up at the next scheduled meeting on **4 July**, Reichwein did, and was duly arrested, along with Saefkow and Jacob. The following day, **5 July**, Leber too was seized at his flat.

Stauffenberg's efficient reports on the state of the Reserve Army had already drawn the attention and praise of Hitler himself, who is said to have remarked, 'Finally, a General Staff officer with imagination and intelligence.' For his part, Stauffenberg was considerably less impressed by the Führer. Their very first meeting took place on the afternoon of **7 June**, the day after D-Day. Fromm and Stauffenberg had been summoned to the Berghof to report on the readiness of the Reserve Army, a question suddenly made less theoretical by the opening of the Second Front in Normandy. Also present were Goering, Himmler, Keitel and armaments minister Albert Speer. Afterwards Stauffenberg told his wife that Hitler had grasped his remaining hand between his two, which were badly shaking. During the meeting he had appeared abstracted, shuffling maps with his shaking hands, and all the while darting nervous, sidelong glances at Stauffenberg from his hooded eyes. Goering, Stauffenberg remarked with distaste, was clearly wearing make-up. All the Nazi leaders, he added, were 'psychopaths' and the atmosphere around them was poisonous and rotten, making it hard to breathe. The only man present who appeared even vaguely normal, he concluded, was Speer.

Stauffenberg made these remarks to Nina during the last weekend he would spend with his family, **24 to 26 June**, at their townhouse in Bamberg. Countess Stauffenberg was full of her plans to take the children with her to their Schloss at Lautlingen – Stauffenberg's own childhood country home – for their annual summer holidays. She was looking forward to the break more than usual this year. In the peaceful rural environment at Lautlingen it was still just possible to forget that there was a war on. Even in the small city of Bamberg there were constant air-raid alarms, and the elder Stauffenberg children had completed their end of summer term tests in underground shelters. Stauffenberg was strangely unenthusiastic about his family's holiday plans. Later, in hindsight, Nina realised that he was worried about them being stranded in such a remote location in the aftermath of what he hoped would be his successful assassination of Hitler. Although Nina knew all about her husband's growing revulsion with the regime – indeed she shared his views – she was unaware how deeply involved he was in plotting against Hitler's life. Naturally, he wished to protect his family as far as possible from such dangerous knowledge and kept his intentions secret. When they parted she had no idea that she would never see her husband again.

On **1 July** Stauffenberg was promoted to full colonel and officially confirmed as Chief of Staff to the commander of the Reserve Army, General Fromm. Taking Stauffenberg's place as Obricht's new aide was balding, bespectacled Colonel Albrecht Mertz von Quirnheim, Stauffenberg's bosom friend and a committed conspirator. Stauffenberg's new job meant that he would now be given regular access to the Führer at his daily military conferences. Of all the plotters, he – despite the handicap of his multiple injuries – would now be best placed to carry out an assassination attempt. He lost no time in doing so.

On **6 and 8 July**, accompanied by his superior, General Fromm, Stauffenberg flew to Salzburg to brief Hitler once again at the Berghof, this time on the latest adjustments to the Valkyrie plan. Since the Normandy landings the High Command were increasingly worried that the Allies might attempt a landing on the almost unprotected north German coastline, and Stauffenberg was ordered to fine-tune Valkyrie to ensure that the 300,000 German soldiers who were at home on leave at any given time could be quickly assembled into scratch units called 'shell detachments' to meet any such incursion. Hitler approved his plan to give military commanders 'executive powers' in the event of an invasion, including authority over Nazi Party officials. Secretly, of course, such powers would mask the army takeover of the state that would follow the dictator's elimination.

Before the second briefing, Stauffenberg saw his fellow conspirator General Stieff, the able little administrative genius who, despite his constant access to the Führer as chief of operations, lacked the great courage needed to attempt the assassination himself. Stauffenberg patted his soon-to-be notorious briefcase and told Stieff: 'I have got the whole bag of tricks with me' – a remark that Stieff interpreted as meaning that he was already carrying a bomb, rather than a heavy hint that Stieff should place the bomb himself. Stieff testified at his subsequent trial that he had dissuaded Stauffenberg from carrying out the attempt that day, though clearly, given the circumstances under which he made this statement, it must be questionable. At all events, and for whatever reason, no attempt was made on this occasion.

Back in Berlin, the pressure to act was becoming intolerable. Stauffenberg's military duties included supervising the supply of reserve troops to the crumbling fronts, and he was well aware of the deteriorating, indeed hopeless situation, exacerbated by the ever-worsening Allied bombing raids. At the same time, the recent arrests of Leber and Rechwein – men who had become his friends, and about whose fate he felt personally responsible – weighed heavily on his mind and conscience. 'We need Leber. I'll get him out,' he had told Adam von Trott zu Solz, one of the few civilian conspirators still at large. Stauffenberg's aide-de-camp, Werner von Haeften, was telling people that his boss had 'decided to do the job himself' and Stauffenberg himself had incautiously told at least two people that he was engaged in high treason, and would be branded a traitor to Germany before history. What would be worse, however, he added, would be committing treason to his own conscience if he failed to act.

On **11 July** Stauffenberg flew back to the Berghof for another afternoon briefing with Hitler. Once again, he was carrying the bomb in his briefcase. However, it had been impressed upon him by Beck and other military conspirators, that it was highly desirable that both Goering – slated to take over command of the Reich's military forces in the event of Hitler's death – and Himmler, whose growing SS would be the chief armed body to be overcome in any post-assassination standoff, should die with the Führer. When he arrived at the Berghof, Stieff, aware of the deadly burden the young colonel was carrying, and nervous as usual, informed him – possibly with relief – that neither Goering nor Himmler would be present. 'Good God,' Stauffenberg responded, 'shouldn't we go ahead anyway?' Yet again, however, Stieff's caution prevailed, and the assassination attempt was once more postponed.

That Stauffenberg was serious about making an attempt on this occasion is evidenced by the fact that he had ordered his fellow conspirators in Berlin to stand by to initiate Valkyrie. He had also ordered the aide who accompanied him to the Berghof, Captain Friedrich Klausing (Haeften was ill), to have a Heinkel HE.III aircraft on standby at Salzburg ready to fly him back to Berlin to take command of the putsch. However, when news of the latest failure reached the capital, Carl Goerdeler, 'half laughing, and half crying' shook his head and predicted: 'They'll never do it.' Following the failure, Stauffenberg, Klausing and the other conspirators present at the Berghof – Stieff, communications chief General Fellgiebel and Lieutenant-Colonel Bernhard Klamroth – met at the Frankenstrub barracks outside nearby Berchtesgaden for an anguished post-mortem before Stauffenberg and Klausing flew back to Berlin. They resolved to make another attempt as soon as possible.

That same night, Stauffenberg's cousin Colonel Casar von Hofacker, a man whose resolution and moral determination matched that of Stauffenberg himself, arrived in Berlin from Paris to report on the catastrophic military situation unfolding in France. Paris, Berlin and Tresckow's Army Group Centre headquarters in the Ukraine, were the three places where the plotters' concentration was strongest.

The military governor of France, General Karl-Heinrich von Stülpnagel, was the leader of the plot there, and Hofacker himself was its liaison man with Berlin. They were ably abetted by several other strong personalities, including the Swabians General Hans Speidel, Chief of Staff to Field Marshal Erwin Rommel – whose Army Group B was currently struggling to contain the Allied bridgehead in Normandy – and Colonel Eberhard Finckh, Stülpnagel's newly appointed Chief of Staff.

The new Commander-in-Chief in the west was Field Marshal Günther von Kluge, who, recovered from the serious injuries he had sustained when his car had overturned in Russia the previous October, had been appointed to succeed the ageing Gerd von Rundstedt, with a brief to save the situation in France. Kluge was as indecisive as he had been when Tresckow had attempted to recruit him to the conspiracy in Russia. Although, as one of Germany's brightest military brains, Kluge knew that the war was lost, he lacked the essential moral courage

Günther 'Hans' von Kluge.

necessary to do what Stülpnagel and Hofacker were urging: to throw in the towel and negotiate a separate peace with the Allies.

Rommel, too, always a simple soldier who steered clear of politics as far as he could, resisted Speidel's wheedling attempts to enlist his heroic name to the conspirators' ranks. After failing to throw the Allies back into the sea on what he called 'the longest day' following the invasion (he had been absent on leave in Germany celebrating his wife's birthday), he also knew that the war was irretrievably lost. He was happy to say as much to Hitler, but he baulked at actually overthrowing, still less assassinating, the Führer. Hofacker had gone to Berlin to meet Beck and Stauffenberg with his pessimistic report of what was really happening on the Normandy front fresh from a face-to-face meeting with Rommel on **9 July**.

On the night of **12 July**, the Abwehr's Hans Bernd Gisevius – who had been in contact with Allen Dulles, the local chief of America's secret service, the OSS, on behalf of the plotters – returned to Berlin from Switzerland, bringing with him more bad news: there was no way, he told his fellow conspirators, that the Western Allies would make a separate peace with Germany against their Soviet ally. Despairingly, Stauffenberg asked Gisevius whether there was any chance of making an 'eastern peace' with the Soviets alone. Gisevius brutally replied that the same applied; there was no hope that either the Soviets or the Western Allies would agree to anything less than Germany's unconditional surrender.

The two men disagreed violently. Gisevius resented Stauffenberg's sudden emergence as the guiding light of the conspiracy in place of his old chief, Oster, forgetting that Oster was now under virtual house arrest. Stauffenberg, for his part, disliked Gisevius's openly expressed ambition to be placed in charge of purging Nazis after the putsch. They parted on bad terms, but Gisevius, for all his post-war sneering at Stauffenberg as a 'military praetorian' who had an inferiority complex about his own injuries, was forced to admire the maimed colonel's courage and his single-minded determination to carry out the assassination, come what may. 'This evening,' he concluded, 'I really had the impression that someone here was going all out.'

On **14 July** Hitler abruptly moved his headquarters from the Berghof to Rastenburg, despite the fact that the advancing Russians were now less than 100 kilometres from his eastern headquarters in the sweltering Polish forests. Fromm and Stauffenberg were summoned to an urgent lunchtime conference with Hitler the next day to discuss the provision of Reserve Army reinforcements for the hard-pressed Eastern Front. This news triggered a flurry of frenzied activity among the conspirators. At a meeting that afternoon attended by the leading figures, Beck, Goerdeler, Olbricht and Stauffenberg, it was agreed that Stauffenberg would attempt the assassination the next day regardless – even without the presence of Goering and Himmler. For their part, the conspirators in Berlin agreed to activate Valkyrie, with Olbricht issuing orders to move troops into the centre of the capital at 11 a.m., two hours before Stauffenberg was due to explode his bomb.

Meanwhile, back in France, at his headquarters in the riverside château of La Roche-Guyon, Rommel – urged on by his fellow Swabian and Chief of Staff Speidel – drafted an 'ultimatum' to Hitler insisting that the position in the west was now hopeless and that peace terms must be sought. His message concluded: 'The troops are fighting heroically everywhere, but the unequal struggle is nearing its end. I must beg you

Stauffenberg (left) meeting Hitler at the Wolfschanze on 15 July 1944.
Stauffenberg had a bomb with him but did not detonate it. He appears not to
be carrying his briefcase – had a nervous Stieff already hidden it?

to draw the political conclusions without delay. I feel it is my duty as commander-in-chief of the Army Group to state this clearly.'

On **15 July** Fromm and Stauffenberg, again accompanied by Captain Klausing, flew out on an early morning flight from Berlin, breakfasted at the Wolf's Lair, and met with Keitel for a preparatory briefing. Stauffenberg also communicated with the conspirators' main men at Hitler's headquarters, Stieff and Fellgiebel. They then met Hitler. At around this time a photographer took the only photograph of Hitler with his would-be assassin. Stauffenberg stands to the left of the picture, rigidly at attention, betraying no hint of the tension he must have been under, his injuries hidden from the camera. Hitler, a small and shrunken figure with his cap pulled low over his eyes, shakes hands with General Karl von Bodenschatz, Goering's Luftwaffe liaison man at Hitler's headquarters. At about 1 p.m. the party proceeded to the briefing hut, a one-storey wooden structure, reinforced by brick supports and a concrete ceiling, with large steel-shuttered windows. This was the eventual location for the explosion of Stauffenberg's bomb on 20 July. That bomb should have exploded now, on 15 July: why didn't it?

Explanations for this latest failure differ. According to one report, Stieff and Fellgiebel were insistent that no attempt must be made without Himmler being present. Stieff, according to this story, was so worried that Stauffenberg was going to go ahead anyway that he sabotaged the assassination by physically removing the briefcase bomb while Stauffenberg was telephoning Berlin to acquaint the plotters in the capital with the unfolding situation. According to another version, Stauffenberg was unexpectedly called to present his report early in the conference before he had a chance to prime the bomb. A third version states that Hitler ended the conference unexpectedly early, while Stauffenberg was phoning Berlin.

At all events, as Stauffenberg ruefully remarked to Klausing as they disconsolately trooped off to lunch on board Keitel's special train, 'It all came to nothing again today.' Stauffenberg had managed to call Olbricht in Berlin to tell him that yet another attempt had failed. It was too late to call off Valkyrie's preliminary moves – the codeword had been issued at 11 a.m. as arranged, and troops from the city's guard battalions and army cadet schools had obediently begun to move into the city centre. Olbricht hastily countermanded the order personally: driving to Potsdam and Gleinicke, and returning the troops to their barracks, but the manoeuvres could not be concealed from his superiors, who were both irritated and puzzled by these unauthorised troop movements.

Olbricht lamely explained that the codeword had been issued merely to test the troops' efficiency and readiness, but a furious Fromm tore a strip off him for issuing the unauthorised command. The same trick could not be repeated – next time, the bomb would have to explode.

**16 July** was spent by the conspirators in another lengthy autopsy on why their latest attempt had failed. Stauffenberg met first with Beck and Olbricht. All their nerves were wound up to breaking point. Beck's housekeeper testified later that the old general, who had recently been operated on for stomach cancer, woke each morning with his sheets soaked through with sweat. Stauffenberg, too, was understandably but uncharacteristically tired, irritable and nervous. Three times now he had keyed himself up to do what he described as 'the dirty deed' and three times had seen his action aborted. Even his deep reserves of courage must have had a limit. Olbricht stated that the issuing of the Valkyrie codeword and its subsequent cancellation had reached the ears of a suspicious Keitel. They must act for real – and soon. Snatching at straws, they argued about whether a collapse of the Western Front and a separate peace with the Anglo-Americans was, after all, possible.

The discussion of the plotters' ever-narrowing options continued that night at Stauffenberg's home in the Tristranstrasse. The core younger conspirators from Stauffenberg's closest circle were present, including his brother Berthold; Mertz von Quirnheim, who, under Olbricht would initiate Valkyrie in Berlin; Casar von Hofacker, Stauffenberg's cousin and the plotters' man in Paris; another cousin Peter Yorck von Wartenburg; Fritz-Dietlof von der Schulenburg and Adam von Trott zu Solz. Talking late into the night they chewed over the hard facts, always arriving at the same conclusion: nothing could be done until Hitler was eliminated, and even then the chances of success were vanishingly slight. Nonetheless, they concluded, the act must be attempted to redeem Germany's honour. Compared to this, as Tresckow had told Stauffenberg, nothing else counted.

Underlining the hopelessness of the Reich's military position, on **17 July** offensives opened both on the Eastern Front and in Normandy, where the Allies appeared on the point of breaking out of their bridgehead and capturing the cities of Caen and St Lô. The same day, the Normandy commander, Rommel, was seriously hurt when his staff car was strafed by an American fighter. The 'Desert Fox' suffered head injuries requiring his hospitalisation in Germany.

On **18 July** more bad news crowded in, confirming the tightening circle within which the plotters were now operating. One of the more unlikely conspirators, the president of Berlin's police, Count von Helldorf, who had an equivocal record as an ardent – if corrupt – former Nazi, tipped Stauffenberg off that a warrant had been issued for the immediate arrest of Carl Goerdeler, nominated by the plotters for the post of Chancellor in the post-putsch government. Stauffenberg immediately passed on the warning to Goerdeler, who went into hiding. Hard on the heels of this disturbing news came even more worrying tidings. A naval officer, Lieutenant Commander Alfred Kranzfelder, told Stauffenberg of a rumour he had heard from a Hungarian nobleman that Hitler's headquarters were to be blown sky-high over the next few days.

The young Hungarian had heard the report from the daughter of General Bredow, murdered by the Nazis in the Night of the Long Knives purge. She in turn had apparently picked it up from Stauffenberg's own indiscreet aide-de-camp, Werner von Haeften. Not only were the Gestapo now breathing down the conspirators' necks, but their own plans were about to become Berlin street gossip. Stauffenberg knew that he must act, and fast; he told Kranzfelder: 'We have crossed the Rubicon.' As if to confirm his resolve, and his fate, another summons arrived from Rastenburg: Stauffenberg was called to attend a conference there on 20 July.

Stauffenberg's aide-de-camp Lieutenant Werner von Haeften who was at his side on 20 July.

The conspirators had less than twenty-four hours to prepare their putsch. **19 July** was spent in frantic checking of their necessarily ad hoc arrangements. Thanks to Olbricht's patient spadework, the basic rudiments were in place but much – too much – still depended on chance: whether individual commanders would remain loyal to the regime or rally to the putsch. Above all, everything depended on whether Stauffenberg would succeed in killing Hitler. One key plotter was Major-General Paul von Hase, the military commander of Berlin. A vital element in Hase's command was the *Grossdeutschland* Guard Battalion, commanded by a Major Otto Remer, a much-decorated veteran of the Eastern Front. Hase failed to establish where Remer's loyalty would lie on the day of the planned putsch, though he could well have guessed. When it was pointed out to him that Remer, among his many other medals, proudly sported a Hitler Youth gold badge on his army uniform, indicating that he was a convinced – not to say fanatical – National Socialist, Hase swept the observation aside, blithely assuming that Remer would obey his orders. He even turned down the suggestion that Remer should be sent on an assignment to Italy to make sure that he was out of the way on the day. It was to prove a fatal mistake.

To support the troops in Berlin, another conspirator, Major Philipp von Boeslager, commanding the 3rd Battalion of the 31st Cavalry Regiment, had been asked by his brother Georg von Boeslager, commander of the 3rd Cavalry Brigade, to move six squadrons of his horsemen, about 1,200 men, to airfields in Poland, ready to fly into Berlin to back up the putsch. Astonishingly, Major Boeslager, in a five-day ride, covering some 600 miles, actually accomplished this manoeuvre, arriving at Brest-Litoskv on **19 July**, ready to board lorries for the airfield the following day.

Stauffenberg, the man at the centre of this gathering storm, spent the day in meetings with his fellow plotters. In the early evening he called on one of them, General Eduard Wagner, quartermaster general of the

Captain Freiherr Georg von Boeslager (right).

Wehrmacht, at his office at the Zossen military base outside Berlin to ask that Wagner's personal Heinkel HE.III plane should be made available next morning to fly him to Rastenburg, and then to return him to the capital after the assassination. Wagner readily agreed to the request. Afterwards, and presumably by way of relaxation, Stauffenberg and Wagner acted as 'beaters' during a hare hunt in the fields around Zossen, driving the frightened animals towards a colleague of Wagner's who killed them with a shotgun. Did Stauffenberg reflect that on the following day he would be hunting rather bigger game?

While this was going on, Stauffenberg sent his personal driver, Karl Schweizer, to obtain the explosive with which he would make the attempt, which had been 'minded' for him in-between his recent trips to see Hitler by a fellow conspirator, Fritz von der Lancken. Schweizer was in blissful ignorance of the contents of the two packages tied with string and neatly packed in a briefcase that he drove back to his master. Returning to Tristranstrasse, Stauffenberg had Schweizer stop outside a Catholic church into which he disappeared. One can only speculate what anguished prayers he offered up: success for his mission? Forgiveness for the lives his bomb would inevitably take? Divine protection for his friends and family?

On arriving home, Stauffenberg showed his brother Berthold the explosives, which he wrapped in a shirt before stowing them away again. Some time that same evening, he attempted to call Nina in Lautlingen, but an Allied bombing raid had severed the phone lines between Berlin and Lautlingen, and he was unable to get through.

**Thursday 20 July 1944** dawned hot and sultry. A sweltering day of high summer heat was in prospect. At No. 8 Tristranstrasse, the Stauffenberg brothers rose early. Schweizer arrived with the staff car at **6 a.m.**, and Stauffenberg, taking Berthold with him for company, drove off through the suburbs of the city showing the ugly scars of recent Allied bomb damage. At Rangsdorf airport they rendezvoused with Stauffenberg's aide-de-camp and co-conspirator Werner von Haeften, the handsome thirty-five-year-old former Berlin banker seconded, like Stauffenberg, to the Reserve Army after suffering severe war wounds. Werner was accompanied by his brother, Berndt, who had come to see him off and whose Christian scruples had originally prevented Werner von Haeften from volunteering for the assassination himself. Such principles had evidently been overcome, for Haeften, like Stauffenberg, carried in his briefcase as backup about two pounds of plastic hexite explosive, into which British-made primers with thirty-minute fuses had already been sunk. Also at the airport, boarding the same flight to Rastenburg, was the irresolute General Stieff and his aide, Major Roll.

Slightly delayed by early morning mist, the Heinkel took off after **7 a.m.** and flew east-north-east across the Prussian plain towards the forests of northern Poland where the Wolf's Lair lay, some 350 miles away. They landed soon after **10 a.m.** and separated; Stieff and Roll driving to their posts, accompanied by Haeften carrying both explosive briefcases, while Stauffenberg was driven the ten miles through two SS checkpoints to the Wolf's Lair, the forbidding forest clearing described by General Alfred Jodl as 'a cross between a monastery and a concentration camp'. As on his last visit on 15 July, Stauffenberg breakfasted with colleagues in the officers' mess known as 'the casino'. He also gave a preliminary run-through of the subjects he would cover in the conference to General Walther Buhle, chief of the army's General Staff.

At **11.30 a.m.** Stauffenberg rejoined Haeften and passed from the Wolf's Lair's outer zone, Sperrkreis 2, into the highly guarded inner zone, Sperrkreis 1, where Hitler lived. Here they went to Field Marshal Keitel's office hut for another preliminary briefing. Haeften, as befitted his junior status, was not admitted to this meeting, but waited outside in a corridor with his telltale heavy briefcase, which he attempted to conceal beneath a tarpaulin. His jumpy manner attracted the attention of a Keitel aide, Staff Sergeant Werner Vogel, who asked who the conspicuously bulky briefcase belonged to. Haeften replied that Stauffenberg needed it for the conference, and promptly removed it from the inquisitive sergeant's presence.

Stauffenberg and Haeften had expected the conference to start at midday, but Stauffenberg learned from Keitel just before **12.00 p.m.** that it had been put off until **12.30 p.m.** while preparations were made to receive Mussolini; the deposed Duce was visiting Rastenburg that same day. Stauffenberg took advantage of the delay to ask Keitel's adjutant, Major John von Freyend, if there was a convenient room nearby where he could change his sweat-soaked shirt, and freshen up for the conference after his long flight. It seemed a reasonable request; the heat of the day was approaching its height, and under the glowering trees and camouflage canopies of the gloomy Wolf's Lair – a place hated by all its forced inhabitants, apart, apparently, from Hitler himself – the atmosphere was oppressively stuffy and muggy.

Stauffenberg's real purpose, of course, was to win a few minutes on his own with Haeften so that they could prime the bomb in the briefcase that he would carry into the conference. He had with him in the pocket of his uniform tunic a small pair of specially adapted pliers that he would use to squeeze the copper casing around the glass phial containing the acid that would eat through the detonator wire which would then ignite the charge. No detail of this operation had been left to chance. Stauffenberg's brother Berthold had encased the pliers in rubber and bent the handles, the better for his brother's remaining three fingers to grip, and Stauffenberg had practised squeezing the phial time and time again, until he could execute the delicate operation practically blindfold in a few seconds.

John von Freyend obligingly showed Stauffenberg and Haeften – ostensibly needed to help the maimed man on with his shirt – to his own quarters. Staff Sergeant Vogel, the nosy NCO who had earlier seen Haeften's suspicious-looking parcel, passed by again and saw the two men bent over some object. At that moment, around **12.25 p.m.**, General Fellgiebel, the communications chief whose job it would be to shut down the Wolf's Lair's links with the outside world after the explosion, telephoned on an internal line and asked to speak to Stauffenberg. Freyend told Vogel to get him and remind him that the conference was starting and that Hitler hated being kept waiting. Obediently, the inquisitive sergeant returned to his boss's sitting room and opened the door.

Stauffenberg, however, was standing with his back against the door, blocking Vogel's entry. The staff sergeant gave his message, and an agitated-sounding Stauffenberg answered that he would be along directly. Vogel's summons was reinforced by Major John von Freyend, who barked from the hut's door, 'Do come along, Stauffenberg!' The two assassins knew they could delay no more, even though their task was only half complete. They had succeeded in priming Stauffenberg's bomb, but had intended to add to the load the explosive that Haeften was carrying. There was now no time for this.

The interruption almost certainly saved Hitler's life, for had the second two-pound explosive slab been added, explosives experts agree, everyone round the conference table would certainly have been killed.

Hastily stowing the single explosive slab, Stauffenberg snapped the tanned leather briefcase shut. Inside, the acid was already eating through the wire that, given the hot conditions, might explode within a quarter of an hour rather than the thirty minutes it normally took. Stauffenberg left John von Freyend's room and joined him and Keitel, who were impatiently waiting outside the hut.

A Time Pencil detonator, similar to the device which Stauffenberg would have used.

Seeing the maimed man weighed down by the heavy briefcase, John von Freyend offered to carry it, put out his hand and gripped the handle. But Stauffenberg, John later testified, practically tore the case out of his grasp, with an energy that even the suspicious Vogel, watching the incident, had to admire. Then Stauffenberg, perhaps worried that his behaviour would arouse suspicion, relented and allowed Major John to carry it, explaining that he wanted to be placed as near to Hitler as possible, as his hearing was not good since his African injuries. Stauffenberg then joined Generals Keitel and Buhle for the rest of the three-minute walk across to the conference hut, while Haeften hurried off to ensure that the staff car would be available for their anticipated hasty departure. During the short stroll to the conference Stauffenberg engaged Buhle in animated talk.

When they arrived, it was about **12.35 p.m.** and the conference had already begun. The four men took their places around the large rectangular oak map table that occupied most of the ten by four metres (thirty three by thirteen feet) space in the briefing room, with a few smaller tables for phones and radios around the walls. The windows were flung open in the stifling heat. There were now twenty-five men gathered around the table. Stauffenberg squeezed in next and to the left of Colonel Heinz Brandt, the General Staff officer who had himself escaped death when he had acted as the unwitting courier carrying Tresckow's and Schlabrendorff's bottle bomb on board Hitler's aircraft the previous year. He would not be so lucky today.

Directly to Stauffenberg's left was Luftwaffe General Günther Korten; then came General Adolf Heusinger, operations chief of the OKH, who was reporting on the critical state of the Eastern Front as they came in.

Hitler was seated on Heusinger's left, three places down the table from Stauffenberg, who slid his deadly briefcase under the table, as close to the Führer as he could. Hitler acknowledged their late arrival with a searching stare, then motioned Heusinger to continue with his report. Another observer who saw Stauffenberg's arrival from his position three places further down the table from Hitler was General Walther Warlimont, Heusinger's deputy chief of operations. Stauffenberg had, recalled Warlimont,

> the classic image of the warrior through all history. I barely knew him, but as he stood there, one eye covered by a black patch, a maimed arm in an empty uniform sleeve, standing tall and upright, looking directly at Hitler who had now also turned round, he was . . . a proud figure, the very image of the general staff officer . . . of that time.

Keitel announced that Stauffenberg would be reporting on the Reserve Army's state of organisation and Hitler shook his would-be assassin's remaining hand. Heusinger's gloomy report on the dire state of the Eastern Front continued. He was just saying that the position around Lemberg was desperate, and would collapse unless reinforced with reserves when Keitel broke in, fussily suggesting that this was a good opportunity for Stauffenberg to report on the readiness of the Reserve Army to supply reinforcements. Hitler demurred, saying that Heusinger should complete his report on the rest of the Eastern Front, and that he would hear Stauffenberg later.

This was Stauffenberg's chance, the window of opportunity he needed to slip away without attracting suspicion. He left his place at the table and whispered to Keitel, who had taken his usual place at Hitler's left hand, that he needed to take an urgent phone call from Berlin on the latest information regarding reserves available for Russia. Keitel, delayed by Stauffenberg for the second time that day, frowned in annoyance but could hardly refuse. He nodded brusquely and Stauffenberg slipped out of the room, beckoning to John von Freyend whose assistance he needed again, this time to get General Fellgiebel on an internal phone. John ordered a telephone operator, Sergeant Adam, to connect Stauffenberg and returned to the conference.

Back in the briefing, Heusinger had resumed his report. As he did so, Colonel Brandt leaned in over the table to get a closer look at the maps and accidentally kicked Stauffenberg's heavy briefcase over. He leaned down to stand it upright, and in doing so pushed it further under the table so that one of the table's two stout wooden supports now stood between the briefcase and Hitler. Heusinger's report was drawing to a close. To his intense annoyance Keitel saw that Stauffenberg had not

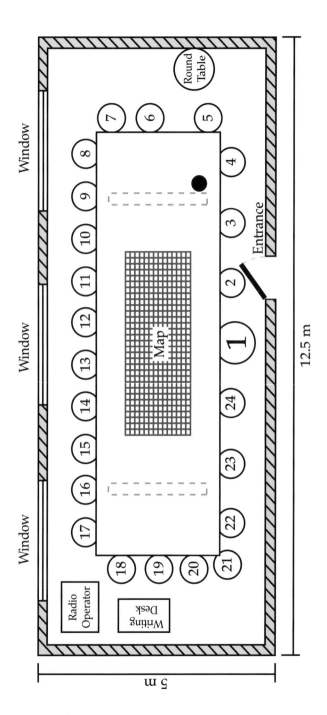

# The Map Room at the Führer's Headquarters, Rastenburg at 12.42 p.m. on 20 July 1944

1. Adolf Hitler
2. General Heusinger
3. Luftwaffe General Korten
4. Colonel Brandt
5. Luftwaffe General Bodenschatz
6. General Schmundt
7. Lieutenant-Colonel Borgmann
8. Rear Admiral Puttkamer
9. Stenographer Berger
10. Naval Caption Assmann
11. General Scherff
12. General Buhle

13. Rear Admiral Voss
14. SS Group Leader Fegelein
15. Colonel Below
16. SS Hauptsturmführer Gunsche
17. Stenographer Hagen
18. Lieutenant-Colonel John
19. Major Büchs
20. Lieutenant-Colonel Weizenegger
21. Ministerial Counselor Sonnleithner
22. General Warlimont
23. General Jodl
24. Field Marshal Keitel

● Bomb in briefcase under the table

returned. He left the conference to find the errant colonel, and to his surprise heard from Sergeant Adam that Stauffenberg had disappeared without making a call. Thoroughly mystified, Keitel returned to the briefing.

Once John had gone, Stauffenberg put the phone down and, in his haste forgetting his cap and belt, crossed to Fellgiebel's communications centre a few hundred yards away, where he had arranged to meet Haeften and Fellgiebel himself. They stepped out of the building to where their car was waiting, so that they could have a good view of the conference hut. Haeften got into the car. Stauffenberg, understandably, nervous, lit a cigarette and distractedly talked to Fellgiebel.

At **12.42 p.m.** the briefcase bomb exploded. A deafening blast roared out and a choking cloud of smoke and dust rose from the hut. So violent was the blast that many of those present thought that a passing Russian plane had dropped a bomb, and Stauffenberg himself compared it to a direct hit from a 150-mm shell. One of those inside the conference, General Warlimont, described the impact:

> In a flash the map room became a scene of stampede and destruction. At one moment ... a set of men ... a focal point of world events; at the next there was nothing but wounded men groaning, the acrid smell of burning; and charred fragments of maps and papers fluttering in the wind. I staggered up and jumped through the open window.

The pandemonium was intense. One man was blown through an open window, but got up unhurt and ran to summon help; others, Hitler included, had their clothes torn to shreds or burned into their bodies. The heavy oak conference table had been shattered into three sections, and segments of the concrete roof had come crashing down. Through the chaos, the stentorian voice of Field Marshal Keitel could be heard demanding: 'Where is the Führer?' Stauffenberg did not hang around to see the full results of his handiwork. Assuming from the force of the blast that Hitler was indeed dead, Stauffenberg chucked his cigarette, leapt into the car alongside Haeften and ordered the driver to head hell for leather to the airfield. Hitler, however, was very much alive.

Fellgiebel, abruptly abandoned by Stauffenberg to his crucial task of closing down Rastenburg's communications, saw with mounting horror the Führer come staggering out of the smoking debris of the conference hut, supported by the ever-loyal Keitel, who was sobbing 'My Führer; you're alive; you're alive!' The dictator presented an appalling spectacle:

The Wolfschanze conference room after the explosion.

his hair had been set alight; his right arm and leg burned and partially paralysed through shock; his black trousers were trailing around his blooded, splinter-flecked legs in tattered ribbons; and both his ear-drums had burst. His buttocks, as he ruefully jested later, had been bruised 'as blue as a baboon's behind' by the impact of him being flung headlong on the floor by the blast. As Hitler staggered away from the carnage, behind him four of his lieutenants lay dead or dying, two others had life-threatening injuries and almost everyone else in the room had suffered burns and/or shock and concussion.

Warlimont, slightly concussed, helped the luckless Colonel Brandt, whose leg had been shattered when the briefcase exploded almost under his feet, and who, shocked, was trying to heave himself across a window ledge. Having accomplished his act of mercy for his comrade, Warlimont's head started to swim, his ears buzzed, and he fainted. Along with Brandt, those who subsequently succumbed to the injuries caused by Stauffenberg's bomb were General Korten, General Rudolf Schmundt and a stenographer named Berger who was killed outright.

At about **12.50 p.m.** Stauffenberg's car was halted at Guardpost 1, the checkpoint separating the inner Sperrkreis 1 from the outer Sperrkreis 2 zone. Although a formal alarm had not been raised, the lieutenant in charge of the checkpoint had heard the bang and seen the smoke and accordingly dropped the barrier. But he recognised Stauffenberg, who told him that he had to get to the airport urgently. As the alarm had not yet been raised, the lieutenant let him pass. Stauffenberg drove on to reach the southern guard post of Sperrkreis 2. By this time, the alarm had sounded and the barriers had been firmly closed by the checkpoint's commander, a Sergeant Kolbe. It looked as though Stauffenberg and Haeften were trapped in the Wolf's Lair. But Stauffenberg's iron nerves and quick mind did not fail him at this critical juncture. Calmly, he told Kolbe the story that had got him through the first checkpoint: that he needed to drive to the

(Top) An SS soldier holding the shredded trousers Hitler wore during the assassination attempt. Hitler sent the trousers to Eva Braun for safekeeping with a note explaining they would be proof of his historic destiny.
(Bottom) A photograph of the conference room, taken on 20 July 1944.

airport as a matter of the utmost urgency. Kolbe was adamant: once the barriers were down, no one could leave. Stauffenberg insisted that Kolbe telephone the Wolf's Lair headquarters, where he spoke to an adjutant, a cavalry captain named Leonhard von Mollendorf who had been one of the officers with whom Stauffenberg had breakfasted that morning. Stauffenberg took the phone from Kolbe and tersely told Mollendorf that he had the permission of Rastenburg's commander, Lieutenant-Colonel Gustav von Streve, to leave the complex, as he had to fly by 1.15 p.m. at the latest. As Streve had been called to the scene of the explosion, Stauffenberg's story could not be verified, but Mollendorf was aware that he was an officer with permission to be at Rastenburg, and was anyway severely crippled, so he ordered Kolbe to let him through. The car tore on to the airport. En route, the driver saw Haeften take a small brown paper parcel and toss it from the car: it was the unused slab of plastic explosive and was later recovered by the Gestapo. At **1.15 p.m.**, heaving huge sighs of relief, Stauffenberg and Haeften took off for Berlin.

Back in the Bendlerstrasse, the conspirators had spent the morning marking time. No news could be expected until about **1 p.m.** Olbricht had been joined in his office at 12.30 by General Erich Hoepner, the former Panzer commander who had been dismissed in disgrace by Hitler in January 1942 for the crime of withdrawing his tanks from before Moscow. Forbidden even to wear Wehrmacht uniform, the humiliated Hoepner, who had not been involved in plotting since the abortive Oster putsch of 1938, had renewed his links with the conspirators in his enforced retirement. Now, carrying his forbidden uniform in a suitcase,

The unused bomb: the parcel of explosive with primer charge thrown from their car by Stauffenberg and Haeften as they fled – would it have made the difference?

The remnants
of Stauffenberg's
briefcase pieced
together by Gestapo
investigators
after the bomb it
contained exploded.

he joined Olbricht for lunch while they awaited news from Rastenburg. Over a bottle of wine they toasted the success of the putsch.

But the first news from Rastenburg was ambiguous in the extreme. Fellgiebel had been speared on the horns of a dilemma as he saw Hitler staggering from the scene of the bomb: if he blocked communications as scheduled, he would immediately attract attention and suspicion. The truth was that the conspirators had made no provision for this eventuality. They were used to aborting putsches at the last minute after the many occasions when an assassination attempt had been planned but had not taken place. What they had not reckoned on was the current circumstance; a bomb had gone off – but Hitler had survived the blast. Fortunately for Fellgiebel, he was temporarily relieved of the terrible burden of his responsibility by the Nazis themselves: Hitler ordered his own communications blackout – although the Nazi leadership and the Wehrmacht's higher command, including Fellgiebel himself, could use the phone, all other phone, radio and teletype communications out of Rastenburg were blocked. Hitler was adamant: until it was discovered who was behind the bomb, no news of it should reach the outside world. Gratefully, Fellgiebel confirmed the blackout. Then, as he walked up and down the path that led by the Führer's personal quarters, unsure of what to do next, he saw Hitler himself emerge and walk shakily around his own compound. He was clearly not even seriously hurt.

Dismayed, Fellgiebel put through a call to the Bendlerstrasse on his personal phone. It was **1.30 p.m.** The call was taken by General Friedrich 'Fritz' Thiele, one of the conspirators. Fellgiebel was brief, and opaque. In a totalitarian state, hostile ears would probably be listening. 'Something terrible had happened,' he reported, then perceptibly paused before adding, 'the Führer is alive'. The news threw Thiele and Olbricht into dithering doubt. Too late, they now realised that no provision had been made for this eventuality. If Stauffenberg's bomb had misfired they could have done nothing – and got away with it. But now that the blast had occurred, there was no chance of covering it up. They conferred with the army's quartermaster general, Eduard Wagner, at Zossen, on board whose plane Stauffenberg was now winging back to Berlin, blissfully believing that his bomb had killed Hitler. Between them, the three generals decided to sit tight and wait for more news from Rastenburg.

The long, hot afternoon wore on. Only one officer in the Bendlerstrasse seemed possessed of the same resolute spirit as his friend Stauffenberg – Colonel Mertz von Quirnheim. At about **1.50 p.m.**, having heard that Stauffenberg's bomb had exploded, Mertz tried to activate Valkyrie. He told another conspirator, General Staff Major Hans-Ulrich von Oertzen, a protégé of Tresckow, to issue the necessary orders to the Armoured School at Krampnitz outside Berlin to send its vehicles into the centre of the capital and prevent the SS from launching a counter-coup out of their barracks at Lichterfelde. Two advance vehicles actually arrived outside the school but, seeing no unusual activity, were redirected to the Siegessaule (Victory Column) near the Brandenburg Gate in Berlin's very heart. Mertz also ordered units from the Infantry School at Dobe-ritz to move into the city centre. At **2 p.m.** Mertz next summoned all available officers from the General Staff of the Reserve Army and told them that Hitler had been assassinated, and that the army was taking control of the country to ensure internal order. The Waffen SS would be incorporated into the Wehrmacht, said Mertz, and Field Marshal Wit-zleben would be the new army commander. Retired General Ludwig Beck would be the new head of state.

Orders for carrying out Valkyrie also reached the conspirators in Paris. Soon after **2 p.m.** Colonel Eberhard Finckh, chief of staff to the Western Command, received a mysterious anonymous phone call at his offices in the rue de Saurene from a source at the Zossen military base outside Berlin. The voice gave the agreed word for launching the coup *'Abgelaufen'* (launched), repeated it, then rang off. Immediately, Finckh called for his car and drove to the St Germain headquarters of

Kluge's deputy in France, General Günther von Blumentritt (left) approved of the plot but was not one of the conspirators. General von Boineburg (centre, with monocle) arrested all 1,200 SS men in Paris on 20 July in a flawless operation.

General Günther von Blumentritt, chief of staff to Field Marshal Kluge, who was away on an inspection trip to the crumbling Normandy front. Blumentritt was a jovial, rotund soldier who – although no Nazi – was not a party to the plot.

Arriving around **3 p.m.** Finckh greeted Blumentritt and got straight to the point. 'Herr General, there has been a Gestapo putsch in Berlin,' he began. 'The Führer is dead. A provisional government has been formed by Witzleben, Beck and Goerdeler.' There was a minute's silence while Blumentritt digested the information.

'I'm glad it's they who have taken over,' he responded, 'they're sure to try for peace. Who gave you this news?' Finckh lied glibly: 'The military governor,' he replied, knowing that Stülpnagel was a fellow plotter.

Without further ado, Blumentritt picked up his phone and was put through to Kluge's forward headquarters at the château of La Roche-Guyon – the building that had been Rommel's headquarters until he had sustained his injuries three days before. General Hans Speidel, another conspirator, answered the phone and said that Kluge was still incommunicado visiting frontline units. Blumentritt was guarded:

'Things are happening in Berlin,' he said enigmatically, then whispered the single word '*Tot*' (dead). At once Speidel was full of questions: who was dead, and how? Blumentritt, knowing that phones were vulnerable to eavesdroppers, refused to elaborate and hung up. After a few moments' chat, Finckh took his leave and returned to Paris. By the time he arrived, it was **4.30 p.m.**

Stauffenberg and Haeften landed back at Berlin's Rangsdorf airfield just before **3.45 p.m.** There was an immediate mix-up: Schweizer was not at the airport to meet them, and there was a delay while another car and driver were summoned. Haeften used the time to call the Bendlerstrasse just before **4 p.m.** He told his fellow conspirators that the assassination had succeeded and that Hitler was dead. They then set out on the thirty-kilometre drive to the Bendlerblock, arriving around **4.30 p.m.**

In the meantime, although Olbricht had sat on his hands, Mertz had not been idle. At **4 p.m.** he ordered the issuing of the second stage of the Valkyrie orders, with the proclamation that began with the words 'The Führer, Adolf Hitler, is dead!' and ended with the announcement of martial law. Mertz, dragging a reluctant Olbricht – who already knew that with Hitler alive the putsch was a lost cause – had crossed the final Rubicon. Olbricht plucked up the courage to get his superior officer on board. He hastened to the office of General Fromm and told him without further ado that Hitler had been assassinated and that he proposed issuing the orders for Operation Valkyrie to begin. Fromm would not be rushed. He insisted on calling Rastenburg to get confirmation of the Führer's death. Olbricht himself picked up the phone on Fromm's desk and Fromm was put through to Keitel.

'What's happening at Rastenburg?' asked Fromm, 'There are the wildest rumours circulating here.'

'Nothing at all,' replied the Field Marshal. 'Everything's normal here. What have you heard?'

'I've just had a report that the Führer's been assassinated.' said Fromm.

'Rubbish,' asserted Keitel, before admitting that an attempt had indeed been made on Hitler's life. 'Fortunately, it failed,' he added. 'The Führer is alive and only slightly injured.' Then Hitler's 'nodding donkey' switched subjects: 'Where, by the way, is your Chief of Staff, Colonel Count Stauffenberg?' Fromm replied that Stauffenberg had not yet returned from Rastenburg and rang off. He told Olbricht that in view of the Führer's survival, it was not necessary to activate Valkyrie. Olbricht,

Heinrich Himmler, feared overlord of the SS.

Ernest Kaltenbruner, Heydrich's successor and in charge of investigating the July plot. Here seen on trial at Nuremberg with Field Marshal Keitel sitting on his right. Both were hanged.

who knew that the plan had already been launched, returned to his office to anxiously await Stauffenberg's arrival.

At Rastenburg, SS overlord Heinrich Himmler had sped from his own headquarters half an hour away to take personal charge of the investigation into the bombing. Suspicion first fell upon foreign construction workers employed at the complex, but when the telephone operator Sergeant Adam spoke up about the peculiar behaviour of Stauffenberg at the time of the blast – including his forgetting his cap and belt in his confusion – others recalled his hurried departure and began to put two and two together. Hitler's ubiquitous private secretary, Martin Bormann, brought Adam to his master for a personal interview. The Führer quizzed the operator closely before quickly coming to the conclusion that Stauffenberg had been responsible for planting the bomb. As yet, however, there was no suspicion of a wider conspiracy.

Himmler lost little time in ordering his No. 2, Ernst Kaltenbrunner – the towering, scar-faced Austrian who had taken over control of the RSHA (Reich Security Main Office) after Heydrich's assassination – to take charge of the investigation into the bombing. Kaltenbrunner was in Berlin and, ironically, flew to Rastenburg from Rangsdorf airfield – the very same destination that Stauffenberg was flying to: their aircraft crossed in flight. Himmler himself took off for Berlin in hot pursuit of Stauffenberg and Haeften.

At **4.05 p.m.** communications with the outside world were restored.

Thrown once again into doubt and confusion by Keitel's blunt assertion that Hitler was alive, the timid Olbricht had returned to his office with the news that Fromm would not sign the Valkyrie order, to find that the more resolute Mertz was already going ahead with the issuing of the orders for Valkyrie II, beginning with the bald and bold words: 'The Führer Adolf Hitler is dead!' Mertz was actively deploying his forces – he had summoned junior officers who were party to the conspiracy to carry out their allotted roles. Captain Friedrich Karl Klausing, the adjutant who had accompanied Stauffenberg to the Berghof and Rastenburg on 11 and 15 July in Haeften's absence, was on his way to secure the Berlin army headquarters. Similarly Major Egbert Hayessen was on his way to the office of the capital's city commander, General Paul von Hase, to take control there. A clutch of young officers – Georg von Oppen, Ewald Heinrich Kleist-Schmenzin, Hans Fritzsche and Ludwig von Hammerstein – had been summoned from the Esplanade Hotel where they had been waiting to act as adjutants in the Bendlerstrasse. Generals Beck and Hoepner, in civilian clothes, had also arrived in the building, and changed into their uniforms – Hoepner using Olbricht's office toilet for the task. All now awaited the arrival of the main actor: Stauffenberg.

Although Mertz had bounced him into action, Olbricht still fussily wanted Fromm to lend his authority to the orders that were already going out under his name. He therefore returned to his superior's office, again asserted that Hitler was dead, and informed Fromm that the orders for Valkyrie II were going out. Furious, Fromm leapt to his feet and demanded to know who had given such an order without his authority. Olbricht replied that Mertz had done so, and when he was summoned, Mertz coolly confirmed it. 'Mertz! You are under arrest!' Fromm barked. It was **4.30 p.m.**

Just at that moment, Olbricht happened to glance out of a window overlooking the courtyard, and was intensely relieved to see a staff car pull up and the unmistakable tall figure of Stauffenberg emerge. Stauffenberg rushed upstairs to Olbricht's office for a hurried consultation. Hitler was certainly dead, Stauffenberg assured the doubting Olbricht, and seeing that the general was still dubious, added the forgivable exaggeration: 'I saw them carrying out his body myself.' Told that Keitel had explicitly denied it, Stauffenberg blurted irritably, 'Keitel's lying as usual!' – a message he would repeat to the growing number of doubters as the long evening unfolded. Other conspirators drifted in – Berthold von Stauffenberg, conspicuous in his blue navy uniform in a crowd of army field grey; Fritz-Dietlof von der Schulenberg; Lieutenant Kleist-Schmenzin and Captain Fritzsche. Stauffenberg repeated the same message to them all: the bomb had killed Hitler, and he had seen his body; he compared the explosion to the detonation of a 150-mm shell. Then Stauffenberg got on the telephone. His first call was to Helldorf, chief of the Berlin Police, summoning him to the Bendlerblock to ensure that he would arrest key members of the SS and Gestapo. Stauffenberg next rang his cousin, Casar von Hofacker, in Paris.

The conspirators in Paris were a small but dedicated group, of which the military governor, General Karl-Heinrich von Stülpnagel, was the titular leader, the equivalent of Beck in Berlin; Lieutenant-Colonel Casar von Hofacker, the only prominent Luftwaffe officer to join the military plot, was, like his cousin Stauffenberg, the dedicated driving force. The other leading figures included Rommel's Chief of Staff,

Colonel Hans
Otfried von Linstow.

General Hans Speidel, Colonel Eberhard Finckh and Colonel Hans Otfried von Linstow, Stülpnagel's Chief of Staff, along with a handful of civilian advisers and administrators. Hofacker had kept this small group abreast of Stauffenberg's previous attempts to kill Hitler earlier that month. On **19 July** he had assembled them again in the Hotel Majestic, to advise them that another attempt would be made the next day. Come what may, he said, this time the bomb would explode. Hofacker had no illusions about the chances of success, telling Baron Teuchert, one of his civilian aides, that they had only a 5 to 10 per cent hope of winning through. He added grimly: 'If this affair miscarries we shall have an appointment with the hangman.' His forecast was to prove all too accurate.

Stülpnagel, too, was fatalistically clear-eyed about the chances. A blonde veteran of the First World War, and an intellectual with a lively interest in history and culture, he had often come close to despair and resignation after the repeated failures of the conspirators since 1938, but Hofacker's iron will had pulled him back into line. Now the strain he was under was beginning to tell: as his friend and fellow officer, the writer and Great War hero Ernst Jünger, stationed on Stülpnagel's staff in Paris, observed in his diary: 'He seemed tired; one of his habitual gestures – he repeatedly presses his right hand against the small of his back, as if to stiffen his spine or thrust out his chest – reveals the sort of anxiety that has taken hold of him, and this can be read clearly in his face.'

Nonetheless, Stülpnagel went through the motions as if 20 July was to be another normal day. At **12 noon** he lunched with his staff as usual at the Hotel Majestic. It was noticed, however, that the general was quiet and abstracted rather than his usual chatty, witty self (as he was when his tongue was loosened by wine). Those present all agreed later that his mind appeared to be on other things. At **2 p.m.** Stülpnagel made an excuse and left the table. Soon after he was observed pacing the Majestic's roof garden. At **3 p.m.** his staff convened a previously scheduled meeting with French officials to discuss the question of housing French refugees from the Normandy fighting. Then the phone in Hofacker's office rang – it was Stauffenberg calling from Berlin.

His cousin gave Hofacker the same urgent message he had broadcast around the Bendlerblock: the bomb had exploded, Hitler was dead, the Valkyrie putsch was underway and government offices around Berlin were being occupied by troops under the plotters' orders. Now Hofacker had to do the same. Eyes gleaming with excitement, Hofacker slammed down the phone and rushed to tell his aide Teuchert, calling him out of the refugees' meeting to say: 'Hitler is dead! The explosion was frightful!' He then hurried off to tell Stülpnagel the good news. Teuchert, dazed with joy, reeled off down a corridor where a civilian greeted him with the Nazi salute and the obligatory 'Heil Hitler!' Hardly able to contain himself, Teuchert burst into hysterical laughter, leaving the civilian staring, aghast and open-mouthed.

Stülpnagel had just received confirmation from Berlin of Stauffenberg's message: the codeword '*Übung*' ('Exercise'*)* was the agreed signal that the assassination had been effected and that the Paris Wehrmacht now had to put Valkyrie into effect in the French capital by arresting all the SS and SD personnel in the city. Quickly, Stülpnagel gathered his available officers together in his office – both those involved in the plot, and those not in the know. His secretary, Countess Sophie Podewils, arrived back in the office from a dental appointment in the midst of all the activity. Her boss, wishing to shield her from the danger of too much knowledge, told her that the fuss was about the latest unacceptable demand from Fritz Sauckel, the Nazis' labour minister, for yet more French workers to prop up Germany's sagging war economy.

Stülpnagel got to his feet and addressed his visitors: 'There has been a Gestapo putsch – an attempt on the Führer's life. All the SS and SD men here in Paris must be arrested. Do not hesitate to use force if there is any resistance.' Stülpnagel called General Baron Hans von Boineburg-Langsfeld, the monocled commander of troops in Paris, over to his desk and spread out a map showing the locations of all the city's SS and SD units. 'They must all be rounded up,' he repeated. 'Is that quite clear?' 'Perfectly clear,' Boineburg answered with a click of his heels. The Paris end of Valkyrie was underway.

Still in blissful ignorance of what was going on in Berlin and Paris, Hitler's staff at Rastenburg, recovering from the initial shock of the bomb, hastily made preparations for the visit from the Duce – Benito Mussolini. As they awaited his belated arrival at the Rastenburg railway siding, Germany's leaders congratulated their Führer on his 'miraculous' escape from Stauffenberg's bomb blast. With the exception of Goebbels, who was at his Propaganda Ministry in the capital, and Himmler, who, promoted to Commander-in-Chief of the Reserve Army in place of Fromm (who was believed to be in league with the plotters), was flying towards Berlin in pursuit of Stauffenberg, most of the top Nazis had gathered at the Wolf's Lair. Goering was there – gaudy as ever in his outsize Luftwaffe uniform and jackboots. Foreign Minister Joachim von Ribbentrop had hastened over from his Schloss at Steinort to offer his unctuous congratulations to his master. There too was foxy-faced Admiral Karl von Dönitz, overlord of the U-boat campaign against Allied shipping and one of the Reich's rising stars.

At **4 p.m.**, some three hours behind schedule, Mussolini's train rolled into the siding. The former dictator, inappropriately swathed in black

Mussolini was greeted by Hitler on 20 July after his train arrived at Rastenburg.

coat and hat against the humid heat, looked all of his sixty years. Hitler, however, looked even worse. White-faced and shaken, his singed hair – 'sticking up like a hedgehog' as one of his secretaries recalled – was concealed by his military cap. His arm in a sling under his military cloak, and with cotton wool sprouting from both of his injured ears, he presented a sorry sight to his comrade-in-arms. Ushering Mussolini into his car for the short drive back to the nerve-centre of the Wolf's Lair, Hitler explained in a few words what had happened just three hours before.

Aghast that Hitler's security had been so easily penetrated, Mussolini allowed himself to be given a conducted tour of the shattered remains of the conference room with Hitler as his guide. 'I was standing right here, next to the table,' recounted the Führer hoarsely. 'The bomb went

(Above) Hitler with Goering and Goebbels.

(Right) Hitler shows the bomb damage to Mussolini three hours after the blast.

off just at my feet! Look at my uniform!' he urged as his tattered and scorched garments were held up for the Duce's inspection. 'Look at my burns!' he exclaimed. Hitler then fixed his fellow dictator with one of his famous hypnotic gazes. 'When I reflect on all this, Duce, it is obvious that nothing is going to happen to me. It is certainly my task to continue on my path and bring my work to completion.' Recalling his previous escape from Elser's bomb, Hitler commented that it was not the first time that Providence had held its protective hand over him. 'Having escaped death in this extraordinary way, I am more than ever sure that the great cause that I serve will survive its present perils and everything will be brought to a good end.' He gazed at Mussolini, as if beseeching confirmation. Obediently, the Duce answered the Führer's cue: 'You are right, Führer,' he affirmed. 'Heaven has helped protect and defend you. After this miracle, it is inconceivable that our cause could come to any harm.'

The two dictators and their respective entourages – which included on the Italian side Marshal Graziani, one of the few Italian military

Hitler massages his injured arm after the bombing. (Left to right) Keitel, Goering, Hitler and Bormann.

leaders to stay loyal to the Duce, and the dictator's son Vittorio; and on the German side Goering, Dönitz, Ribbentrop and the omnipresent Martin Bormann – then adjourned for tea at **5 p.m.** before settling down for their formal talks. The discussions had been due to cover such subjects as the defence of Italy's Gothic Line against the steady Allied advance up the peninsula, and the fate of thousands of Italian soldiers who were reluctant to fight further for their sawdust Caesar and were being held in deplorable conditions in German camps. The meeting was, however, entirely overshadowed by the repercussions of Stauffenberg's bomb.

With communications with the outside world having been restored, it was becoming all too apparent at Rastenburg that Stauffenberg's attack had been part of a much wider conspiracy. Anxious inquiries as to whether Hitler was really dead were flooding in from German army bases where the Valkyrie orders had been received, along with confused reports of unauthorized troop movements in Berlin, Paris, Vienna, Prague and even occupied Norway. These all showed that Valkyrie was underway, and that under its cover some sort of attempted putsch was in progress. Hitler himself appeared distracted over his tea, fiddling with the multi-coloured array of pills prescribed for his various ailments by his quack physician Dr Theo Morell, and occasionally swallowing a lozenge in-between his favourite cream cakes. As messengers scurried in and out with news of the condition of those injured by the bomb, or reports of what was going on in the rest of Germany and Europe, the Führer remained silent and strangely abstracted.

The awkward hiatus was filled with interjections from the competing Nazi bigwigs around the table, who, much to the embarrassment of their Italian guests, began to squabble and shout one another down in their protestations of loyalty, indulging in ever more accusatory finger-pointing as they endeavoured to apportion blame for the bombing. Goering opened the attacks, opining that the true reason for the recent reverses in Russia was now all too obvious. 'Our brave soldiers have been betrayed by their generals!' he cried, before asserting that his loyal Luftwaffe could and would save the day. Not to be outdone, Dönitz chimed in, protesting the navy's utter loyalty. The U-boat packs would yet strangle Britain's sea lanes, he pledged. Ribbentrop and Bormann added their voices to the chorus: the one claiming that Germany's deteriorating international position could yet be restored by the efforts of his diplomats; the other assuring his boss that the Party, purged of all disloyal elements, would re-double its efforts to win the war on the home front.

In the face of this mix of boot-licking and mutual recrimination, the presence of the embarrassed Italian visitors was apparently forgotten. 'We noted a growing reciprocal animosity, as if each of them intended to accuse the other of having protected or allowed the plotters to act,' recalled Filippo Anfuso, Mussolini's ambassador in Germany. 'For us Italians it was all frankly unpleasant and disturbing . . . at a certain point Mussolini looked to me as if to ask what we should do.' As the chorus of loyalty descended into a babble of shouted mutual hatred, with Goering and Dönitz attacking each other for the shortcomings of their respective services, and Goering screaming at Ribbentrop that he was just 'a failed champagne salesman' before threatening him with his brandished Reichsmarschall's baton, the appalling animosities at the heart of the Reich were laid bare for all to see. They were fighting like rats in a sack.

Suddenly, Hitler awoke from his trance. Roaring and spitting, he ignored his squabbling underlings as he unleashed the full force of his fury against the 'miserable traitors' who had dared raise their hands against him. He vowed a fearful vengeance against them – and their families. 'They have deserved ignominious deaths and that is what they will get,' he hissed. 'This nest of vipers who have tried to sabotage the greatness and grandeur of my Germany will be exterminated once and for all.' It was a pledge that he would carry out to the last, terrible letter. As Mussolini took his leave from his partner in crime for what would prove to be the last time, he must have been full of foreboding for the fate that lay in store for them all.

Back in the Bendlerblock in Berlin, even more dramatic scenes were taking place. Stauffenberg headed a delegation of conspirators who marched into Fromm's office at about **4.45 p.m.** Olbricht informed Fromm that he now had confirmation from Stauffenberg – who had been at the scene himself – that Hitler was dead. Stauffenberg agreed – indeed, he added, after witnessing the explosion he had seen Hitler's body being carried away with his own eyes. Fromm responded that he had spoken to Keitel, who had assured him that the Führer had been only slightly hurt and was definitely alive. 'Keitel is lying as usual,' repeated Stauffenberg. Fromm commented that someone in Hitler's entourage must have been involved, to which Stauffenberg responded quietly: 'I know that he is dead because I placed the bomb myself.'

Apparently thunderstruck, Fromm exploded. With real or feigned rage he stormed that Stauffenberg had committed high treason as well as murder and must take the consequences. He asked if Stauffenberg had a pistol and would know what to do as a German officer. Stauffenberg coolly replied that he was unarmed, and that in any case he had no intention of committing suicide. Fromm turned to Mertz von Quirnheim and told him to fetch a pistol, to which Mertz pointed out that as the general had recently put him under arrest, he was unable to fulfil that order. At this point, the burly Fromm squared up to the tall Stauffenberg with red face and raised fists, bellowing that he was under arrest along with Olbricht and any other officer involved in the plot. Stauffenberg, despite all that he had already been through that day, remained calm and collected. On the contrary, he told Fromm, it was he who was under arrest.

Alerted by the commotion, Haeften and Kleist-Schmenzin came in from the adjoining map room, and Kleist-Schmenzin pushed a pistol into Fromm's substantial belly. Accepting the inevitable, Fromm said that he considered himself relieved of his commission by force and asked to be given a bottle of brandy to console himself. He was placed under guard and locked in the office of his adjutant, Captain Heinz-Ludwig Bartram. Hoepner, an old friend of Fromm, was appointed Commander-in-Chief of the Reserve Army in his place by his fellow conspirators. He went along to the office to console Fromm, who told him: 'I'm sorry, Hoepner, but I can't go along with this. In my opinion the Führer is not dead and you are making a big mistake.' Hoepner disconsolately trailed back to the others to relay Fromm's request to be allowed to go home.

Although this request was denied, there was an air of laxness at the Bendlerblock that typified the haphazard, almost half-hearted nature of the operation. At that stage, resolute action might still have saved the day, but confusion, timidity and irresolution ruled in the offices and corridors where the seconds were ticking away and control of events was slipping irresistibly away from the conspirators. Hans Bernd Gisevius, although not an officer, had always been clear that forceful action – up to and including the violent deaths of their Nazi enemies – was the only policy that would bring success. Arriving in the Bendlerblock, he was horrified by the slackness he saw all around him, which even seemed to be infecting Stauffenberg himself. Forgetting rank and decorum, Gisevius fired off a series of questions at a harassed General Beck, to which there were no satisfactory replies:

Why was Fromm not shot at once, rather than merely locked in an office? Why was Goebbels still at large in his Propaganda Ministry, doubtless already busily organising the Nazi fightback? Had the radio station been seized? Or the Gestapo headquarters? Why were there no troops defending the Bendlerstrasse itself? The old general's hesitant, equivocal replies told their own story.

Right on cue, as if to demonstrate the conspirators' helplessness, the door was flung open and an SS Oberführer (colonel), Humbert Piffraeder, in full black uniform and flanked by two plainclothes Gestapo detectives, marched into the room. Piffraeder had been directly tasked by Himmler to detain Stauffenberg and, missing him at Rangsdorf airport, had followed him back to the Bendlerblock. Clicking his heels 'like a pistol shot' and giving Gisevius the Hitler salute, he demanded to speak to the colonel about his activities at Rastenburg. Piffraeder was speedily disarmed and he and his accompanying policemen joined Fromm and other loyalist officers in the plotters' 'bag'. Outraged at such softness, Gisevius turned to Stauffenberg, demanding to know why the SS man had not been shot out of hand. Stauffenberg assured him that he would be 'dealt with' later, and agreed to consider Gisevius's suggestion that a hit squad of young officers be formed at the Bendlerstrasse to shoot Goebbels and any SS leaders they found at large. But meanwhile he turned to what he considered the more urgent task – shoring up Valkyrie.

More conspirators were trickling into the Bendlerblock, although there was still no sign of the man the plotters had designated as the new Commander-in-Chief of the Wehrmacht, Field Marshal Erwin von Witzleben. As Stauffenberg resumed his self-imposed task of organizing the putsch by telephone, calling garrisons throughout German-occupied Europe, the other leading plotters gathered in Olbricht's office for a crisis meeting. Already it was clear that things were not going according to the putschists' plan. The unforeseen event of the bomb having exploded without killing Hitler had thrown the plotters onto the back foot, and the rest of the army into confusion. The Valkyrie II orders had slowly been transmitted, telling local commanders that Hitler was dead, a Gestapo coup had misfired and that Beck and Witzleben had taken control of the country. Already, however, the conspirators' orders were being countermanded by commands from Rastenburg, where the switchboard was busy sending out messages assuring all and sundry that the Führer was alive and 'in perfect health', and that Reichsführer Himmler had been appointed to command the Home Reserve Army.

'Only his orders are valid,' the message concluded. 'Orders from General Fromm, Field Marshal Witzleben and Colonel-General Hoepner [are] not to be executed! Maintain contact with Gauleiters [provincial Nazi party chiefs] and senior SS and Police commanders.'

Faced with these flat denials, even the most committed conspirators began to waver in their belief that Hitler was indeed dead. The first to give in was one who knew the Führer had survived for a certainty: one of the plot's two main men on the spot in Rastenburg – the ever-wavering chief of the General Staff's Organisation Branch, the diminutive General Stieff. Faced with the failure of Stauffenberg's bomb, Stieff called the army's quartermaster general, General Wagner – with whom Stauffenberg had been shooting game barely 24 hours before – at Zossen, outside Berlin, to tell him that the putsch must be called off. 'It's madness,' said Stieff, before promptly going to see Keitel to tell all he knew about the plot and the plotters in a misplaced bid to save his own skin. The craven betrayal did not save Stieff from a slow and agonising death.

Beck took the line that it did not matter whether Hitler was alive or dead. He did not care whether it was true that the dictator had survived the bomb, he declared, since: 'For me, Hitler is dead.' He incorporated such sentiments into the broadcast he was dictating to deliver as the conspirators' designated new head of state: 'A Führer who engenders such conflicts among his closest associates that it comes to an assassination attempt is morally dead.' These weasel words were symbolic of the confusion that reigned in the conspirators' minds: instead of openly declaring that he had approved Stauffenberg's bomb, Beck appeared to be distancing himself from the attempt and adopting some sort of neutral stance. This cannot have come as any surprise to Stauffenberg, who knew full well that he who wields the dagger never wears the crown. He had ruefully predicted before the bombing that even if the attempt succeeded he would be disowned by his comrades in the conspiracy – and so it would prove.

Suddenly, another visitor arrived at the Bendlerblock. General Joachim von Kortzfleisch, deputy commander of the III Corps, had been summoned in Fromm's name. When he arrived, however, he was received by Beck, Olbricht and Hoepner, who told him that Hitler was dead and invited him to place his troops under their command. Kortzfleisch, although a distant relative of the Stauffenberg brothers – they had attended a family wedding as recently as October 1943 – was a Hitler loyalist who refused to believe the news and tried to escape. Although he was detained and joined the growing number of Nazi loyalists in the conspirators' makeshift office cells, the fact that none of the plotters – including Stauffenberg, who must have known of the general's true views – had ascertained where Kortzfleisch's real loyalties lay, spoke volumes about how ill-prepared they were for their putsch. An even worse blunder, and one that was to prove ultimately fatal to their plans, was about to be exposed.

As soon as he received his Valkyrie orders, Berlin's city commandant, General Paul von Hase, who was party to the conspiracy, called his key officers to his office in Berlin's central Unter den Linden boulevard. Present were Brigadier-General Walther Bruns, head of the army's ordnance school; Colonel Helmuth Schwierz, head of the explosives school; and Major Otto Ernst Remer, the highly decorated and much-wounded Eastern Front hero who had recently been assigned to Hase's command as commander of the *Grossdeutschland* Guards battalion, and who – although clearly a Nazi loyalist – Hase had refused to send away. The idea that a young (Remer was 31) and relatively junior officer would refuse to obey a general had clearly never occurred to Hase. 'The

Major Otto Ernst Remer.

Führer has met with an accident – possibly even a fatal accident,' Hase told Remer. 'We don't know exactly what has happened, but we must occupy the city centre.' Hase showed the young officer a map with key objectives circled in red in the government quarter of central Berlin – including Joseph Goebbels's Propaganda Ministry opposite the Reichs Chancellery on the nearby Wilhelmstrasse. He instructed him that no one – not even ministers – were to pass in or out of his cordon once established. 'You don't know the Führer's condition then?' queried Remer, who, though brave, was none too bright. 'No. But as soon as we hear we'll tell you,' replied Hase reassuringly.

Obediently, Remer headed off to collect three companies of his battalion, which had been made up to regimental strength. He felt a faint stirring of suspicion, aroused when he had noticed Major Egbert Hayessen, Hase's adjutant and another conspirator, furtively shuffling some papers into a briefcase as if to hide them from Remer. He confided his feelings of unease to his own adjutant – a Protestant pastor in uniform, Siebert – who shot back the query: 'Military putsch?' Such suspicions were heightened when Dr Hans Hagen, one of Goebbels's cultural commissars attached to the battalion to keep its morale and party loyalty high, told him over lunch that he had seen retired General Brauchitsch – sacked by Hitler in 1938 – riding in a car through Berlin in full uniform, which he was certainly not entitled to wear. Although Hagen was mistaken in his identification – Brauchitsch played no part in the events of 20 July and he had probably seen either Beck or Witzleben – the 'uneasy feelings' that the sight had aroused in Hagen had certainly not been allayed by the mysterious orders Hase had issued. Now he badgered Remer into letting him go and see his boss Dr Goebbels to find out what was going on.

Goebbels – the most senior Nazi leader in Berlin – had heard the bald announcement that Hitler had survived the bomb in the early afternoon, but the master of news and public enlightenment knew no more than other Germans, thanks to the Rastenburg information blackout, until about **5.30 p.m.**, when he succeeded in getting through to Hitler himself by phone. The Führer was still closeted with Mussolini, and kept his orders brief. There were mounting indications that a military putsch was underway in Berlin, he said. Unauthorised orders to initiate Operation Valkyrie were going out and must be countered without delay. The plot had to be nipped in the bud, and the plotters arrested. As a first step he ordered Goebbels to broadcast an emergency communiqué confirming that Hitler was alive and well – and would himself address his people that night.

The little minister had just begun to draft the broadcast in his usual inimitable style when he was interrupted – Dr Hagen had arrived on a motor-cycle provided by Remer and insisted on speaking to the minister. Irritated at the interruption, Goebbels grumpily agreed to receive Hagen, who babbled out a confused story of having seen Brauchitsch, clearly bent on launching a putsch. When Goebbels expressed scepticism that the weak and elderly Brauchitsch had been involved in anything so daring, Hagen responded: 'I'm neither drunk nor crazy. Now that the Führer's dead the generals are taking over . . .' Goebbels assured him that Hitler was alive, and that he had just been speaking to him. He admitted that there had been an assassination attempt, but said that all was well at Rastenburg. But what was happening here in Berlin? It was **6 p.m.**

'Just look outside your windows, Herr Reichsminister,' replied an excited Hagen. 'There are the troops carrying out the putsch.' Goebbels twitched his curtains, and in the gathering twilight of the summer evening saw Remer's men gathering in their trucks. Hagen suggested that the minister send for Remer and assert his authority. Goebbels saw the sense in that – but this most canny of the Nazi politicians had not got where he was by not insuring against risks. He picked up the phone and got put through to the main SS barracks in Berlin, in the leafy southern suburb of Lichterfelde, the scene of mass executions during the Röhm purge exactly ten years before. He told the commander of the elite Leibstandarte *Adolf Hitler* – the Führer's own bodyguard unit – to prepare to move his men the five miles into central Berlin, then steered Hagen to the door. 'Go get your commander,' ordered Goebbels, as he limped across the office and took Hagen's elbow. 'But is Remer a reliable man?' he asked anxiously. 'I can vouch for him with my life!' swore Hagen passionately.

As Hagen roared off on his motor-bike to find Remer, Goebbels returned to the task of drafting Hitler's communiqué, spurred on by another call from the Führer in Rastenburg demanding to know why the good news had not already been broadcast. Worried that Hitler might be beginning to doubt his own loyalty, Goebbels set to his task with a will and within a few minutes had completed a short text and had it sent to the national radio broadcasting station – the Deutschlandsender – whose premises had still not been secured by the putschists. All the hard work they had put into drawing up their sententious and idealistic proclamations about Hitler's tyranny being ended had gone to waste and their hopeful words would never be heard. Instead, listeners all over

Germany heard the following short broadcast – the first public word of what had happened at Rastenburg. It was **6.45 p.m.**

'Today an attempt was made on the Führer's life with explosives,' Goebbels's brief announcement began. After listing the names and conditions of those injured, he continued: 'The Führer himself suffered no injuries beyond light burns and bruises. He resumed his work immediately and – as scheduled – received the Duce for a lengthy discussion. Shortly after the attempt he was joined by the Reichsmarschall [Goering].'

Meanwhile Remer, having carried out his orders and cordoned off the government quarter, had twice returned to Hase for fresh instructions – each time becoming more convinced that the general was involved in something subversive. After overhearing another unit get the order to arrest Goebbels, it finally dawned on Remer that he was the man in the middle between both sides, and that the plotters distrusted him despite using him to execute their orders. He withdrew to brief his own officers about what was afoot: 'Our heads are at stake. It seems to be a military putsch after all,' he said. He decided to go and see Goebbels, defying Hase's orders not to do so.

Remer arrived at the Propaganda Ministry at about **7 p.m.** and was ushered into Goebbels's office immediately. He was just in time to see a fellow army major – Martin Korff from the explosives school – receiving a tongue-lashing from the minister for having the temerity to attempt to arrest him. Korff was the officer tasked by Hase with the job because of Remer's increasingly apparent loyalty to the regime. After sending Korff packing, Goebbels turned to Remer. The Propaganda Minister's first question was whether Remer was a convinced National Socialist. The young Major answered in the affirmative, adding that

Hitler with an injured Jodl (right) and Bormann (smiling on left).

he was 100 per cent behind Hitler. He then inquired anxiously as to Hitler's condition. Goebbels assured him that he was well, and suiting the action to the words, picked up his phone and got put through to Hitler once again. The familiar harsh voice came rasping down the line from Rastenburg. Remer had met Hitler when the Führer had invested him with the Knight's Cross and Oak Leaves, but it did flash through his mind that the man on the line might be an imposter imitating the Führer's familiar, raucous voice. As their conversation went on, however, he became convinced that he was actually being addressed by his leader.

Hitler began by telling Remer that he was unhurt, and asking the young Major if he recognized his voice. *'Jawohl, mein Führer!'* he barked, stiffening to attention. He was awaiting his orders.

Without further ado, Hitler explained in a few short sentences what had happened and what measures the situation required. He promoted Remer to full colonel on the spot – and gave him immediate plenary powers over everyone in Berlin to do what he thought fit to crush the conspirators' coup and restore order. Reichsführer Himmler was on his way to Berlin, added Hitler, but until he arrived, Remer was in complete charge. From this moment, the coup in Berlin was doomed.

In Paris, Operation Valkyrie was unfolding according to the plotters' plans. At **6 p.m.**, having arranged for the arrest of all SS and SD men in the French capital, General Stülpnagel took a call from the Bendlerblock in Berlin. Beck was on the line. The old General came straight to the point:

'Stülpnagel, are you aware of what's happened in the last few hours?'

'Yes.'

'In that case, I must ask you if you are still with us?'

'General, I only await the opportunity,' Stülpnagel answered unhesitatingly.

'The blow has been struck – but we still don't have any exact information on the outcome . . . are you still with us, no matter what happens?'

'Yes,' Stülpnagel repeated. 'I've ordered the arrest of all the SS and SD men in Paris. We can rely on our troops here – as well as on their commanding officers.'

Thinking aloud, Beck continued: 'In any event, the die is cast. It's impossible to turn back now.' Striving to reassure the hesitant old general, Stülpnagel reiterated that he was with the revolt, come what may.

La Roche-Guyon.

Stülpnagel's next call came from Field Marshal Kluge's headquarters – the Seine riverside chateau of La Roche-Guyon that he had taken over from Rommel only two days before. General Hans Speidel, Rommel's aide, whom Kluge had inherited, told his fellow conspirator that Kluge wanted to see him at the Chateau no later than 8 p.m. that night. Stülpnagel promised to be there and hung up. Before departing for La Roche-Guyon, Stülpnagel wanted to check with General Boineburg on how the roundup of SS and SD officers was going. Boineburg told him that he had put the 1st Guards Regiment at the *Ecole Militaire* on readiness to carry out the arrests, but had decided to delay implementing the detentions until nightfall. 'In order', he explained, 'that we won't gratify the Parisians with the spectacle of Germans arresting their fellow countrymen.'

Stülpnagel had to be satisfied with this. Time was ticking on, and he should already have set out from the Hotel Majestic for his appointment with Kluge. He left another conspirator – Colonel Hans Otfried von Linstow, posted to Paris from the Eastern Front because of a heart condition – in charge as his liaison man at the Majestic. Stülpnagel's secretary, Countess Podewils, had ordered up two staff cars to convey him, Colonel Casar von Hofacker, and two aides – Dr Baumgart, Stülpnagel's orderly officer and Dr Horst (by coincidence, General Speidel's son-in-law) – to La Roche-Guyon. At **7.20 p.m.** Stülpnagel's party appeared in the hotel's doorway. Sentries snapped to the salute as Stülpnagel called out their destination and got into the car.

Kluge had been on his first familiarisation tour of his new command's front when a message had come through that afternoon from General Blumentritt, relaying the news that Colonel Eberhard Finckh had brought him: that Hitler had been killed by a bomb and that a junta led by Field Marshal Witzleben and General Beck had taken power. Displaying a singular lack of curiosity, Kluge had acknowledged the news without reacting. Yet again, 'Clever Hans' was waiting to see which way the cat would jump before committing himself. He continued this passive and neutral stance later that afternoon when Beck called from Berlin to demand his support for the putsch: 'Kluge, listen to me,' said Beck urgently. 'It's essential that you support the operation that's been launched in Berlin.' But before supporting anything or anyone, Kluge demanded to know one essential fact: was Hitler dead? As Beck began to answer, one of the field marshal's staff officers appeared with the text of Goebbels's brief radio communiqué, which had just been broadcast at **6.30 p.m.** assuring the world that although there had been a bomb explosion inside his headquarters, the Führer had escaped unharmed and resumed his duties.

After reading it without comment or apparent emotion, Kluge resumed his questioning of Beck. What exactly was happening at Rastenburg, he demanded. Impatiently, Beck brushed the query aside: 'That will have little consequence as long as we take action,' he assured Kluge. 'I'm going to put the question to you unequivocally, Kluge: do you approve of what we're doing here, and will you agree to be led by me?' Kluge continued to equivocate, citing the radio communiqué's assurance that Hitler was still alive. Beck went on pressing him, reminding this most reluctant of Hitler's opponents of previous commitments he had made to the opposition, and once more appealing for his unconditional support. Kluge had had enough. Making an excuse that he needed to consult with his staff and promising to call Beck back in half an hour he rang off. He never did call back.

Kluge's next caller was General Alexander von Falkenhausen, who, until a few days before, was Stülpnagel's opposite number as military governor of occupied Belgium and Holland. Although he had been dismissed a few days before on Martin Bormann's insistence for his supposed softness towards the occupied populations and lukewarm attitude to the regime, Falkenhausen was still at his post near Brussels and he wanted to know what was happening. He told Kluge that he too had been called by Beck soon after **6 p.m.** on a crackling line from Berlin. Although their conversation had been cut short, he had understood Beck to say that Hitler was dead and that reports of his survival were false. What had Kluge heard, he asked. Kluge answered that he personally doubted if Hitler had been killed, and then rang off, only to receive two more contradictory pieces of information in the form of telegrams. The first was signed by Field Marshal Erwin von Witzleben, styling himself 'Supreme Commander of the Wehrmacht', insisting that Hitler was dead and that Kluge should 'Carry out instructions as planned'. The other came from Keitel, insisting that Hitler was alive and had just been conferring with Mussolini. Kluge, who had been on the point of finally committing to the conspiracy when he had received Witzleben's telegram, now plunged once more into the familiar waters of terminal indecision.

Kluge was joined by General Blumentritt, who, after vainly trying to reach someone in a responsible position at Rastenburg, managed to place a call to another hesitant conspirator, General Stieff. Speaking from the headquarters of his Organisation section of Oberkommando des Heeres (OKH, Army High Command) at Mauersee, a short distance from Rastenburg, Stieff confirmed that Hitler had survived the bomb with superficial wounds. This last conversation apparently made up Kluge's uncertain mind. 'Well then,' he told his staff, 'the plot has failed.' As they waited for Stülpnagel to arrive, Kluge confided to Blumentritt his tangential involvement in the conspiracy, dating to the previous year when Tresckow, backed by Beck and Witzleben, had made persistent if unavailing efforts to recruit him to their ranks. After giving the matter some thought, Kluge claimed, he had turned the plotters down – but not turned them in. 'Of course I should have reported them to the appropriate authorities,' he added. 'But what man of honour would have done that?' At any rate, he concluded, 'If it made no sense then, it makes none at all now.'

Stülpnagel's party arrived at the chateau soon after **8 p.m.** Kluge greeted them coldly and formally. Hofacker, as the driving spirit of the conspiracy in Paris, spoke first, briefly outlining the history of the plot, and what they knew of that day's events in Rastenburg and Berlin. 'But,' concluded

Stauffenberg's cousin, 'it doesn't matter what happens in Berlin. What counts are the decisions we are about to make here in France. I appeal to you, Field Marshal Kluge, to act as your predecessor Rommel would have done had he been here. Free yourself from Hitler's spell and place yourself at the head of our movement in the West.'

Kluge seemed at first to reflect on Hofacker's eloquent appeal. He stood up, took a few hesitant steps, and then brutally declared: 'But, gentlemen, the attempt on the Führer's life has failed.' Stülpnagel gulped. 'Herr Field Marshal,' he interjected, 'I thought you were already aware of that.' 'I had no idea,' Kluge answered stonily. And then smoothly, as though nothing untoward had taken place, he invited them all into the dining room for dinner.

The atmosphere around the candlelit table was described later by Speidel as 'funereal'. There was a strange misfit between the attitudes of the field marshal – full of false jollity and an eagerness to speak of anything but the pressing subject that was uppermost in all their minds – and that of his guests who sat in strained silence, picking at their food while Kluge devoured the meal with every appearance of enjoyment, while regaling the company with tales of his experiences on the Eastern Front.

Eventually, Stülpnagel, his nerves jangling at the thought of what was happening in Paris, could stand the strain no longer. 'I'd like to have a word with you in private,' he told Kluge. The field marshal frowned with displeasure, before accompanying the military governor into the adjoining room. There followed a few minutes of silence, before the dining room door was flung open and Kluge, stuttering and red-faced with rage, was framed in the doorway. 'Blumentritt!' he yelled. 'General Oberg and the rest of the SD are about to be arrested – if they haven't been already. Stülpnagel ordered it before leaving Paris. He did not see fit to ask me – his commanding officer – which is an unprecedented act of sheer insubordination!' Stülpnagel, hands clasped behind his back as though he were already manacled, stood silently to one side as the field marshal ordered Blumentritt to phone Paris at once to countermand the arrest order, 'Or I shall not answer for the consequences.'

Blumentritt hurried off to do as he was bidden, but he was too late. Linstow told him that the arrests were already underway, and the troops could not be recalled. Kluge swung round and ordered Stülpnagel to return at once to Paris and free his prisoners. Adopting his usual Pontius Pilate stance, Kluge washed his hands of the whole distasteful business, telling Stülpnagel: 'You and you alone must bear responsibility for what you've done.' Stung by Kluge's cowardice, Stülpnagel at last found his voice. 'Quite impossible!' he snapped. 'We cannot turn back. What's done is done.' Hofacker chipped in with a final appeal to Kluge's honour: 'Herr Field Marshal,' he said, 'your own and the army's honour are at stake and the destiny of millions of men rests in your hands.' Kluge, perhaps for the first time that day, at last said what he really felt openly.

'Yes,' he said, as though in a daze. 'If only the swine were dead . . .' Then, as if recalling where and who he was, he escorted Stülpnagel down the steps to the chateau's courtyard where the general's car was waiting. 'Consider yourself suspended from duty,' he said, adding *sotto voce*, 'Get changed into civilian clothes and disappear until this has blown over.' Without deigning to reply, or express the contempt he felt, Stülpnagel snapped a smart military salute and climbed into his car. Kluge bowed in response. The cars drove away into the night. It was **11 p.m.**

While this drama was in progress at La Roche-Guyon, the Paris part of Operation Valkyrie proceeded like clockwork: a textbook example of impeccable military planning, executed without a single hitch and without bloodshed. If matters had followed a similar course in Berlin, the outcome of 20 July would have been very different. The troops carrying out the arrests assembled under the trees of the Bois de Boulogne, the huge park in the west of the city, at **10 p.m.** before driving to the headquarters of the SS and Gestapo at 82–86 Avenue Foch, a five-storey building on a wide, leafy boulevard close to the Arc de Triomphe. The handsome building in a wealthy quarter of the city had been the first station of the cross for many British Special Operations Executive (SOE) and French Resistance agents picked up in Paris and taken there for initial interrogation accompanied by brutal torture. From there they had often been taken to Fresnes Prison on the outskirts of the city, before later transportation to Germany and certain death. Now it was the turn of the interrogators and torturers to briefly taste their own medicine in the same grim buildings.

The soldiers did not know why they were arresting the SS – but the men in black were unpopular with most ordinary soldiers, whose general view was that if it hastened the end of the war it was a good thing – so the arrest orders were obeyed without question. Under the command of General Boineburg, his deputy General Brehmer and Colonels Kraewel and Unger, the arrests were carried out swiftly and smoothly. There was no resistance from the startled SS and SD men, who, shocked to be held at gunpoint by their own military countrymen, nevertheless tamely submitted to the same ordeal to which they had subjected so many victims. Now the jackboots were on the other foot.

The heads of the SS and SD in Paris who had presided over a veritable reign of terror during the occupation were respectively Obergruppenführer Carl-Albrecht Oberg and Standartenführer Helmut Knochen. Both were convinced Nazis who had been responsible for: the rounding up and deportation to their deaths of thousands of French Jews; the execution of hundreds of French hostages in reprisals for Resistance actions; and the detention, torture and killing of scores of Allied agents. Not for nothing was the cold and bespectacled Oberg called 'the butcher of Paris' by the city's terrified people. Because the July night was so sweaty and sticky, Oberg was in his shirtsleeves in his office on the Boulevard Lannes when the troops, led personally by the city's deputy military governor, General Brehmer, came for him. He was on the phone to Otto Abetz, the silky German ambassador to France, when Brehmer burst in, gun in hand. Bawling with indignation, Oberg leapt to his feet and demanded an explanation. Brehmer, unabashed, replied that there had been a putsch in Berlin and he had orders to arrest him. Oberg, assuming that there had been a misunderstanding, submitted to force of arms.

At the Avenue Foch, and the SS and SD subsidiary stations throughout the city, trucks pulled up, disgorged troops who entered the offices and rounded up their prey. But the kingpin – Knochen – was not there. One of his men told Lieutenant-Colonel Kraewell that he was spending the evening at a nightclub, and offered to call him. Knochen obediently returned to the Avenue Foch and was immediately arrested and comfortably confined with Oberg in a superior suite at the Hotel Continental. The lesser security men were swiftly disarmed, hustled on to the lorries and driven out to Fresnes prison, which had already been cleared of its occupants to make room for the new arrivals. By **midnight** no fewer than 1,200 SS, Gestapo and SD men were detained at the jail and at an old military fort at St Denis. At the *Ecole Militarie* in the city centre and at the military college of St Cyr on the edge of the capital, Boineburg had given orders for sandbags to be piled high to prevent bullet ricochets, and firing squads had been detailed for the execution of those senior SS thugs whose death sentences were due to be decreed by drumhead military court martials in the morning. In Paris at least, the conspirators had beaten the Nazis at their own brutal and deadly game.

\* \* \*

# BERLIN
## JULY 1944

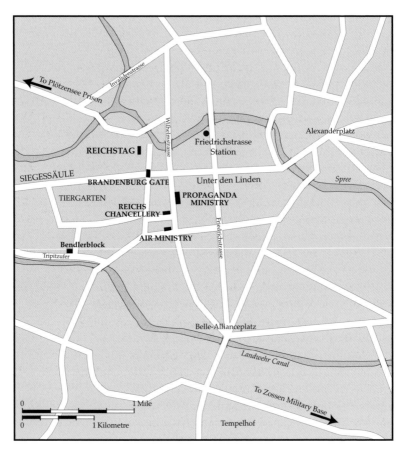

To Plötzensee Prison

Invalidenstrasse

Alexanderplatz

Wilhelmstrasse

Friedrichstrasse
Station

**REICHSTAG**

Spree

SIEGESSÄULE

**BRANDENBURG GATE**

Unter den Linden

TIERGARTEN

**REICHS
CHANCELLERY**

**PROPAGANDA
MINISTRY**

Friedrichstrasse

**AIR MINISTRY**

**Bendlerblock**

Tripitzufer

Belle-Allianceplatz

Landwehr Canal

To Zossen Military Base

0                    1 Mile

0              1 Kilometre

Tempelhof

Elsewhere in Germany and occupied Europe, the Valkyrie orders had met with more mixed results. Because the orders had gone out so belatedly from the Bendlerblock, some military commands received the countermanding orders from Rastenburg first, causing much bewilderment. At Breslau in the far east of Germany, the local military commanders met and decided not to support the putsch. At Hamburg, in contrast to Paris, local Nazi party and SS officers gathered at the office of the district Wehrmacht commander, General Wilhelm Wetzel, to drink mutual toasts in sherry and Martini, and assure one another that they would not be arresting each other.

Closer to Berlin, at Cottbus, the elite *Grossdeutschland* motorised infantry training brigade under Lieutenant-Colonel Werner Stirius obeyed its Valkyrie orders to occupy the radio stations and transmitters at Herzberg and Königs Wusterhausen, along with the local Nazi party headquarters and SS barracks. All this was accomplished without resistance. At Krampnitz military base the officer commanding the army's riding school – a pre-war equitation champion, Colonel Harald Momm – indulged in some premature celebration, which would soon cost him dear, when he heard from the Bendlerstrasse that Hitler had been assassinated. 'Orderly! Champagne! The swine is dead!' he is reported to have said. After the plot had failed, he was arrested and interrogated and only his friendship with the loyalist General Heinz Guderian saved him from a death sentence. As it was, his outburst cost him demotion to the rank of captain, and forced service in the notorious SS Dirlewanger punishment battalion. He would survive this and five years as a Russian prisoner, to write his memoirs and resume his riding career after the war. At Doberitz, troops under Major Friedrich Jacob succeeded in occupying the broadcasting station on Berlin's Masurenallee, but lacking technical expertise were deceived by the station's staff and were unable to stop Goebbels's announcement of Hitler's survival going out on the airwaves. The same thing happened at the transmitter stations at Nauen and Tegel, which, although successfully seized, continued broadcasting.

But if the coup around Berlin was collapsing under the weight of the dawning realisation that Hitler had indeed survived, events in Vienna and Prague – the capitals of occupied Austria and Czechoslovakia – followed the pattern set in Paris. The Wehrmacht commander in Vienna, a grizzled Panzer commander from Rommel's North African campaign, Lieutenant-General Baron Hans-Karl von Esebeck, obeyed the Valkyrie orders when he received them, arresting all the SS and Gestapo men in

Vienna at their headquarters on the Danube canal. Their brief captivity was quite convivial however, and they were plied with Cognac and cigarettes while their fate was decided. By **10 p.m.**, Esebeck – told in a call from Keitel that Hitler was alive – had reverted to loyalty to the regime and released his captives. The same thing happened in Prague where Lieutenant-General Ferdinand Schaal, assured by Stauffenberg in a call from the Bendlerblock that Hitler was dead, obediently arrested all the SS men he could find in the city – only to free them again when the true state of affairs became plain. For his pains, Schaal spent the rest of the war in Nazi detention.

The failing putsch had become a war by telephone. Between **6 p.m.** and **10 p.m.**, backed up on others lines by Beck and Olbricht, Stauffenberg himself was almost continuously on the phone – pleading, cajoling, ordering, persuading, promising – to district commands throughout Germany and abroad in the occupied territories. He had attempted to counter Goebbels's broadcast with a signal of his own: 'The wireless communiqué is incorrect. The Führer is dead. Previous orders are to be carried out with all possible speed.' But dauntless though he was, even he was beginning to acknowledge the possibility that the putsch would fail. One officer heard him say soon after **6 p.m.**: 'The fellow [Hitler] isn't dead after all, but the machine is still running. It's too early to say how things will turn out.' At Rastenburg 'the fellow', watched by the omnipresent Bormann, had himself joined the telephone war – ringing trusted officials throughout the Reich to assure them that he had survived and was about to broadcast to the German people.

One by one, the weaker links in the conspiracy, discouraged by the confusion and incompetence around them, but above all disheartened by the growing certainty that Hitler was alive, began to sheer off and try to save themselves from the Führer's vengeance. At Rastenburg, as Hitler visited those seriously injured by the bomb in hospital, Fellgiebel followed Stieff, telling his fellow plotters at Bendlerstrasse that it was all up. On hearing that one of the senior Bendlerstrasse conspirators – his fellow communications expert General Fritz Thiele – had vanished and was nowhere to be found, Fellgiebel scoffed: 'If he thinks he can extricate himself like that, he's very much mistaken.' It transpired that Thiele had gone to see Heydrich's former protégé, the mastermind of the Venlo Incident, Walther Schellenburg, at Reich Security Headquarters and try and talk his way out of trouble. Fellgiebel's prophecy proved all too accurate: Thiele would replace the arrested Fellgiebel as communications

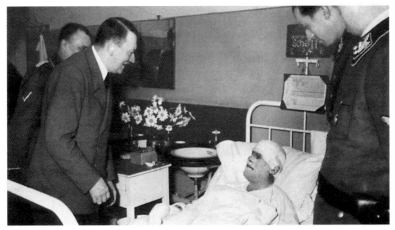

Hitler visiting the injured victims of the blast in hospital.

chief at Rastenburg, but after a few days his true role in the plot would be exposed and he would follow his co-conspirators to Gestapo captivity and death.

Hoepner, never the most resolute of the conspirators, now sat gloomily irresolute, telling Beck that if Hitler had really survived, 'Everything we are doing makes no sense.' General Fritz Lindemann, in charge of the Home Army's artillery division, was another conspirator who chose to make himself scarce. Closeted with Quartermaster General Wagner at Zossen, he disappeared with the proclamations that the new regime should have been reading over the radio in his pocket. One of the few remaining robust conspirators, Hans Bernd Gisevius, was assigned the laborious task of drawing up a new proclamation, while Beck fretted about the failure to seize and neutralise the radio network. Where were the troops assigned to the task? Answer came there none.

Earlier Gisevius had left the Bendlerstrasse on a mission to see his old boss, the Berlin police chief, Count von Helldorf. He found him sipping coffee with Arthur Nebe, chief of the city's Criminal Police. Both Helldorf and Nebe were highly dubious figures to find among the conspirators: as early Nazis both were deeply implicated in the crimes of the regime. Nebe had been involved with the *Einsatzgruppen* carrying out mass executions in Poland and Russia; while Helldorf had made a fortune extorting money in return for providing exit visas from Jews desperate to escape Nazi persecution. Both had become involved with the opposition – Nebe had reportedly become sickened by what was happening in the east, while Helldorf had been piqued that his career had been eclipsed by other top cops in the Nazi hierarchy – Himmler, Heydrich, Schellenberg and Kaltenbrunner. The conspirators themselves could not afford to be choosy about enlisting these two dodgy characters into their ranks, since the support of the Berlin Police would clearly be crucial to the success of their coup. But Helldorf and Nebe, whom Gisevius found sitting in an atmosphere of frigid calm, had heard nothing. No troops had come to seek their support; not even a single liasion officer had appeared as arranged. Now, they understood, the dreaded Reichsführer Himmler was flying back to the capital to take charge of repressing the half-cocked coup. With every shrug and second of painful silence, Gisevius got the impression that the two unprincipled policemen were distancing themselves further and further from the whole misbegotten enterprise. As hastily as he could, he fled back to the Bendlerstrasse. It was **7 p.m.**

As the long, hot summer day began to fade over the capital, the conspirators' hopes darkened with every lengthening shadow. The first person Gisevius saw when he re-entered the massive block was Olbricht, who invited him into his office for a 'private chat'. Tentatively, the general raised the question to which he already knew the answer: was it too late, he wondered aloud, as they had done on previous occasions, to pull back, call off Valkyrie and deny that the past six hours since Stauffenberg's bomb had exploded, had ever happened? The embarrassing silence that followed the popping of the futile question told its own story. Both men looked at each other and read the putsch's doom in their faces.

At **7.45 p.m.** Field Marshal Witzleben, the conspirators' designated new Commander-in-Chief of the Wehrmacht, at last arrived at the Bendlerstrasse in full uniform. He had come from the army base at Zossen, where he had expected to find a disciplined force ready to seize the state, but had encountered only confusion and irresolution. If the hard-pressed plotters in the Bendlerblock were hoping for a new impetus from this senior source, they were to be sorely disappointed. With a face as red as the stripes along his trousers, Witzleben was in a towering rage. Furiously shaking his field marshal's baton, he ignored Stauffenberg, who had snapped to attention and reported for duty. 'A fine mess, this!' Witzleben hissed before disappearing into Fromm's old office for a meeting with Beck that turned into an angry post-mortem on the dying putsch. Periodically pounding the desk in rage, the old soldier fired a stream of questions to which neither Beck – nor Stauffenberg when he was summoned to join them – had any adequate answers: Where were the battle-ready units? Why had the broadcasting stations not been seized from the Nazis? What was happening in the rest of the country? After more than half an hour of noisy grumbling and grousing, Witzleben left the way he had come and returned to Zossen, where he announced that he was 'Going home' – and did just that. The conspiracy had been deserted by its own Commander-in-Chief.

With sinking hearts, Beck, Stauffenberg and Olbricht returned to their hopeless task of attempting to shore up the rapidly crumbling support for Valkyrie by telephone. Anxious, angry and frightened callers were still being told that Hitler was dead and that the military takeover must go ahead, even as the radio, in-between bursts of blaring Wagnerian music, was announcing that Hitler would address the nation later that night. Losing heart, Hoepner went to see his old friend General Fromm and, without telling the other plotters, agreed to allow the general to go to his apartment on the floor above his office. Hoepner was clearly convinced that only by attempting to curry favour in this way could he hope to save his own skin. Fromm used his limited freedom to contact officers of the Reserve Army still working in the Bendlerblock and countermand the orders of the putschist plotters.

Nothing illustrates the dwindling morale of the conspirators, as their chances of success and/or survival sank to zero, more than Olbricht's behaviour at this juncture. Lacking Stauffenberg's leadership qualities and his flair for marrying thought and action, the self-effacing, bespectacled general was still a tireless and unwavering opponent of Nazism. Nevertheless his conversation with Gisevius is symbolic of the fatal mixture of incompetence and half-hearted irresolution that had doomed the putsch from the outset. Now, alerted by Fromm, the Reserve Army's branch heads converged on Olbricht's office to demand to know what was going on. Olbricht repeated the increasingly incredible line that Hitler was dead, and when General Karl-Wilhelm Specht, acting as spokesman for the other officers, retorted that the radio was reporting the opposite, Olbricht had no answer. Specht declared that he was not about to betray his oath to the Führer on mere rumours, and he and the others announced their intention of quitting the building. Olbricht meekly let them go.

Even more serious – indeed the final blow that crushed the conspiracy – was the revolt by Olbricht's own staff. Several of these men, because they were believed to be loyal to the regime, had not been recruited to the conspiracy and remained in ignorance of the true significance of the Valkyrie orders that they had obediently executed. Growing increasingly suspicious, however, a group led by Lieutenant-Colonel Franz Herber, in charge of the Reserve Army's arms and ammunition, and comprising Lieutenant-Colonel Bolko von der Heyde, a Hitler loyalist so besotted with the Führer that he had sat immobilized with shock in his office for half an hour after hearing the first reports of his master's death; Major Herbert Fliessbach, Olbricht's ordnance officer; Major Fritz Harnack and Lieutenant-Colonel Karl Pridun, cornered their chief and demanded to know what was happening. Once again, Olbricht provided no coherent answer. Herber then held a private meeting with his fellow officers who decided that a treasonable coup was in progress, which they must crush. Herber ordered Fliessbach to call the Reserve Army's Berlin arsenal and have them deliver a truck full of small automatic arms, grenades and ammunition to the Bendlerstrasse.

At **9 p.m.** Lieutenant Ewald Heinrich Kleist-Schmenzin returned to the Bendlerblock with the first solid news that the troops who had previously carried out the plotter's orders were changing sides. The city commandant, General Hase, he said, had gone to negotiate with Goebbels after Remer had begun to withdraw his Guards battalion from the positions they had occupied around the government quarter. Goebbels had invited Hase to dinner, and had then summoned the Gestapo to arrest him. Armoured vehicles from Krampnitz, which had taken up position in the central Tiergarten park, had also been stood down by their loyalist commander, Colonel Wolfgang Glaesmer, when he realized what was really happening. Although arrested by Olbricht, Glaesmer had easily escaped.

Newly promoted to colonel by Hitler, Remer had lost no time in standing down the scattered formations of his Guards battalion, but his work was hampered by being continually recalled to the Propaganda Ministry to make personal reports on the unfolding situation to Goebbels. By mid-evening, however, he had assembled most of his men in the ministry's garden, where Goebbels made a typically rousing pep-talk speech, denouncing the 'villainous traitors' who had dared lift their hands against the leader, and urging Remer's men to crush the coup with all possible speed.

Remer had worked out that the Bendlerstrasse was the conspirator's headquarters and he sent one of his most trusted officers, Lieutenant Rudolf Schlee, to spy out the land and withdraw the troops guarding the block. Schlee and another loyal lieutenant, Herbert Arnds, arrived and spoke to the captain guarding the main entrance, who advised Schlee to see Olbricht. Telling Arnds to form a combat patrol and storm the building if he had not returned within twenty minutes, Schlee agreed 'despite my reservations' since he wanted to see for himself what was going on inside the Bendlerblock. He was taken to Olbricht's ante-room where Mertz asked him his business. Schlee replied that he had come to remove the guards around the Bendlerblock, at which Mertz angrily told him to disregard the orders and commanded him to stay where he was. Mertz then departed to fetch Olbricht. Seizing his chance, Schlee left the room and marched off down the corridor past Fromm's office and out of the main entrance, passing 'a knot of generals' as he did so. As he rejoined Arnds, another captain approached who told them he was a signals officer working in the Bendlerblock who has seen through what was really going on there. A clique of generals and other officers were carrying out a putsch, he said, but he was not transmitting their orders. Schlee promised that help was on its way, and leaving Arnds behind to withdraw the guards, he drove off at speed to report back to Remer.

By **9.30 p.m.** Arnds had cleared the Bendlerstrasse, and with only the sentries under Olbricht's command still at their posts, the conspirators' headquarters were denuded of its defences just as worrying reports were coming in that SS and loyalist Wehrmacht units were mustering to re-take control of central Berlin. Nervously glancing into the darkened street, Olbricht observed that it looked as though they would soon have to defend the Bendlerblock against a loyalist attack. Pistols were procured, and half a dozen conspirators armed themselves – including Stauffenberg, who had a Belgian pistol, holding it against his body with the stump of his left arm while he loaded it with his remaining three fingers. These weapons were not the only ones available to the desk warriors in the Bendlerstrasse: the munitions ordered by Fliessbach had now arrived and been allowed into the building by Olbricht's sentry, who believed them to have been obtained by his chief to defend the building. Instead they were to be used to deliver the *coup de grâce* to the putsch.

Events now moved speedily to their climax. Around **10 p.m.**, at about the same time that a despairing Stauffenberg was telling the conspirator's leader in Vienna – Captain Karl Szkoll, who had reported that Esebeck was having second thoughts about supporting the coup – 'Don't you people break down as well', Herber's group demanded to see Olbricht again. This time they were in a much more belligerent mood. Why had orders gone out to defend the building, demanded Herber, aggressively stepping up to Olbricht's desk, and against whom were they defending it? The business of the Reserve Army was to supply troops to the fronts, and anyway what was all this Valkyrie plan about? Olbricht was the soul of vagueness: he made a little speech, explaining that for some time 'we' had been observing 'the situation' with 'growing anxiety'. The situation was heading towards catastrophe, he said, and measures had to be taken against it. Those measures were now being carried out. 'Gentlemen, I ask you to support me,' he lamely concluded.

Herber and his group had heard enough. They went downstairs to the second floor room where the newly arrived weapons were stored, and armed themselves. While they were doing so, the conspirators briefly experienced one brief last ray of hope amidst the encroaching gloom. A Colonel Müller, deputy commander of the Infantry School at Doberitz, arrived and asked for belated authority for his men to seize Berlin's main broadcasting station and post guards around the Bendlerstrasse. Gratefully, Olbricht signed the order at **10.45 p.m.** – but it came much, much too late.

After leaving the Bendlerstrasse, Lieutenant Schlee had found Remer closeted with Goebbels on the second floor of the Propaganda Ministry. He reported that he had uncovered the centre of conspiracy where the traitors had built their nest – the Bendlerblock – and asked for authority to take a strong force to storm it.

Goebbels put in yet another emergency 'Blitz' call to Rastenburg, got Hitler on the line, and obtained the Führer's authority for the assault. Immediately Schlee gathered the most available troops – thirty-five of his own men, a couple of platoons from the Guards' 5th company and a platoon of bicycle-borne troops – and took them back to the Bendlerblock, where he deputed another of his officers, Lieutenant Werner Schady, to throw a seventy-man cordon around the building. It would not be the last duty that Schady would perform on that fateful night.

Inside the offices, the final drama had begun. At **10.50 p.m.** Olbricht's loyal secretary, Delia Ziegler, heard a huge commotion in the corridor outside her office. There were shouts of 'For the Führer!' and the clattering of running boots on parquet. Her door burst open and Herber and his colleagues, pistols in hand, pushed past her and her colleague Anni Lerche, and confronted Olbricht in his inner sanctum with weapons cocked. The general was talking to three fellow non-military conspirators: Peter Yorck von Warternburg, Eugen Gerstenmeier and Stauffenberg's brother Berthold. 'This time we want the truth!' demanded Herber harshly. 'It seems that some action against the Führer is taking place. Me and my comrades remain loyal to our oath. We demand to see

General Fromm.' Olbricht said he was unavailable, and referred them to Hoepner who had taken over Fromm's functions.

While this confrontation was taking place, Delia Ziegler had run into the corridor to alert Beck and Hoepner who were in Fromm's office. Instead, she ran into Stauffenberg and Werner von Haeften in deep conversation. The two plotters, comrades in arms as they had been ten hours before at Rastenburg, ran into Olbricht's office. One of the loyalist officers, Austrian Lieutenant-Colonel Karl Pridun, tried to seize Stauffenberg. At that point, the mounting tension cracked, and someone opened fire. There was an exchange of shots, one of which, fired by Pridun, hit Stauffenberg from behind in the left shoulder. Delia Ziegler saw him grimace with pain. Scarlet blood staining his white summer jacket, Stauffenberg staggered into the ante-room to Fromm's office.

He was not followed immediately. As Olbricht and Herber's party set off to find Fromm, Stauffenberg asked one of the secretaries to call Stülpnagel's headquarters in Paris. It would be the last of the many calls he had made that day, and it was a call of despair. When he got through to Colonel Linstow at the Hotel Majestic he heard with grim satisfaction that the SS and SD were under lock and key, but had to report the failure of the putsch in Berlin. 'All is lost,' he told a dismayed Linstow. 'My assassins are at the door.' While Stauffenberg was making this final call, Haeften squatted on the office floor attempting to burn incriminating papers. Stauffenberg told Delia bitterly: 'They've all left me in the lurch.'

As the room filled with acrid smoke, the doorway framed the bulky shape of General Fromm, grinning with gloating satisfaction that the tables had been so comprehensively turned. He was accompanied by Beck, Hoepner, Olbricht and Herber's loyal squad brandishing their weapons, supported by other Reserve Army officers who had decided to throw in their lot with the winning side. Outnumbered and outgunned, the conspirators allowed themselves to be disarmed, Stauffenberg restraining Haeften, who attempted to draw his gun. 'Now gentlemen,' announced Fromm, unable to keep the smug satisfaction out of his voice, 'I'm going to do to you what you wanted to do to me. You are all under arrest.'

Beck plaintively requested to be allowed to keep his pistol 'for personal use'. 'Do so, but make it quick,' was Fromm's callous response. As Beck loaded the gun with shaking hand, he inadvertently pointed it towards Fromm, who sharply told him to take care. Beck's final thoughts turned to the past: 'At times like this I remember the old days . . .' he began. But Fromm was in no mood for military sentiment. Only by acting swiftly and ruthlessly, he had decided, could he decisively demonstrate his loyalty to the Führer and at the same time conveniently silence the men who might have their own tales to tell of his ambiguous determination to back the winning horse. Brutally, he cut Beck's reminiscences short and urged him to get on with the job in hand. The old man, hand still visibly trembling, drew himself to attention, pointed the pistol at his temple and fired. But the bullet missed its mark, merely grazing his forehead and burying itself in the floor. Beck collapsed with shock into an armchair, demanding dazedly: 'Did the gun fail to function?' When he realized what had happened, he pleaded for a second chance, but sank into a stupor, blood pouring down his face. Fromm ordered two officers to 'help the old man' and they attempted to take his pistol. Reviving, Beck pointed the gun at his head again, but although the second shot hit him in the head, it only rendered him unconscious.

Coldly ignoring the old man's suffering, Fromm left him dying on the floor while he turned to the other five conspirators. 'Now you, gentlemen,' he said. 'If you have any last letters to write, you have a few minutes in which to do so.' Olbricht and Hoepner asked for paper, and Fromm himself showed a touch of sentimentality, inviting Olbricht to sit at the round table, 'Where we so often sat opposite each other'. As they sat at the table writing final farewells to their families, Stauffenberg, Haeften and Mertz stood silently to one side, the sleeve of Stauffenberg's jacket soaking with blood. Fromm withdrew from the room to organise a firing squad.

In the courtyard he met Lieutenant Schlee, whose troops, under Lieutenant Schady, had by now sealed off the building and begun to scour it for any conspirators who had not already succeeded in escaping. Schlee ordered Schady to command the firing party, which consisted of ten NCOs armed with their K98k service rifles. A truck was driven in to illuminate the scene with its headlights, and a pile of builders' sand in a corner of the courtyard, kept in readiness to douse incendiary bombs, was selected as a suitable place of execution.

Satisfied, Fromm returned to his office. His old friend Hoepner, craven as ever, cornered him and pleaded for his life. He was sure, he said, that he could explain his actions if he were allowed to go to trial. Fromm relented, but there was no mercy for the others. 'In the name of the Führer, I have convened a court martial that has pronounced sentence of death on the following: General Olbricht; Colonel Mertz von Quirnheim; this colonel and this lieutenant' – indicating Stauffenberg and Haeften – 'whose names I will not speak,' Fromm bellowed sanctimoniously.

Now Stauffenberg, faint with loss of blood, roused himself to say a few short sentences. As ever he was ready and willing to take personal responsibility for everything, claiming that he had been the commander of the putsch, and the others had been carrying out his orders as subordinates. When he had finished speaking, Fromm did not respond, but merely stood silently to one side as the quartet filed out under guard. Once they had gone, Fromm noticed that Beck was still alive. He ordered an officer to give him the *coup de grâce*. Unwilling to carry out the distasteful task, the man delegated an NCO to do it. Beck's unconscious body was dragged into the office ante-room and finally dispatched with a single shot.

Downstairs in the courtyard at **12.21 a.m. on 21 July**, the last scene was played out. Under the glare of the lorry's lights, one by one the four condemned men were led before the rifles of the firing squad. Olbricht fell first, followed by Stauffenberg, then Haeften, whom some reports say threw himself into the path of the shots that cut down Stauffenberg, and lastly Mertz. As Stauffenberg died, witnesses clearly heard him summon his last reserves of courage and energy to cry: '*Es lebe heilige Deutschland!*' ('Long live sacred Germany!') It was **12.30 a.m.**

# 10 Retribution
## Hitler's Revenge

Hardly had the echoes of the shots died away when Fromm, glowing with self-satisfaction and having sent a teleprinter signal to Rastenburg reporting his 'violent suppression' of the attempted putsch and the execution of its leaders, swaggered across the courtyard, mounted a truck and delivered an impromptu speech to the assembled troops. It was full of thanks for the Führer's survival and congratulations to the soldiers for their role in saving the day. Fromm ended by calling for a triple 'Sieg Heil!' Behind him in the Bendlerblock, Beck's body was unceremoniously dragged down the stairs and thrown into the back of a truck along with those executed in the courtyard. They were driven to the St Matthias cemetery in the suburb of Schoneberg in the south of the city, and hastily buried with their uniforms and decorations. Only a day later, the bodies were exhumed on Himmler's orders and cremated. Satisfied with his night's work, Fromm went off to report to Goebbels.

He could have saved himself the trouble. The Nazis were furious that he had presided over the centre of the conspiracy without apparently noticing what was going on under his nose, or, still worse, had let the conspiracy ripen without denouncing it just in case the plot succeeded. The Nazis were also enraged that by ordering the hasty executions and covering up his true role, Fromm had deprived them of their chief prey. Condemned for cowardice and incompetence, the treacherous Fromm was shot by firing squad at Brandenburg prison on 12 March 1945 after Hitler had acceded to his request for a 'soldier's death' rather than the usual hanging. Presumably in gratitude Fromm died shouting out a hearty 'Heil Hitler!'

The aftermath of 20 July was savage in the extreme. The revenge exacted on the surviving plotters and their associates and families by an increasingly vicious and desperate Nazi regime was bloody, cruel and pointlessly vindictive. It was presaged by the radio broadcast that Hitler himself made from Rastenburg while the final scenes at the Bendlerstrasse were still being played out. Speaking in a low, solemn voice, Hitler, in self-pitying tones, put the credit for his survival on Providence, which, he said, had saved him for more of the thankless toil, worry, care and sleepless nights that he had suffered on behalf of the German people since the war had begun. He swore vengeance on what he called 'a very small clique of ambitious, wicked, and stupidly criminal officers' who had forged a plot to eliminate both him and the entire leadership of the Wehrmacht. Ominously he vowed to 'settle accounts with them in the way we National Socialists are accustomed to settling them'.

Among those listening to the speech was the literally captive audience of the surviving conspirators in the Bendlerstrasse. A few – Gisevius and Kleist-Schmenzin among them – had managed to slip away in the confusion, but the core of surviving, mainly civilian, conspirators were rounded up and locked up in Stauffenberg's and Mertz's old offices. Among them were Berthold von Stauffenberg, Peter Yorck von Wartenburg, his friend Count Schwerin von Schwanenfeld, the Protestant theologian Eugen Gerstenmeier, and Robert Bernardis, an Austrian officer whose friendship with Stauffenberg had pre-dated the *Anschluss*. Within minutes of the executions, two more Austrians – Heydrich's

Hitler watches Admiral Dönitz broadcast the navy's loyalty on 20/21 July.

successor Ernst Kaltenbrunner and Otto Skorzeny, the scar-faced Waffen SS commando leader who had masterminded the rescue of Mussolini after his overthrow in 1943 – arrived at the Bendlerblock to supervise the suppression of the putsch. Without a word, Skorzeny went from prisoner to prisoner, ripping off their decorations and badges of rank and tossing them into an upturned steel helmet on the floor. Then the office radio was switched on and they all – victors and vanquished in the deadly power game that had played out that day – listened in silence as Hitler spoke.

Simultaneously, in Paris, the final act of the tragedy that Valkyrie had become was underway. After Colonel Linstow had taken the last despairing call from Stauffenberg, the leaders of the conspiracy in France assembled in their officers' mess at the Hotel Majestic. Stülpnagel and Hofacker had just arrived back from their fruitless attempt to win Kluge – the Fromm of France – over at La Roche-Guyon. They had just received Fromm's signal announcing the execution of the coup's ringleaders in Berlin and they knew with sinking hearts that what had happened in Germany spelt death for them also. Switching on the radio, they also heard Hitler's speech, swiftly followed by sycophantic addresses from Goering and Dönitz pledging the undying loyalty of the Luftwaffe and Kriegsmarine respectively.

The Wehrmacht in Paris had good reason themselves to know that the loyalty of the Luftwaffe and navy was not mere empty words. The naval commander in France, Admiral Theodor Krancke and the Luftwaffe commander, General Friederich-Karl Hanesse, outraged at the arrest of the SS and suspicious that the army was about to surrender to the Allies, were threatening to mobilise their men in a counter-coup. Resolute as he was, Stülpnagel knew, as he listened to Hitler's voice, that the game was up. Quietly, he gave orders for Oberg and Knochen to be freed and brought to the Hotel Majestic, while their underlings at Fresnes and St Denis were also released. 'Providence', said Stülpnagel, 'has decided against us.'

The ticklish job of explaining to the SS and SD chiefs that their detention had all been an unfortunate misunderstanding was entrusted to the man who had supervised those arrests in the first place: the hoarse-voiced General Boineburg, who, with his monocle, looked like a caricatural German officer, but was a shrewd and honest man for all that. Boineburg went to the Hotel Continental in the Rue Castiglione where he found the two Nazis drinking Cognac in some comfort in one of the hotel's luxuriously appointed suites.

'I have good news, gentlemen,' he began. 'You are free to go'.

An outraged Oberg was not to be mollified. 'What's the meaning of this filthy business, Boineburg?' he demanded. Boineburg replied that he would have to ask Stülpnagel, and after collecting their personal sidearms which had been confiscated from them, Oberg and Knochen returned with him to the Hotel Majestic.

Army officers and SS men, never bosom buddies at the best of times, now stared at each other in silent fury. The German ambassador to France, the smooth and cultivated Otto Abetz, tried to pour emollient oil on truly troubled waters. 'No matter what happened in Berlin today,' he said, 'here in France – with the battle for Normandy raging on our doorsteps – we Germans must stand shoulder to shoulder.' Abetz explained to Oberg that Stülpnagel had acted in good faith after receiving apparently reliable information than it was the SS who were behind the attempt on Hitler's life. Then the conciliatory diplomat called for champagne, and under the influence of the wine, the tension began to relax.

General Blumentritt, who had been appointed by Kluge as Stülpnagel's successor, arrived with a plan to fix the embarrassing impasse. The arrests – since they had taken place at dead of night and would have been reversed by dawn – could be explained as a simple 'mistake', he said, and few Frenchmen would even know they had taken place. Disunity in the face of the enemy, added Blumentritt, would be fatal. A cover-up would be the order of the new day. Blumentritt's scheme was received with relief on all sides apart from Admiral Krancke, who continued to rant about Stülpnagel's 'perfidious treason'. It clearly suited the army, since it meant that their officers stood a better chance of escaping the inevitable post-putsch purge if it could be shown that they had acted in good faith rather than as rebels; but it would also be in the interests of the SS, since their tame acquiescence in their detention hardly helped their image as the hard men of the Reich. In the end, as the champagne flowed and the night wore on, and the slightly surreal spectacle of recent captors and captives carousing together unfolded, all agreed that it was a case of least said, soonest mended.

Stülpnagel knew there would be no reprieve for him. His courage and dignity mirrored that of Stauffenberg as he gave his closest aides the same advice that Kluge had given to him at their final farewell: to lie low and wait until the storm had blown over. He himself, he added, had no intention of trying to evade the consequences of last night's actions. Those consequences did not take long in arriving. The cowardly and treacherous Kluge, like his counterpart Fromm in Berlin, had attempted to ensure his own survival by 'shopping' Stülpnagel. After the latter's departure from La Roche-Guyon, he had promptly denounced him in a phone call to Rastenburg. His next action was to send an obsequious telegram of effusive congratulations to Hitler on his survival. But the Führer was not fooled: 'Kluge knew all about the plot,' he said to General Heinz Guderian.

When the sleepless Stülpnagel went to his office on the morning of **21 July**, his secretary told him that there was a message from Keitel summoning him back to Germany to explain his actions. He knew what the summons meant: disgrace, imprisonment, torture and death. Replying that he would report to OKH at 9 a.m. the following day, Stülpnagel told his orderly, Corporal Fischer, and his driver, Sergeant-Major Schauf, that they would be leaving Paris at **11.30 a.m.** for home. Then, only pausing to send a typically courteous message to his writer friend Ernst Jünger, explaining that he would have to break their dinner date that evening as he had been unexpectedly summoned home, Stülpnagel set out on his final journey.

Schauf set a cracking pace eastwards along the valley of the River Marne, but at Meaux the car broke down. While waiting for a replacement vehicle from Paris, the general – exhausted after more than twenty-four sleepless hours – flung himself on a couch in the garage and slept. After the new car arrived, they resumed their journey, and soon the thick beech glades of the Argonne Forest – scene of some of the last battles of the First World War – closed about them. Stülpnagel professed to be worried that the forest might be hiding men of the Maquis French Resistance, and stopped the car to check their weapons. In reality, he had another purpose in mind.

As they neared the town of Verdun, infamous for the battles that had raged there for months in 1916, Stülpnagel ordered Schauf to leave the main road for a side turn leading north towards Stenay – the German headquarters in the battle – and Sedan, scene of France's military collapse in both the war of 1870 and in 1940. Although the road was off their route, Schauf and Fischer humoured their boss. The general had fought here as a young officer of the Darmstadt Grenadiers in 1916, and now told them stories of the terrible attrition as they drove through a landscape still scarred by the ruins of villages that had never been re-occupied by their former inhabitants.

They passed one such wretched hamlet, Samogneux, under the looming hill known ominously as Le Mort Homme, scene of some of the battle's most desperate fighting. As they approached the village of Champ on the Meuse canal, Stülpnagel ordered Schauf to stop the car. He wanted, he said, to stretch his legs and get some air after the long drive. He would catch up with them in the village. The two NCOs were uneasy about leaving the general alone. A German soldier wandering alone in the depths of the occupied French countryside was at risk at the best of times, but at this stage in the war, with Maquis attacks on the occupiers a daily occurrence, it seemed suicidal. As Stülpnagel scrambled down the canal embankment, Schauf and Fischer decided to stop the car and wait around the next bend.

No sooner had they driven off than a gunshot echoed through the still summer air. They looked at each other, did a U-turn and drove back. Stopping where they had halted before, they followed the general's footsteps down to the canal bank. Suddenly, they spotted his body floating in the water. Schauf flung himself into the shallow canal and they fished Stülpnagel out. The general was semi-conscious and bleeding from a gunshot wound in the right temple. The bullet had passed laterally through both eyes, blinding him. Assuming that Stülpnagel had indeed been the victim of an attack, the two men lost no time in carrying him back to the car and driving to the nearest German military hospital at Verdun. Here, Schauf called Colonel Linstow in Paris and reported that Stülpnagel had been gravely wounded in a terrorist attack.

However, the nature of the wound, and the smoking gun with which Stülpnagel had shot himself told their own tale. On **25 July** Oberg arrived at Stülpnagel's hospital bedside in Verdun to conduct his own investigation. The general told his former captive little – beyond the fact that he assumed all responsibility for the misbegotten putsch in Paris. Having hoped for a full confession from the blinded general, Oberg left empty-handed.

On the same day, Stauffenberg's cousin, Casar von Hofacker, was arrested at his hiding place in Paris by a Gestapo agent named Maulzer who had tracked him down. Hofacker, Linstow and Eberhard Finckh all showed exemplary courage in the face of Gestapo intimidation and torture. As a result of their bravery, details of the Paris plot remained hidden from the Nazis and many of those implicated in the conspiracy in France – including Generals Speidel and Blumentritt – survived the war.

Henning von Tresckow in Russia was more fortunate than Stülpnagel in France. On 20 July he and Fabian von Schlabrendorff had been told in a phone call from Mertz in the Bendlerblock that Stauffenberg's bomb had exploded, and that Hitler was dead. However, as the day wore on, it became ever clearer that the assassination attempt and the subsequent putsch had both failed. Tresckow had gone to bed by the time Hitler spoke after midnight, but Schlabrendorff woke him to tell him the bad news. 'I am now going to shoot myself, for they are bound to find out about me in the investigation,' Tresckow – this most tenacious of conspirators – told his right-hand man. He explained that he feared he would be forced to reveal names under torture and would take his own life in order to prevent this. Schlabrendorff attempted to dissuade his chief, saying that he should wait on events before taking the final, drastic step. They spent the rest of the night arguing, but Tresckow remained firm in his resolve – although he urged Schlabrendorff to stay alive as long as he possibly could. His final words as they parted were:

> Now they will heap abuse on us all. But I am convinced, now as much as ever, that we have done the right thing. I believe that Hitler is the arch-enemy, not only of Germany, but of the entire world. In a few hours' time I shall stand before God and answer both for my actions and the things I neglected to do. I think I can with a clear conscience stand by all I have done in the battle against Hitler. Just as God once promised Abraham that he would spare Sodom if only ten just men could be found in the city, I have reason to hope that, for our sake, he will not destroy Germany. No one among us can complain about his death, for whoever joined our ranks put on the poisoned shirt of Nessus [in Greek mythology, the fiery shirt the dying centaur Nessus tricked Hercules into wearing, that could not be removed until it had killed him]. A man's moral worth is established only at the point when he is prepared to give his life for his convictions.

So saying, Tresckow bid farewell to Schlabrendorff and drove to the front at Ostrow near Bialystock where the 28th Rifle Division were holding the line. He drove on into No Man's Land. Out of sight, but within earshot of German troops, he used two pistols to fake a duel, and then killed himself by blowing his head off with a rifle grenade. The charade was initially successful, and it was assumed that Tresckow had been killed in action by partisans. Schlabrendorff bore his body back to Germany where it was buried near Tresckow's parents' grave in Brandenburg. It would not rest in peace for long.

*  *  *

An atmosphere of suspicion and terror spread like some poisonous miasma through the land in the wake of 20 July. The officers of the Wehrmacht were the chief target of Hitler's wrath. Once it had become clear that the conspiracy had encompassed much wider circles in the Wehrmacht than the 'small clique' he had blamed in his radio speech, the net spread by the Gestapo and Kriminalpolizei ('Kripo') investigators spread wider and wider, catching the guilty and the innocent alike in its meshes. The cases of two lieutenant-colonels on the General Staff, Karl Rathgens and Günther Smend, were typical of many. Smend was arrested on **21 July** at Rastenburg on suspicion of links with the plot. Released after several days of intensive interrogation, he took a train to Berlin. However, Gestapo officers were waiting for him on the platform: fresh allegations had been made against him. Re-arrested and taken to the feared cells of the Gestapo's headquarters on Prinz Albrechtstrasse, this time Smend was subjected to severe torture. Under this pressure, he recalled a conversation with his friend Rathgens, a nephew of Field Marshal Kluge, at a casino in the summer of 1943, in which they had agreed that in view of the reverses on the Eastern Front, Hitler had to be got rid off. This casual conversation was enough to earn both officers the death penalty.

The finger of suspicion even pointed at those injured by Stauffenberg's bomb. General Adolf Heusinger, the Wehrmacht's operations chief, had been standing a few feet away in the conference room when the bomb had exploded. Like Hitler, he had suffered burns and burst eardrums, which had required his hospitalisation. Arrested at the Rastenburg district hospital on **23 July** on Himmler's direct orders by two Gestapo investigators, Heusinger was held at Prinz Albrechtstrasse. Though not tortured, he was closely questioned about his connections with the plotters. On one occasion he found himself being quizzed by the fearsome SS chief Ernst Kaltenbrunner, when they were both seeking shelter from an Allied air raid in the building's bomb shelter. As the Gestapo found no direct evidence of his involvement, Heusinger was released from Ravensbrück concentration camp in September and even received a sort of grudging apology from Hitler himself, but the Führer remained suspicious, and Heusinger was demoted to take charge of the army's mapping department.

An element of class warfare came into play as the investigation proceeded. The drunken Nazi labour leader Robert Ley had already denounced the 'blue-blooded' officers behind the plot on the night of its failure – this was a theme eagerly taken up by Goebbels's propaganda machine. The fact that there were so many 'vons' and 'Grafs' among the plotters fuelled Hitler's already lively suspicion of the Wehrmacht's upper-class officer caste, and he leant a ready ear to radical Nazis like Goebbels and Himmler who wanted to purge the conservative, aristocratic, Prussian hierarchy that had traditionally dominated Germany's army, and promote more humbly born Nazi soldiers such as Field Marshals Walter Model and Ferdinand Schoerner, the sons of a music teacher and a policeman respectively. It was also noted that the ranks of the conspirators had only contained army officers, rather than the much more Nazified services of the Luftwaffe and navy – Casar von Hofacker and Berthold von Stauffenberg being the only representatives of those services among the plotters.

On **24 July**, as the wave of arrests were stepped up, Major Bernd Freytag von Loringhoven, a young officer recently appointed aide-de-camp to the tank warfare specialist, General Heinz Guderian, attempted to protect his cousin from the SS terror. Colonel Baron Wessel Freytag von Loringhoven, was, as Bernd strongly suspected, involved with the plot, having procured the explosive which comprised Stauffenberg's bomb. His cousin thought a lunch with the loyal Guderian might burnish Wessel's loyalist credentials. At the meal, Guderian talked volubly, but Wessel, 'as white as a sheet', said next to nothing even though he was usually very sociable. Two days later, on **26 July** at **7.30 a.m.** Guderian himself burst into Bernd's office and demanded to know Wessel's whereabouts as he was being sought. Bernd guessed that his cousin was about to be arrested, and set off in search of him along the forest paths around the Rastenburg complex. Almost a kilometre away he came across Wessel's body: his cousin had shot himself with his service pistol, leaving a last letter for his wife on his knees. As a horrified Bernd stood beside the body, an SS man emerged from the trees and demanded to know what he was doing. Bernd replied that he had been searching for his cousin on General Guderian's orders and hastened away. On his return, Guderian, 'with blue eyes blazing' asked his aide-de-camp what he knew of the plot. Bernd convinced his chief that he had had nothing to do with the conspiracy, and the general protected him – along with a trio of generals, Speidel, Heusinger and Kilmansegg, who also came under suspicion – after receiving this assurance, though simply sharing a surname and close family ties with a conspirator would normally have been enough to earn him arrest and quite possibly death.

Wessel was not the only conspirator to seek a more merciful death by his own hand rather than those of Hitler's blood-besotted henchmen.

Major Bernd Freytag
von Loringhoven.

General Eduard Wagner, the Wehrmacht's quartermaster general who had provided the plane for Stauffenberg's fatal flight to Rastenburg, knew that he was a marked man. Hearing of Stülpnagel's bungled suicide bid, Wagner took no chances. On **21 July** he held a pistol in each hand to both temples and fired. Major Hans-Ulrich von Oertzen, one of the officers who had transmitted the Valkyrie orders from the Bendlerblock, was held and questioned after the putsch's failure. But a senior member of the plot whose involvement had not yet been revealed, Baron General Karl von Thungen, managed to cover for him and he was allowed home. The reprieve was to be brief – the next day the Gestapo came for Oertzen again. He saw them coming. His wife Ingrid watched in horror as he reached into a sandbag kept on their window sill as a defence against air raids. Oertzen pulled out two small grenades, one of which he detonated. The blast ripped his hand off. Bleeding and in agony, he placed the second grenade in his mouth and pulled the pin just as the Gestapo burst in.

Worn out and dispirited by the failure of the putsch, many of the civilian conspirators who would have held high places in government had the coup succeeded, made little effort to escape . On **24 July** Ulrich von Hassell, the disillusioned diplomat who had been slated to replace Ribbentrop as foreign minister, met Gisevius – on the run in Berlin's

Grunewald forest. Gisevius was determined to flee Germany and survive, but Hassell was tired and depressed. After a final dinner with his two sons at Berlin's luxury Adlon Hotel on **26 July** Hassell simply went to his study desk and awaited the inevitable visit from the Gestapo. It came on **28 July**. The same day, his wife Ilse and daughter Almuth were arrested under *Sippenhaft*. His son Wulf, mixing bravery with despair, went to the Gestapo himself and demanded to share his family's fate. For once the Gestapo declined to oblige, and Wulf went to Munich where he successfully lobbied for his mother and sister's freedom – although the whole family were placed under house arrest.

On **31 July** Carl Goerdeler, who would have served as chancellor in Beck's government, celebrated his sixtieth birthday hiding in Berlin. He had been on the run since before 20 July, when he had been tipped off that his arrest was imminent. Thanks in part to his own garrulous indiscretion, his projected role in the conspirators' future was widely known – and had even been broadcast by the BBC, which had helpfully added that there was a reward of a million marks for anyone turning him in. Nonetheless, loyal friends hid him, and allowed him to sleep under their roofs. One, Dr Fritz Elsas – like Goerdeler, the pre-Nazi mayor of a major German city: in Elsas's case, Berlin – paid with his life for his humanity and the 'crime' of sheltering the wanted old man. Fatalistically certain that he was doomed, yet continuing to evade arrest, Goerdeler – always an opponent of removing Hitler by violence – saw the failure of Stauffenberg's bomb as the 'judgement of God' on his fellow conspirators, and passed his time underground writing yet another of his innumerable papers on Germany's future, this one calling for a Christian re-birth to purify its people from the stain of Hitlerism.

Hitler himself understandably took a deep personal interest in the fate of the plotters who had come so close to killing him. He personally decreed the scope and details of the new 'blood purge' he had unleashed across the Reich, insisting that he be given a daily report each evening on the investigation's progress. It was delivered by his future brother-in-law – and last victim – the loathsome SS liaison officer on his staff, Hermann Fegelein, who was married to the sister of the Führer's mistress, Eva Braun. Briefing the four-hundred-strong SS investigation team, set up under Himmler, Kaltenbrunner and SS Obersturmbannführer Georg Kiessel to ferret out all the details of the plot, Hitler denounced the conspirators as: 'The basest creatures imaginable . . . riff-raff from a dead past . . .' and vowed, 'This time I'll fix them. There will be no honourable

Roland Freisler, Hitler's hanging judge in action.

bullet for these traitors; they will hang like common criminals. We'll have a court of honour expel them from the army and then they can be tried as civilians. And above all; no long speeches at the trials. Freisler will take care of that . . . he's our Vyshinsky.'

In comparing Roland Freisler to the Soviet Union's notorious public prosecutor Andrei Vyshinsky – the bespectacled legal terrorist who had presided over the show trials of Stalin's leading victims in the 1930s – one sadistic dictator was paying tribute to the brutality of another. Indeed, Freisler, the ferret-faced president of the Nazi People's Court, had learned his contempt for humanity and justice as a captive of, and convert to, the Bolsheviks in Russia in the First World War. Returned to Germany, he swiftly switched allegiance to the Nazis and rose rapidly within the party's legal hierarchy. Though never fully trusting the man he called 'that old Bolshevik' and passing him over for the post of justice minister, Hitler appreciated Freisler for his malign skills as a twisted jurist whose main speciality was heaping vitriolic, venomous abuse on his victims, bawled out in a raucous, ranting roar that rivalled Hitler's own.

The People's Court was a special institution set up by Hitler in the wake of the Reichstag Fire and designed to by-pass the existing legal system, with its inconvenient lingering legalistic concepts of justice and fairness, by administering speedy and savage punishment to political opponents and minor malefactors. As president of the Court, Freisler was quite literally a hanging judge. In fact he was judge and jury too. The almost invariable verdict was 'Guilty' and the all-too-frequent sentence was death.

Now Hitler summoned 'our Vyshinsky', along with Berlin's official executioner Wilhelm Roettger, to Rastenburg to spell out exactly how he wanted the July plotters dealt with. 'I want them hanged. Hanged up like slaughtered cattle in an abattoir,' Hitler commanded the repellent Roettger, a shopkeeper who 'moonlighted' as a hangman and had guillotined or hanged more than 1,300 people in Berlin since taking up his grisly office in 1942. Roettger needed no further encouragement. A chain-smoking drunken sadist who delighted in the suffering of his victims, he would do his best to ensure that their last moments were as undignified and pain-filled as inhumanly possible. To Freisler, Hitler underlined that he wanted the victims systematically degraded and ritually humiliated as part of the punishment process. Having been expelled from the army, the soldiers were to be shabbily dressed, dirty, unshaven and still bearing the marks of the savage tortures they had undergone. Above all, said the fiendish Führer, they must be shouted down and given no chance to explain or justify their actions. He knew he could rely on Freisler to browbeat and bully his victims as they were dispatched to their deaths – which would take place, said Hitler, immediately after their 'trials'.

On **3 August** Reichsführer Heinrich Himmler called the Gauleiters – the Nazi party's district leaders – to Posen to acquaint them with a novel concept of justice he had dreamed up: *Sippenhaft* ('kin punishment'). As usual, the SS overlord harked back to his own notions of what the pagan, pre-Christian Germanic tribes would have done to those who betrayed the *Volk*. 'According to the sagas when they proscribed a family . . . they had no mercy,' he said in his speech. 'They outlawed the entire family. They proclaimed: "This man is a traitor; there is bad blood in the family, the blood of traitors and the whole lot must be exterminated."' What Himmler was proposing, in his usual outlandishly inhuman fashion, was to extend the guilt of the men of 20 July to their wives, children and siblings – and even their distant relatives. Not one must be left alive – men, women, children and even the elderly – and when they had been eliminated, he pledged, they would be cremated and their ashes mixed with sewage so that no trace of them was left to defile the earth. The first to suffer, piped Himmler in his high-pitched squeak, would be the family of the arch-traitor himself: Stauffenberg. 'The name Stauffenberg will disappear from the pages of history. The family will be exterminated root and branch,' Himmler proclaimed to wild applause from the assembled party hacks. As frequently happened, even Hitler was slightly embarrassed by Himmler's crazy extremism. But he did authorise the implementation of *Sippenhaft* in a patchy, ad hoc fashion. The Stauffenberg family – including children, old people and distant relatives – were arrested, separated and held in detention, along with many other relatives of the conspirators, most of whom had no knowledge of the plot (see Afterword).

The next day, **4 August**, the Wehrmacht's 'court of honour', set up on Hitler's orders to drum the conspirators out of the army, went about their demeaning business. Presided over by the elderly Gerd von Rundstedt, the army's most senior field marshal, along with Keitel and loyalists such as General Guderian, the tribunal obediently expelled a total of twenty-two officers, depriving them of the last shreds of legal protection that they would have enjoyed at a court martial of their peers and turning them over to the tender mercies of Freisler's People's Court. The kangaroo court echoed the trumped-up tribunals that had expelled Ernst Röhm – clearing the way for his murder in the 1934 purge – and

An official stenographic record, marked 'Secret', of Gestapo interrogation of the conspirators.

the 1938 framing of Fritsch. As such it represented the final humiliation of the Wehrmacht, signalling its abject prostration at Hitler's feet.

The first prisoners went before the People's Court on **7 August** and were sentenced and executed on **8 August**. They were mainly the men who had been at the Bendlerblock on July 20: Field Marshal Erwin von Witzleben; Generals Erich Hoepner, Hellmuth Stieff and Paul von Hase; Colonel Peter Yorck von Wartenburg; Lieutenant Frederick Klausing, the aide-de-camp who had accompanied Stauffenberg on his first two abortive bombing missions earlier in July; Lieutenant Robert Bernardis and another young Lieutenant, Albrecht von Hagen. The sixty-four-year-old Witzleben, whose torturers had no respect for his age or former rank, had been humiliated by having his belt, braces and false teeth removed. Led into court in manacles, he was forced to hold his trousers up with his hands. A delighted Freisler, resplendent in his blood-red judicial robes, screeched to the hoots of the hand-picked Nazi audience: 'You dirty old man! Why do you keep fiddling with your trousers?' In the face of this obscene provocation, the old soldier retained his dignity, defiantly roaring '*Ja!*' when Freisler mockingly asked him whether he and Beck could have managed things better than their Führer.

Hoepner, dressed in an old cardigan, appeared depressed, dazed or even drugged. Following Hitler's orders, Freisler immediately silenced Stieff – the first accused to come before him – when he tried to explain the motives that had prompted the conspirators. Refusing to listen, Freisler let loose with a torrent of un-judicial abuse: damning the defendants as 'rabble', 'criminals', 'traitors' and 'pigs'. The entire ghastly proceedings, also on Hitler's orders, were broadcast on radio and recorded on full-

Deprived of belt and braces, Field Marshal Witzleben is forced to hold up his trousers at his trial in a deliberate humiliation ordered by Hitler.

Cowed and dressed in a shabby cardigan, General Erich Hoepner faces the People's Court.

length newsreel films to be shown in German cinemas as a warning of what became of those who dared raise their hands against the Führer. Under Erich Stoll, the top cameraman of the *Die Deutsche Wochenschau* newsreel team, every second of the degrading spectacle was recorded on camera for the Führer's sick delight. The camera crew had to ask Freisler – in vain – to tone down his bawled bullying, which at some points made the soundtrack inaudible.

After this brutish charade, Freisler sentenced all eight of the accused to death by hanging. Having done so, he pompously vowed to 'follow the Führer until final victory . . . now that we have freed ourselves from *them*'. Witzleben's reaction to the sentence was typical of the acid-tongued field marshal: 'You can have us hanged,' he told Freisler defiantly, 'but within three months the people will drag you through the filth of the gutter.' His prophecy was not that far wrong. The condemned men were handcuffed after the sentence and then driven to the Plötzensee Prison in the north of the city where, denied the last comforts of religion on Hitler's spite-filled special orders, they were put to death that same afternoon. One by one they were led into the execution shed – a bleak and bare whitewashed room, twenty-six foot by thirteen foot, with two tall windows. It was furnished with the ghastly implements of execution: a guillotine and, at the end of the room, a steel girder lined with eight butcher's meat hooks, along with a small table laid with Cognac and glasses for the refreshment of the hangmen while they went about their ghastly work.

The chamber of Plötzensee Prison where the plotters were executed has been preserved as their memorial.

Judicial hanging had been introduced to Germany only recently – replacing the guillotine, which was found to be too slow to deal with the growing number of victims consumed by the rising tide of terror as the Nazi state neared its final days. On one single night at Plötzensee in 1943 more than 180 people had been hanged. The first to suffer in this way had been the members of the Red Orchestra spy ring the year before. Earlier 'traitors' condemned by the Nazis – such as the man blamed for the Reichstag Fire, Marinus van der Lubbe, and the Scholl siblings who had formed the 'White Rose' Christian resistance group – had all been beheaded. The hanging method used was the 'Austrian' 'short drop' as opposed to the British 'long drop' which was designed to break the neck and cause instantaneous death. With the short drop, the condemned had a noose placed around their necks and were then hoisted into the air, allowed to fall and slowly strangled. Persistent legend has claimed that the July plotters were throttled by steel piano wire, but this is untrue. A cameraman named Sasse who was one of those ordered to film the awful proceedings, has testified that the ropes were thin hemp cords. It is also likely, though German law proscribed that the condemned be left hanging for twenty minutes, that a merciful unconsciousness ensued within seconds of suspension.

Despite Hitler's ban on religious consolation, the Plötzensee Prison chaplain, Harald Poelchau, did manage to murmur a few words of spiritual help to Witzleben and Hase as they stood on the brink of eternity. But as he approached Yorck von Wartenburg, he was interrupted by SS men storming into the cell with floodlights to film Yorck von Wartenburg as he was led to his death. Witzleben was the first of the eight to die. In an ante-room, he was handed over to his killers by the Reich's senior prosecutor with the words: 'Defendant, you have been sentenced by the People's Court to death by hanging. Executioner, perform your function.' Witzleben, in prison garb but with his head held defiantly high, was then led through a black curtain into the execution chamber by Roettger and his assistant. They cruelly taunted the old man and urged him to walk faster. Watched by the cameramen and a couple of warders, they led him to the end of the shed, which was illuminated by a battery of blinding film lights and reflectors. They made him perform an about-turn, stripped him to the waist and lifted him up to place the noose round his neck. The upper loop of the short rope was attached to the meat hook and the field marshal was dropped 'with great force', causing the noose's slipknot to instantly tighten the rope around his throat. As an extra obscenity, the executioners ripped the struggling man's trousers from his legs, letting him dangle naked. Although Witzleben, his arms pinioned behind his back, writhed helplessly for five minutes, he was apparently unconscious, and, added Sasse, 'In my opinion death came very quickly.'

Another black curtain was then drawn, hiding the hanged man from sight, and the horrific procedure was repeated. Each of the eight men, said Sasse, walked to their deaths, 'with assurance . . . upright and manly, without a word of complaint'. The dignified way in which the conspirators met their terrifying and lonely deaths was in stark contrast to the constant litany of jeers, leers and obscene jokes cracked by the appalling Roettger, and made an appropriate comparison between the system of nihilism and death that he served, and the hope of civilisation that they represented. Within an hour, all eight condemned men had been dispatched and the film of the atrocity was being processed, ready to be rushed to Rastenburg for an impatient Hitler's eager viewing that very night. Although the trials of the more prominent plotters continued to be filmed, Sasse stated that further filming of the executions was refused as 'I could not expect my cameramen to film any more such cruelties. All the cameramen were with me on that.'

As well as the films – from which no footage has apparently survived the war – still photographs of the satanic scenes were taken by the staff of Hitler's personal photographer, Heinrich Hoffmann. They too were

rushed to Rastenburg. A sickened Bernd Freytag von Loringhoven was
with his boss General Guderian when they appeared:

> I was present at the daily briefing at the Wolf's Lair and was listening to
> Guderian reporting the situation on the Eastern Front when Fegelein
> burst into the room, brutally interrupting the proceedings, and tossed
> a bundle of photographs on the Führer's map table. I realized with a
> shock that these were pictures of the 8 August executions. Hitler put
> on his spectacles, eagerly grabbed up the macabre images and gazed
> at them for an eternity, with a look of ghoulish delight. The close-up
> shots of the victims' death throes were soon being passed from hand
> to hand. I recognized my old regimental comrade Peter Yorck von
> Wartenburg. His face had preserved its expression of nobility, serene
> and transfigured even in death. It was a terrifying moment. Guderian
> shrank back and I guessed that this vile episode filled him with shame.
> Unable to stand the sight, I hurried from the room.

According to Albert Speer, these disgusting images were left casually
lying around the Wolf's Lair for several days – nothing could better
illustrate the utter depravity of the Hitler regime.

The rounds of show trials and executions continued with remorseless
savagery. On **10 August** Berthold von Stauffenberg was executed, along
with General Erich Fellgiebel and Fritz-Dietlof von der Schulenberg.
With contemptuous courage, Fellgiebel told Freisler that he had better
hurry up and get on with the hangings, or he would find himself hanged
first. The same cool courage in the face of Freisler's obscene mockery was
shown by the Catholic lawyer Josef Wirmer a few weeks later, when told
by the judge that he would soon be roasting in hell. Wirmer bowed and
remarked: 'It will be a pleasure to welcome you there soon afterwards,
your honour!'

On the same evening that Witzleben and his seven companions in
suffering met their deaths, Carl Goerdeler set out from Berlin on his
final journey. Fearing that he was doomed to discovery, and no longer
wishing to endanger those who had risked their lives to shelter him, he
dressed like any other summer hiker in a light summer suit, carrying
a rucksack and alpenstock, and travelled by a series of local trains to
Marienwerder in West Prussia, where he had grown up. Not having any
of the papers with which the totalitarian Reich increasingly burdened its
citizens – a passport, ration card or even a permit to travel – and with his

Berthold von Stauffenberg, the elder brother of Claus, faces the People's Court.

picture staring out from 'wanted' posters like any common criminal, the conservative economist who had been nominated as chancellor in the Beck government knew that his days were numbered and that he could be recognised and picked up at any time. But before he was arrested he wanted to make one last visit: to the grave of his parents.

It took Goerdeler two days to reach his destination, sleeping like a tramp on the benches of waiting rooms. On **11 August** he set out to walk to the cemetery where his parents lay, but he was followed by a woman whom he thought he knew. As he reached the graveyard gate he realised that she had recognized him too, and he made off through the woods and fields, finally pausing, exhausted, to sleep on the ground by the shores of a lake. Awakening ravenous with hunger on the morning of **12 August**, Goerdeler ventured into a guesthouse in the village of Konradswalde to have breakfast. A group of Luftwaffe personnel came in and sat at the next table. Goerdeler glanced up and met the eyes of

Helene Schwarzel, a woman who had visited his family home and knew him. Once again, without waiting for his breakfast, Goerdeler set off across the open countryside. Unthinkingly, without wishing the hunted man any malice, the excited Schwarzel told her companions that the man they had taken for an old vagrant was Germany's most wanted outlaw fugitive. Their heads full of the million-mark reward, the Luftwaffe group took off in hot pursuit of Goerdeler and easily caught him. He did not resist, and capture must have come as some sort of relief after the tension and discomfort of nearly a month in hiding. The relief would not last long – Goerdeler would now endure long months of starvation and harsh interrogation before he was granted the brutal quietus of death at the hands of the hangman.

We know in excruciating detail what some of the tortures endured by those conspirators who fell into the Gestapo's hands entailed, from the testimony of Fabian von Schlabrendorff, one of the tiny number of active conspirators who survived the persecution. True to his promise to Tresckow on the last day of the latter's life not to take his own life, Schlabrendorff waited passively for the inevitable arrest. It came when he was awoken from sleep early on **17 August** at the Polish village of Mackow, where his unit was billeted. The following day he was taken under military guard by train to Berlin. Some instinct told him neither to escape nor attempt suicide, although he had the chance to do both. (He even had to show his escorts, new to Berlin, the way to the Gestapo's headquarters.) On the night of **18 August** they arrived at the terrible terminus on the Prinz Albrechtstrasse. Handed over by his 'correct' army captors to the 'crude and rude' Gestapo, Schlabrendorff's long Calvary began.

Among his fellow captives in the Gestapo's cells, Schlabrendorff encountered: Admiral Canaris, the fallen Abwehr chief; General Hans Oster, mastermind behind the abortive 1938 putsch; Carl Goerdeler; Ulrich von Hassell; the pastor Dietrich Bonhoeffer; and 'many, many more'– all waiting for Nazi 'justice' to take its inevitable course. Forbidden to talk, when the prisoners met in the prison washroom, a glance or a whispered word had to suffice to encourage, warn or pass on some snatched titbit of news. Of their Gestapo guards, Schlabrendorff found the most sympathetic to be the older policemen who had been serving prior to the Nazi takeover in 1933. There was also sympathy from fellow political prisoners from the other end of the political spectrum to these chiefly conservative men – the Communist 'trusties' who carried out the jail's menial tasks.

In their initial questioning, the Gestapo tried to link Schlabrendorff to Count Heinrich Lehndorff, a courageous East Prussian aristocrat and landowner who had been an avowed opponent of Nazism from the outset, and who had indeed met him in company with Tresckow. Learning from Lehndorff, who was in an adjoining cell, that the Gestapo had no proof of such connections, Schlabrendorff decided to tough things out by flatly denying every accusation. His Christian conscience was troubled by having to lie, but he justified it to himself by reflecting that his tormentors were criminal liars themselves. Lehndorff, who had twice escaped the Gestapo's clutches after 20 July, living off the land on his estates until he was hunted down by dogs, finally admitted his participation in the plot and was swiftly condemned to death. In his last letter to his wife, who had also been arrested with their children under *Sippenhaft*, Lehndorff wrote movingly:

> I have always had the firm impression that you were walking by my side, and this feeling shall remain with me to my last hour . . . The Christian faith and belief in a 'Kingdom of Heaven' are the only help in distress. The road to it, however, seems to lead only to sorrow, and all our old habits must first be removed by force – only then can one become a 'new being'. In any case, I shall die in this faith without fear or dread.

Schlabrendorff endured long hours of interrogation and brutal insults and abuse without cracking. Steadily, however, the pressure and the coercion increased. His tormentors worked in teams of three, two of them employing the 'hard cop, soft cop' technique, while the third appealed to his soldierly sense of honour. When this, too, failed to elicit any names of fellow officers whom he knew to be plotters or just anti-Nazis, the pressure suddenly became physical. In the midst of one of his interrogations, without warning, the Gestapo commissioner who was questioning him, a man named Harbacker, struck him in the face. Schlabrendorff deliberately failed to react, which seemed to enrage his tormentor. Soon after, he was led at night into a room where Harbacker was waiting, together with his young female secretary, a uniformed sergeant of the Security Police, and an assistant in civilian clothes. After Schlabrendorff refused a final chance to confess, the torture began.

Major Fabian von Schlabrendorff on trial.

Firstly his hands were chained behind his back and his fingers forced into gauntlets lined with pins which, when tightened with a screw, were driven into his flesh. Though the pain was atrocious, Schlabrendorff still held out. Next, he was hooded with a blanket, chained down on a bedstead-like frame and had his bare legs forced into 'stovepipes' which turned out to be a larger version of the spiked gauntlets. Once again a screw was used to constrict the pipes, forcing the nails inside them into his legs 'from ankle to thigh'. Again, Schlabrendorff held firm against the agony, so the ante was upped once more. The frame was revealed to be a medieval-style rack, and with his head still hooded, his chained body was stretched, both gradually, and in a series of excruciating jerks. When even this failed to make Schlabrendorff speak, cruder methods were resorted to.

He was bent over and tied so tightly that any movement was impossible, while Harbacker and the Sergeant took turns to belabour him from behind with heavy clubs. Each blow made Schlabrendorff fall forward on his face with full force, but as his hands were still tied behind him, he was unable to break his fall. Even Harbacker's secretary joined in, spitting on him and screeching vile insults. Mercifully, his torments were ended when he passed out. He was dragged back to his cell by guards who looked at his battered and bleeding body 'with undisguised expressions of horror and pity'. Utterly exhausted, he lay on his cot in his blood-stained underwear, and the following day suffered a heart attack.

When he had recovered, he was subjected to a second similar torture session, again without extracting the results his tormentors required. Only when Harbacker threatened that the next session would be truly 'horrible', with yet more appalling methods employed, did Schlabrendorff realise that he was approaching the limits of his physical endurance, and that, rather than reveal the names of any of his co-conspirators, he would take his own life. While considering how to achieve this in his shackled state, an inspiration struck him: he decided to admit that the dead Tresckow had once planned to replace Hitler's rule with that of a field marshal. Knowing that Tresckow was beyond even the Gestapo's reach, he thought that by throwing his torturers this meagre bone he would at least temporarily relieve some pressure on himself. Somewhat to his surprise the ploy worked, and for the time being his tormentors left him alone.

Instead of more physical torture, the Gestapo resorted to psychological shock tactics. They brought Schlabrendorff to Sachsenhausen concentration camp outside Berlin, where, after being shown and threatened with execution on the camp's firing range, he was taken to the camp crematorium. Here he was confronted with the exhumed coffin containing the body of his old commander, Tresckow. It seemed that having discovered the extent of Tresckow's 'treason', the Gestapo believed that he was such a wily customer that he had actually faked his own death and defected to the Russians. Schlabrendorff, they imagined, had been party to this trick and had placed the body of a dead Russian soldier in the coffin that had been buried at Brandenburg.

When the coffin lid was removed and the decomposing body in German uniform exposed, it was the Gestapo's turn to be shocked: the corpse was unmistakably that of Tresckow after all. 'Half-imploring and half-threatening', they made a final appeal before the open coffin for Schlabrendorff to fully and frankly confess his part in the plot. Still he steadfastly refused. In the final act of this gruesome scenario, the coffin and Tresckow's body were cremated before Schlabrendorff's eyes and he was returned to his jail cell.

The same day that Schlabrendorff was arrested, **17 August**, fate finally knocked on Field Marshal Kluge's door. It came in the shape of the cold, monocled Field Marshal Walter Model, who was known as the 'Führer's fireman' for his ability to pull the fat out of the fire in several desperate situations on the Eastern Front. Model was fast becoming Hitler's favourite soldier. Given command of German forces in the west, he turned up unannounced at Kluge's La Roche-Guyon headquarters and politely announced his deposition. Hitler had not thought to tell 'Clever Hans' that he had been removed after just a month in command. Kluge simply sat at his desk, too stunned to move. The evidence of

Kluge's failure to stop the Allied advance from Normandy could clearly be heard in the chateau, where the menacing drumbeat of shellfire was alarmingly audible. Now he was being summoned home in the wake of Stülpnagel to explain not merely his military inadequacy, but his ambiguous behaviour before and during 20 July. Hitler's doubts about Kluge's loyalty were now so marked that when the field marshal disappeared on another inspection tour of the front in mid-August, at a Führer conference, General Alfred Jodl openly expressed the belief that he would go over to the enemy.

Before leaving for Germany, Kluge wrote a series of letters – to his wife and son, and to Hitler, entrusting them to aides before he departed. At dawn on **19 August**, accompanied by his driver, orderly officer and an armed escort vehicle, the disgraced field marshal set off. Following the route Stülpnagel had taken a month before, they neared Verdun – the haunted battlefield where Kluge had also fought in the previous war.

Kluge ordered the small convoy to halt for lunch. His staff spread a rug under some trees in the midday August heat and left Kluge alone with some picnic food. The field marshal was clearly preoccupied, as his driver had heard him muttering to himself on the journey. He asked for some stationary and wrote another letter – this time to his younger brother, a lieutenant-general. He gave the letter to his orderly officer, ordering him to make sure that it reached its destination, then instructed the party to get ready to continue their journey. Left alone for another moment, Kluge took out a phial of potassium cyanide. He was dead within seconds.

His last letter to Hitler was an odd mixture of his usual fawning obsequiousness and some uncharacteristically blunt advice:

> My Führer, I have always admired your greatness . . . your iron will to maintain yourself and National Socialism . . . You have fought an honorable and great fight . . . Show yourself now also great enough to put an end to a hopeless struggle when it is necessary . . . I depart from you, my Führer, as one who stood nearer to you than you perhaps realized and firm in my conviction that I have always done my duty to the utmost of my powers. Heil, Mein Führer!

After reading it, Hitler handed the missive to Jodl with the cynical comment that had Kluge not committed suicide, then he would have probably been arrested anyway.

On **30 August**, it was the turn of the Paris plotters to face Freisler's 'justice'. Stülpnagel had been patched up in the Verdun hospital, before being sent on to Berlin to face first the Gestapo torturers and finally Freisler. The blinded General, it was said, conducted himself with dignity and endured his ordeal with 'soldierly stoicism'. Tried with him were Casar von Hofacker, Hans Otfried von Linstow, and Eberhard Finckh. All the Paris conspirators had held out courageously against their tormentors, and as a result their collaborators in France largely escaped detection. Hans Speidel was detained, but the wily Swabian, partially protected by his friend Guderian, managed to talk his way out of trouble without implicating anyone, and survived the war to resume his military career in the post-war West German army – as did Adolf Heusinger – both retiring as top NATO commanders.

Hofacker showed the same dauntless spirit as his cousin Stauffenberg, refusing to be cowed by Freisler, and claiming that he had had as much right to revolt against Hitler on 20 July as Hitler had to rise against the Weimar republic in Munich on 9 November 1923. His only regret, he said, was that his maimed cousin, rather than he, had been chosen to place the bomb, since, had it been him it would not have failed. When an outraged Freisler tried to silence Hofacker, he replied: 'Be quiet now, Herr Freisler, because today it's my neck on the block – but in a year's time, it will be yours.' Possibly because of this insolence, Hofacker was kept alive for more months of torture until he was finally hanged on 30 December 1944. The others died as soon as their trial ended.

During his torments, Hofacker was finally forced to reveal to his torturers the conversations he had had with Rommel, just before the famous field marshal had suffered his near-fatal injuries on 17 July. Hofacker alleged that Rommel had agreed to demand that Hitler seek an end to the war, and if he refused, that Rommel would join the plotters in deposing him. Rommel had also apparently been named as a member of a future post-Hitler government in papers drawn up by the ever-indiscreet Goerdeler; and hospital sources claimed that immediately after the devastating attack in July he had criticised the Führer's conduct of the war from his sickbed. All three factors added up to the same thing: Germany's most celebrated and successful soldier was wobbly at best, traitorous at worst. He had to be silenced.

But the Nazis were faced with a dilemma: if Rommel were arrested and arraigned before the People's Court like the rest, it would create a terrible public impression and amount to a PR disaster. The charismatic and popular 'Desert Fox' could not be seen to be among the July traitors, since if *he* thought the war was lost, many loyal Germans might come to agree. Instead, Rommel's severe wounds offered a way out of the dilemma. Hitler deputed Keitel to offer Rommel a choice: either he would be dragged through the People's Court to suffer public disgrace and a lingering death, or he would commit suicide, which would be publicly explained as death due to the delayed results of the wounds he had suffered in July. He would be given a funeral with full military honours, his wife would receive a field marshal's widow's pension, and the name of Rommel would live on in imperishable glory.

Hitler's adjutant, General Wilhelm Burgdorf and another Nazi general, Ernst Maisel, were dispatched to Rommel's house in the small Swabian town of Herrlingen, near Ulm, where, on **14 October**, they arrived to offer Rommel this stark choice. After a hurried and doubtless strained consultation in Rommel's study, the field marshal, understandably upset, emerged to tell his wife Lucie and teenage son Manfred that he was about to die to spare their family disgrace and penury. Taking his farewells, he was driven off into the countryside in Burgdorf's Opel staff car, to be given a cyanide capsule. Fifteen minutes after leaving his home, his wife was told by phone that her husband was dead. Hitler kept his side of the cynical bargain: it was given out that Rommel had died of wounds; a day of mourning was proclaimed; and a solemn military funeral was held. The biggest wreath was sent by Adolf Hitler.

Once he was in the Gestapo's hands, Goerdeler began to sing like a bird. Always loquacious, now the garrulous politician would not stop talking. The reasons were twofold: the man who had sent Hitler lengthy memos on economic policy at the same time as he was attempting to persuade the Allies to help in his overthrow, always held an absurdly optimistic view of human nature and his own powers of persuasion. Now, by naming as many conspirators as he could think of, along with those people who had merely made mildly critical comments about the regime, he hoped to convince the Führer – even at this late stage – that the conspirators were no tiny band of malcontents, but a huge popular movement with a presence in every sector of German society. Finally, Goerdeler believed, Hitler would discover how unpopular he was with the public, and that he was on the wrong track and should alter course. Moreover, by talking the talk, Goerdeler hoped to spin out his interrogations as long as possible – perhaps until the Allies arrived in Berlin to put an end to his ordeal. It was his last and wholly misplaced piece of optimism.

In fact, Goerdeler's careless talk cost lives. His fellow conspirators began to shun him like the plague. New waves of arrests followed every fresh confession. Hardly believing their luck, his Gestapo interlocutors spared Goerdeler the worst tortures, but he was kept under continuous pressure, chained hand and foot, and subjected to a starvation diet with harsh lights kept on in his cell continually. His neighbour in the next cell and future biographer, the historian Gerhard Ritter, would hear Goerdeler literally groaning with hunger, and the man who took the stand before the People's Court on **7 September** – alongside Hassell, the lawyers Josef Wirmer and Paul Lejeune-Jung and the Socialist Wilhelm Leuschner – was a shrunken, wizened, prematurely aged figure, still wearing the now-shabby summer suit in which he had been arrested. Although he was sentenced to death along with the others after Freisler had raged at him as a 'cowardly, contemptible traitor', and his co-defendants were hanged at the conclusion of their trial on **8 September**, Goerdeler was kept alive for a further five months. This was partly in the hope that he would reveal even more names and details of the plot, and partly because Himmler, hoping to save his own skin and knowing of Goerdeler's international contacts, wanted to use him as a bargaining chip with the Allies.

During this time, it finally dawned on Goerdeler that he had made a ghastly mistake and involved many innocents in the wreckage of the conspiracy. Among those implicated and sent to their death by his foolish gabbing was Goerdeler's own younger brother. At last, and far, far too late, he stopped talking. The Führer that he called a 'vampire' and 'disgrace to humanity' had finally sucked even his incorrigible optimism dry. When Ritter saw him in January, Goerdeler's once-luminous eyes had become 'like those of a blind man'. Finally, at the insistence of Otto Thierack, the Nazis' justice minister, he was dragged from his cell to the

Carl Goerdeler, the conspirators' candidate for chancellor, faces the People's Court.

gallows by the SS on **2 February 1945**. After stringing him along for so long, now his killers did not even give him time to write a farewell note to his family before rushing him to his death.

It was partly Goerdeler's revelation of the plot's wide ramifications that prompted a new wave of arrests in October, and partly the discovery of new documentary evidence of the plots against Hitler's life, stretching back as far as the Oster conspiracy of 1938. On **15 September**, Kaltenbrunner, whose regular reports of the investigation were presented to Hitler each night by Fegelein, reported that the investigation was nearing its conclusion. Most of the plotters had been rounded up and were either dead or being dealt with, he said, and no further major revelations could be expected. A week later, a chance discovery made him eat his words.

An army driver, despondent at the death of his boss, Lieutenant-Colonel Werner Schrader, a plotter who had committed suicide on 28 July, went to one of the leading police investigators, Franz Xavier Sonderegger. The chauffeur told him that he had seen Schrader hide a suspicious bundle of papers in a safe at the military base of Zossen. His policeman's curiosity aroused, Sonderegger followed up the tip and discovered a documentary gold mine. The Zossen papers, carefully collected and filed by the Abwehr lawyer Hans von Dohnanyi, gave the Nazis details of the 1938 conspiracy; of the involvement of top generals including Brauchitsch, Halder and Thomas; and of the wide range of discontents that had prompted the plotters' actions: anger at the Fritsch affair, resentment of the growing power of the SS and moral revulsion at the persecution of the Jews.

The revelations of Zossen both alarmed and angered Hitler. He ordered hundreds more arrests, including Halder and Schacht and even old enemies from the distant 1920s, such as the Social Democrat Gustav Noske, the strongman who had crushed the Spartacist revolt in 1919, and Hermann Ehrhardt, the Freikorps leader who had escaped the Führer's wrath during the Röhm purge. At the same time Hitler closed down the publicity mill surrounding the investigation. No longer would Freisler's ravings be filmed and broadcast; Halder's detention was kept strictly secret – even from other prisoners. Sometimes relatives were not told that their loved ones had been executed until weeks after the event. The Führer even thought briefly of sweeping the whole affair under the carpet for fear that the public would find out the extent and the antiquity of the opposition. But then his psychopathic rage got the better of him, and the arrests, tortures, trials and executions continued. By the end of 1944, thousands were crowding the Gestapo's cells. Housing the prisoners was becoming a problem. After one of the increasingly frequent Allied air raids on the capital severely damaged the Gestapo prison on Prinz Albrechtstrasse, they were dispersed, with many finding themselves incarcerated in various concentration camps: Buchenwald, Sachsenhausen, Dachau and Flossenbürg.

One of those transferred to Sachsenhausen was the collater of the Zossen papers, the Abwehr lawyer Hans von Dohnanyi, a close collaborator of Oster. Dohnanyi had been in the Gestapo's hands since he had been picked up at the Abwehr's offices as early as April 1943. Since then he had suffered unspeakable tortures at the Gestapo's hands, which had left him paralysed with a broken spine, and with severe internal injuries. In an effort to escape his tormentors he had deliberately infected himself with diphtheria bacilli brought to his prison cell by his wife. Brought to the sickbay at Sachsenhausen on a stretcher, the dying Dohnanyi was cared for by a medical orderly, Max Geissler, and a Norwegian doctor-prisoner, Sven Oftedal – later a post-war minister in Norway. The discovery of the Zossen papers only spurred the Gestapo to fresh cruelties, and Geissler heard the results through the thin sickbay walls as 'those uneducated thugs really tore into him unspeakably.' Despite his suffering Dohnanyi continued to run intellectual rings round his captors, and from the answers Geissler overheard, he believed that the lawyer had got the better of the encounter even in his extreme condition.

Meanwhile, the trials and hangings ground on. August had seen the second tier of the military conspiracy brought before Freisler and the condemned victims had included: the slippery former Berlin Police chief, Count von Helldorf; Hans-Bernd von Haeften, brother of the aide who had been with Stauffenberg on 20 July; Major Egbert Hayessen, aide to General Hase, whose behaviour on 20 July had attracted the suspicion of Remer; Colonel Fritz Jäger, whose armoured troops had taken to the Berlin streets in support of the putsch; and Adam von Trott zu Solz, the Anglophile diplomat and Oxford Rhodes scholar who had attempted in vain to build foreign support for the plot. On **20 October** the Socialist leaders Julius Leber and Adolf Reichwein went courageously to their deaths.

As a scholar and diplomat thoroughly at home in England, Trott would not have been surprised by the cold contempt displayed towards the plotters by Britain. Having had its fingers thoroughly burned in

Julius Leber and Adolf Reichwein, Socialist leaders executed for participating in the plot.

the Venlo Incident, Whitehall had definitively washed its hands of the German Resistance. The international isolation of the conspirators was emphasised by the reaction in Britain to the assassination attempt and its aftermath, where it was widely seen as an internecine struggle between the extremists around Hitler and the army who wished to bring the war to an end without Germany's sacred soil being invaded. In a brutally cynical memo, the British historian and Foreign Office mandarin Sir John Wheeler-Bennett – later to become an early historian of the Resistance – even suggested that the Gestapo and SS were doing the Allies 'an appreciable service' by removing many who would 'pose as "Good Germans" after the war and cause us endless embarrassments'. Wheeler-Bennett even mocked Freisler's victims for the 'pitiable' impressions they had made before the People's Court, apparently without considering the Gestapo's ministrations that had reduced them to that state.

Christmas 1944 was bleak. The Battle of the Bulge, Hitler's last-gasp offensive in the Ardennes, where he had broken through in 1940, had petered out after an initial success, and the New Year offered only the prospect of further failure. The borders of the Reich were shrinking daily, and in **January 1945** Hitler was forced to abandon the Wolf's Lair

A memorial to Adam von Trott zu Solz, the diplomat who sought in vain to raise foreign support for the Resistance.

– many of whose buildings resisted the attempts to blow them up in the face of the advancing Russians – and take refuge in his last hiding place, the bunker warren below the Berlin Chancellery. With the Western Allies closing in from France, the Low Countries and Italy, and the Red Army moving into the ancestral Prussian heartland – while Allied planes droned unchallenged over the cities of the Reich day and night with their deadly loads – the bombed and bedraggled German populace knew that the end could not be far off.

But still the senseless persecution continued. On **10 January** came the trial of members of Helmuth von Moltke's harmless Kreisau Circle, who had always forsworn violence despite their criticism of the Nazi regime. Ironically, one of the very few members of the circle who advocated assassination – the lawyer Eugen Gerstenmeier, who had been in the Bendlerblock on 20 July – defended himself so skilfully that he became one of the very few to appear before Freisler and escape death. He got seven years, and survived to become a leading politician in post-war Germany. After a two-day intellectual tussle with Freisler, a duel from which both men seemed to draw a strange satisfaction, Moltke and the Jesuit priest Father Alfred Delp were sentenced to death. The execution of the sentence was delayed for a fortnight, leaving the sweet-natured Moltke time to take a last Holy Communion with his wife Freya,

Count Helmuth
von Moltke during
his trial before the
People's Court.

and describe to her the exultant joy he felt in being about to enter the presence of God.

On **23 January**, the same day that Moltke went to his death at Plötzensee, Hans Bernd Gisevius at last succeeded in escaping from Germany. After months in hiding, he had managed to procure a forged Gestapo passport with which he crossed the border to Switzerland. Fabian von Schlabrendorff, despite the tortures he had suffered, also managed to survive – by a miraculous deliverance that encompassed the death of the fiendish Freisler. His trial having been repeatedly postponed, Schlabrendorff was finally brought before the People's Court on **3 February**, the day after Goerdeler's execution. As he sat waiting to appear before Freisler, the hanging judge was interrupted in mid-tirade by the wail of Berlin's air-raid sirens. As lawyers, warders, spectators and prisoners alike scrambled for the safety of the court's underground shelter, Freisler remembered that he had left Schlabrendorff's file behind in his haste to escape the court. He returned to collect it. At that moment the courtroom received a direct hit from a bomb dropped by a US B-17 in the heaviest raid that the city had ever suffered. A beam crashed down, crushing the sadistic Freisler's skull.

When his body was discovered, he was still clutching Schlabrendorff's file. As Freisler's corpse was brought to a hospital morgue, the wife of General Jodl happened to be there. She later testified that she heard a witness say aloud: 'It is a judgement of God.' Nobody disagreed.

The bomb that killed Freisler saved Schlabrendorff. The same air raid also damaged his cell on Prinz Albrechtstrasse, and like Dohnanyi he was sent to Sachsenhausen, before coming before the court on **16 March** under a new and more moderate judge who – astonishingly – acquitted him on the grounds of Schlabrendorff's complaint that torture had been used against him. But the Gestapo were not to lose their prey so easily. Promptly re-arrested, Schlabrendorff was told that as he could not be hanged, he would be shot instead – in a piece of ludicrously German bureaucracy, he was required to sign an official form certifying that he had been acquainted with this fact.

By now, in the closing weeks of the war, the persecution of those plotters who remained alive had become a macabre race between Hitler, Himmler and their fanatical SS minions determined to hunt down and extirpate every last internal enemy, and the Allies and Russians, as they pushed into the Reich from east, west, north and south. Schlabrendorff joined the shifting convoys of VIP prisoners, the so-called 'Prominenten', being moved from camp to camp by the Nazis within the shrinking pocket of territory that they still controlled. His companions in adversity were a mixed bag who included, at various times: relatives of Stauffenberg and Goerdeler; relations of the royal houses of Europe; famous names such as General Franz Halder and Hjalmar Schacht; the former premier of France, Leon Blum; the chancellor of Austria deposed by the Nazis, Kurt von Schuschnigg; the industrialist Fritz Thyssen, whose millions had helped bankroll Hitler's rise to power, but who, like so many, had finally become disillusioned with the regime; and the British secret agents captured at Venlo – Sigismund Payne-Best and Richard Stevens – who had spent most of the war in a VIP block at Sachsenhausen.

But their former power and privilege availed the Prominenten little in the grim battle to survive. Starved, harried by their brutish SS captors, and under constant threat of death, they moved in convoy from camp to camp along a tortuous route towards the mountainous south of Bavaria and the Tyrol. On **3 April**, the night they arrived at Dachau, near Munich, another prisoner in the camp met his end. Georg Elser, the humble locksmith whose bomb in the Munich beerhall in 1939 had come almost as close as Stauffenberg's in killing Hitler, was led away and shot. He had been kept alive throughout the war with the aim of using him along with Payne-Best and Stevens as witnesses in a show trial to expose the machinations of the artful British Secret Service. That trial would never take place, but Elser would not escape Hitler's memory.

The following day, **4 April**, another documentary discovery was made at Zossen camp by Kaltenbrunner's investigators: the long-sought secret diaries of Admiral Canaris. The black notebooks were brought to Hitler the next day, and threw him into a frenzy with their revelations of the

Abwehr's secret plotting, sabotage and even betrayal of his covert plans. He seized on their revelations as an explanation for the whole disastrous course of his war – he had been betrayed from the beginning by Canaris, Oster and the other 'gentlemen' of the Abwehr, and this, not his own blunders, had brought Germany to disaster. Late in the day as it was, they would pay for their crimes. Orders were sent from Berlin – almost encircled by the Russian advance – and in the far south of Germany, the dark deed was done.

With the exception of Dohnanyi, the chief Abwehr prisoners – Canaris and Oster among them – had been at Flossenbürg camp in the wooded hills of northern Bavaria since February. They had been subjected to particularly harsh treatment – kept in fetters twenty-four hours a day and continually tortured. It appears that Oster had broken under the regime and made a full confession. The tough little admiral, by contrast, had held out, piously denying all accusations levelled against him, and stonewalling Oster's incriminating evidence. After the discovery of his diaries the two former colleagues were brought together for a 'trial' on the afternoon of **8 April**, where Oster was made to repeat his charges while Canaris still stoically refuted them. Canaris was then apparently taken away for more torture. That night, his cell neighbour, a Danish agent named Lunding, heard the rattle of the

Flossenbürg concentration camp crematorium.

admiral's chains as Canaris was brought back to his cell. Both he and Oster, along with the other Abwehr officers, had been sentenced to death for high treason.

They communicated in code by tapping on each other's walls. Canaris's last message was brief: 'Nose broken at last interrogation. My time is up. Was not a traitor. Did my duty as a German. If you survive, remember me to my wife.' That night another former Abwehr colleague joined them at Flossenbürg. Dietrich Bonhoeffer had been brought with the convoy taking Payne-Best and other Prominenten to the south. After conducting a prayer service and giving a short sermon that, according to Payne-Best, 'touched the hearts of us all', the young pastor was led away by the Gestapo. As he left, he asked Payne-Best to give his greetings to Bishop George Bell, the English cleric who had attempted in vain to persuade the British government to recognise the Resistance and help them overthrow Hitler. Bonhoeffer added: 'This is the end – [but] for me the beginning of life.'

At 6 a.m. on **9 April**, with the sound of the guns of General Patch's advancing US Seventh Army already audible, Lunding heard a commotion in the cell next door, followed by a voice bellowing 'Out you come!' The executioners had come for Canaris, along with Oster, Bonhoeffer and three other Abwehr officers. They were roughly ordered to undress, and Lunding caught a glimpse of the Admiral's bare feet padding along the stone corridor. Bonhoeffer was last seen naked, kneeling in prayer. Then amidst the frenzied barking of the camp guards' dogs, their SS killers led them to an execution shed similar to that at Plötzensee, with a stepladder under each noose. Canaris was the first to die – and suffered longest, his body jerking and twisting as he was slowly strangled. Even the SS physician attending the cruel spectacle paid tribute to his 'staunch and manly death'.

The prisoners' belongings were thrown into a heap on the guard room floor. Bonhoeffer left a Lutheran Bible and a volume of Goethe behind – his burning faith and his German culture his passports to eternity. Canaris's last reading matter was a biography of Frederick the Great – a literary taste he shared with his nemesis, Hitler. The dead men's bodies were cremated behind the cell block. A smell of burning flesh and flakes of charred skin drifted into Lunding's cell. Canaris's prophecy that Hitler's war would mean *Finis Germanae* had been horribly fulfilled.

Within days of the killings at Flossenbürg, the war in Europe ended, and Hitler, trapped like a cornered rat beneath the rubble of Berlin, took the life that the July plotters had tried so desperately to take before doom engulfed their 'sacred Germany'. Now, at last, it was the turn of the Nazis to die as their world imploded. On **30 April**, with his new bride Eva Braun sitting beside him on a sofa, Hitler simultaneously shot himself and bit into a cyanide capsule. Most of the other denizens of the bunker – Goebbels and his family, Martin Bormann, Wilhelm Burgdorf – did not long survive him. Keitel and Kaltenbrunner were hanged after the Nuremberg trials. It was a bitter end for all Germans, a zero hour appropriate in its savage nihilism to the men who had brought it about.

The conspirators, too late, had learned the lesson of those who accept or tolerate evil. Such passivity, as another survivor, Pastor Martin Niemöller, recognised in a famous poem, is all too likely to end with the innocent being drawn into the abyss along with the guilty. In a frenzy of insensate bloodshed just before the end, the SS had emptied Berlin's prisons and shot many of the surviving plotters 'while attempting to escape'. One of these victims was the geopolitical theorist Albrecht Haushofer. When his body was found, a poem was among the papers in his pocket:

### GUILT

I am guilty
But not in the way you think.
I should have recognized my duty earlier.
Should more strongly have called evil evil.
I reserved my judgement for too long.
I did warn. But not early, nor clear.
And today, I know,
Of what I am guilty.

In a last letter to his wife, Peter Yorck von Wartenburg, a gentle but determined man from one of Prussia's oldest and noblest families, and one of the first conspirators to die, had written: 'It seems that we are standing at the end of our beautiful and rich life together . . . I hope my death will be accepted as an atonement for all my sins, and as an expiatory sacrifice . . . By this sacrifice our time's distance from God may be shortened by some small measure . . . we want to kindle the torch of life; a sea of flame surrounds us.' The Phoenix born from the ashes of the conspirators and their hopes lives and inspires still.

# Afterword

## with Count Berthold Schenk von Stauffenberg

15 November 2008 marked the centenary of Claus von Stauffenberg's birth. The anniversary was the signal for a series of commemorative celebrations. The events included a Bundeswehr exhibition in the Count Stauffenberg Barracks at Sigmaringen; the foundation of a memorial association in Stuttgart and Albstadt-Lautlingen on 25 October; a military tattoo of the Bundeswehr at Jettingen in Bavarian Swabia, Stauffenberg's birthplace; the opening of an exhibition at Lautlingen and a memorial ceremony attended by the German defence minister at the Bendlerblock.

These events reflect the fact that in Germany today Stauffenberg is rightly regarded as a national hero and that more than sixty years after the war, the events of 20 July 1944 remain a source of fascination for people worldwide. Indeed, as this book is being published, trailers for a new film on the subject are being screened and the release of the film, starring Tom Cruise in the lead role, is imminent. The historian Guido Knopp is also working on a documentary on the subject. There will doubtless be many other attempts to re-tell the story to new audiences over the coming years.

One aspect of the plot's aftermath that has not been explored by writers or filmmakers is the extent to which conspirators' families were persecuted. Perhaps surprisingly, the Nazis did not carry out their *Sippenhaft*, or 'Detention of kin' policy, thoroughly or consistently.

In 1944, Stauffenberg's family was living in Bamberg, in the house of his wife Countess Nina's parents. Although this was a Catholic town through and through, it was entirely in the grip of the Nazis. At school, as well as the compulsory 'Heil Hitler!' at the beginning of each day, there were weekly National Socialist 'prayer meetings' conducted by elderly and retired teachers who wore the party badge and were greeted on the streets with the compulsory Nazi salute and a 'Heil Hitler!' Nazi

Count Berthold
Schenk von
Stauffenberg, eldest
son of Claus.

propaganda was becoming much more strident and noticeable. Posters were pasted everywhere with the slogan: 'The enemy is listening too.'

Even as late as 1944 Bamberg did not suffer air raids: only twice, a couple of bombs fell on the town's outskirts. Nevertheless, air-raid sirens sounded incessantly, and the '*Drahtfunk*' – a sort of cable radio transmitted over the telephone network – was constantly switched on. Most children's exams were held in the underground air-raid shelters. And the casualty lists of the fallen were growing ever longer. Many schoolchildren – including many bomb evacuees, mostly from Hamburg – were already war orphans and their numbers increased inexorably.

The Stauffenberg family were only together for a few periods. In 1943, Claus returned home to Lautlingen on convalescent leave. After that, his children saw him just three more times: for two days at Christmas 1943, at the funeral of his father in January 1944, and for a week's holiday in June 1944.

The children had no idea what their father was planning and preparing, neither did they know that their mother knew what was due to take place. Nina had to conceal her real opinions, and let fall no hint of her opposition to the Nazis, which was not an easy task. One knew in general terms, even if not specifically, what could happen if one did not co-operate with the authorities. The newspapers were full of reports about the special trials for those caught listening to enemy broadcasts, or illegally slaughtering animals, and similar 'crimes', which mostly ended with death sentences. The family knew that concentration camps existed but no one knew what happened in them, and no one wanted to know either.

In mid-July 1944 the family – Nina and her four children – left Bamberg for Lautlingen and their annual summer holidays with their paternal grandmother. Berthold von Stauffenberg, the eldest of Nina's children, has recalled, 'We now know my father was not in accord with our holiday plans, but my mother no longer wished to change them.'

On 21 July, the day after the plot, according to Berthold, 'I heard on the radio about a criminal attack on the Führer, but my questions about this were answered evasively, and the adults tried to keep me and my next-youngest brother Heimaren away from the radio.

'My great-uncle, Count Nikolaus von Üxküll, a former General Staff officer in the Imperial and Royal Austrian Habsburg Army, was deputed to take us on a long walk, during which he told us about his adventures as a big game hunter in Africa. Naturally we didn't know then that he too was a member of the conspiracy, and I ask myself today what was really going through his head on that walk.'

On 23 July, Nina explained to her children that it was their father who had carried out the attack on Hitler. 'To my question as to why he had wanted to kill the Führer, she said that he had believed that he had to do it for Germany. She also told us that she was expecting another child. For me the news was a shattering shock – the end of my world. We had loved our always cheerful father unconditionally and above everything. He was an absolute – if often absent – authority, and now this!

'From this moment until early in 1945 I was unable to think clearly, and simply absorbed the blows that would fall on us. And they fell quickly and hard.'

On 23 July, Üxküll and Nina were arrested and taken to Berlin. The next night, Nina's mother and her sister, who was a senior official in the Red Cross, were also arrested and detained in the local court jail in Balingen. Nina's sister was soon released, but not allowed to return to Lautlingen. Nina's mother was freed in November but kept under house arrest. The village stood by her, and there never were so many repairs carried out in her house – the repairs being a pretext for people to see her, despite an official ban on such visits.

The children stayed on alone at their house with their nanny and grandmother's housekeeper, along with two Gestapo officials. On the radio and in papers there were reports about the conspiracy and the first conspirators' trials before the People's Court. Berthold recalled, 'It was fortunate that we were now in Lautlingen, since the village for the most part stood opposed to the regime, albeit in secret. Nevertheless we felt ourselves to be outcasts, and this is a feeling that I will never forget.'

On 16 August came the order that the children – Berthold, ten years old; Heimeran, eight; Franz-Ludwig, six, and Valerie, three and a half; along with their cousins, aged six and five – were to be taken to a children's home. The few belongings they had were quickly packed. The housekeeper took the children to the priest who gave the children his blessing. The priest warned them that bad times probably awaited them, but that we should never forget why their father had done what he had. Only later did the family realise how courageous these words were.

The next morning the children were taken to Stuttgart, which had been heavily bombed the night before. That evening, accompanied by a female Gestapo official, they boarded the night train for Berlin, changed in Erfurt, and at about noon arrived at Nordhausen. From here they were taken by car to the children's home in Bad Sachsa in the south Harz mountains. The home, at Bornetal on the town's outskirts, with its Black Forest style wooden houses seemed picturesque and idyllic. It had been founded by the Bremen businessman Daniel Schnackenberg, and in 1936 had been taken over by the Bremen Nazi party as the 'Bremen' children's home.

Apart from its working and administrative buildings, the home consisted of seven wooden houses, each equipped to hold about thirty children, divided by age group and gender. The location may have been selected for its position – it was a secure, easily sealed-off area that lay just outside the administrative district boundary. Moreover, the staff came mainly from Bremen and were not tied to the locality. The political background made the choice comprehensible too, since Bad Sachsa was the most proudly Nazi-supporting area in the entire district of the Hohenstein/Nordhausen county, to which it belonged at that time.

Stauffenberg's children were the first arrivals. Berthold found himself alone in Haus # 1, the house for boys over ten; his brothers and his cousin were in House # 2 for boys of six to nine years. His sister and his cousin were in the house for girls of two to five years. Since the houses were isolated and widely spaced apart they met only occasionally and by chance. In the days and weeks that followed more children arrived but the houses were never filled to capacity.

Looking back, Berthold said, 'I have no bad memories, nor have my brothers. We were well, even lovingly, treated; we were taken care of and our lives seemed very simple and, given the material shortages of the time, we were no worse off than the mass of the German population. Unlike hundreds of thousands of our contemporaries, we were spared air raids and the terrors of enforced flight, exile and Soviet conquest – even our home village of Lautlingen suffered more than we did from the depredations of the French-Moroccan troops.'

By Christmas 1944 there were so few children being held that they were concentrated together in a single house. Early in 1945 the home was taken over by the Wehrmacht, and it became the top-secret 'Unit 00400', the staff headquarters for the nearby V-weapons rocket programme.

Bad Sachsa was very close to the notorious Mittelbau forced labour underground rocket factory and the Dora concentration camp. There were now only fourteen children remaining: six Stauffenbergs, with the children of Claus's brother Berthold von Stauffenberg and his cousin Casar von Hofacker, who were both executed for their part in the conspiracy; along with the daughter of General Lindemann who was the same age as Berthold; two grandchildren of Carl von Goerdeler and two little girls, the daughters of Leutenant-Colonels Robert Bernardis and Henke, step-daughter of the Abwehr conspirator Dr Captain Ludwig Gehr.

The children were all transferred to a former villa that had been converted to serve as a clinic called 'Iso'. At Easter they were due to be taken to the Buchenwald concentration camp, where they had been informed their relatives were being held. They never reached the camp, because just as they were put in a Wehrmacht transport vehicle and reached the outer suburbs of Nordhausen – where they were due to be put aboard a train – a terrible air raid began. Along with the rest of the town, the railway station was completely destroyed. The children therefore had to return to Bad Sachsa and continue to live there as before.

Finally, on 12 April 1945, the Americans arrived. In the woods over in the Bornetal valley fighting continued until the German forces retreated. The Americans had threatened during negotiations to completely destroy the town unless it surrendered.

Berthold recalls, 'Our house was thoroughly searched by the Americans, who naturally did not know what they would find there. Afterwards, things continued much as they had gone on before. We plundered booty from what had been left behind by Unit 00400, and were able to take longer walks in the neighbourhood.

'After some time we were visited by the newly-appointed mayor, who explained to us that we were now free. He also, as I only discovered at a meeting in the year 2000, ensured that we were properly registered as local residents. Nothing else changed for us, though; as far as we were aware things continued as they had before. Our two remaining kindergarten nurses went home to Bremen, naturally travelling, in the absence of other means of transport, only by foot and by cadging lifts.'

Without warning, on 11 July 1945, the children's Great Aunt Alexandrine arrived in a car with French number plates. She had been a prisoner, together with other *Sippenhaft* detainees and many other prominent prisoners of the Nazis.

Akexandrine organised transport by bus and drove the children back through a devastated Germany to Lautlingen, where they arrived on 13 June 1945. All the talk locally was of the occupation of the area by French-Moroccan troops, who were given free rein for one long day to plunder, during which time the local population, with the permission of their conquerors, were allowed to seek sanctuary in the castle garden and in the church in order to protect themselves from assault and rape.

Also in the castle was a small German-run clinic and a large number of evacuated Gestapo family members. The French pursued a harsh occupation policy, but had very little themselves, so there was a thriving black market. The neighbourhood was also made unsafe owing to the presence nearby, on the army exercise area known as 'Heuberg', of 'liberated' soldiers belonging to General Vlasov's Russian army.

At the beginning of July 1945 the family discovered that Nina was stranded near Hof. After she had been taken into the initial investigative custody in July 1944 in the Berlin Police Presidium on Alexanderplatz, she had been taken to Ravensbrück, the Nazi concentration camp for women, to an annex kept by the Gestapo.

For the birth of her fifth child Konstanze on 17 January 1945, Nina was brought to a maternity home in Frankfurt an der Oder. Soon after the birth she was forced to leave by the rapid advance of the Soviet army, and evacuated by hospital train. She and Konstanze picked up an infection and were therefore taken under false names and with Gestapo guards to a Catholic hospital in Potsdam.

After recovering their health they were escorted by a *Feldgendarme* – a military policeman – to join the other *Sippenhaft* prisoners, who were at that time in Schönberg. The policeman, who considered such a 'political' duty beneath him, wanted to go home, and so simply deposited Nina and Konstanze in a village near Hof after obtaining from Nina a written certificate that he had more then performed his duty. Shortly afterwards, the Americans arrived in the village and Nina, quite by chance, became the first of the *Sippenhaft* prisoners to be liberated.

The family were only able to return to their home in Bamberg in 1953. The house had been requisitioned by the SS, then vacated as the Americans approached and damaged the property with artillery fire and plundering. Nina had to fight hard not only to bring up her five children, but also to rebuild the house and to regain legal possession of it. The family jewels were first stolen by the Gestapo, and then by members of the American Counter Intelligence Corps (CIC). They were only returned from the US in 1948.

Berthold chose to pursue a career in the army. Not surprisingly, he has been asked many times why he decided to become a soldier. The answer he has given was that 'it was not for reasons of tradition, as we are not a particularly military family. It was also not because of my father; rather in spite of him, as naturally I knew that I would spend my entire career in his shadow. I simply thought that it was the right career for me, and that the burden of bearing the Stauffenberg name would be worth it. I was not disappointed. I have never regretted my choice of career for a single day.'

It is true, however, that he came to hate the awkward question, 'Are you your father's son?' but he has said, 'I learned to live with it. And I must also live with 20 July. Contrary to the official "line" at the beginning this was by no means uncontroversial. No one ever uttered any criticism to my face, but naturally I heard nevertheless of plenty of outspoken mess-room discussions. Among other things there were discussions about the Oath of Allegiance that all soldiers had had to swear and which in 1934 had been changed from general loyalty to the Reich to personal allegiance to Hitler. Some used the argument that they had been bound by this oath in good faith, but with others I had the suspicion that they used it in order to have an alibi to excuse them from taking part [in the conspiracy].'

In 1999 the family were unexpectedly forced to confront the past again: the Sword of Honour, awarded to Claus in 1929 by the head of the army for being the best cavalry graduate of that year, reappeared. It had vanished after 20 July 1944, probably looted by the Berlin Gestapo. It then found its way by an unknown route to the hands of Max Reimann, the post-war chairman of the Communist Party of Germany (KPD). By

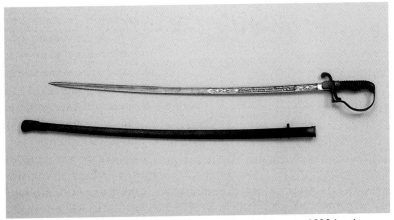

The Sword of Honour, awarded to Claus von Stauffenberg in 1929 by the Chief of Staff of the army for being the best cavalry graduate of that year.

the 1960s it was in the hands of the chairman of the (West) German Communist Party (DKP), Herbert Mies.

Mies said he had never been able to locate a single member of the Stauffenberg family to return the sword. He eventually found such an opportunity, and at last the sword found its way back to Nina who treasured it as a precious memento until her death in 2006. It is now on display in the Stauffenberg exhibition in Stuttgart's Old Castle.

Berthold has explained that, 'In hindsight, the months from July 1944 to June 1945 marked me indelibly for the rest of my life, and for this reason I would not have missed them. The same goes for the materially even more difficult post-war time. Like most of my contemporaries, especially the war orphans, these times taught us the seriousness of life through our own eyes in a manner that today's younger generation – on whom I would never wish it – must fail to understand.

'We certainly grew up faster, and were continually aware that we had to stand on our own two feet rather earlier than normal. And that we did, yet from all of us something upright grew. I have been ever thankful since 1945 above all for one thing: that practically all our family were finally and happily re-united. We certainly mourned my grandmother who died in a concentration camp, even though she had never borne the name Stauffenberg; and also grieved for my shot-down aviator aunt, but we still came through it all. Among our regular evening prayers was the sentence: "Dear Lord, we thank thee that thou has reunited us again."'

# Dramatis Personae

**Beck, General Ludwig (1880–1944)**: An upright soldier of the old school and probably the most technically brilliant staff officer in Germany, Beck's movement from strong sympathy for National Socialism to outright opposition is symptomatic of many of the military conspirators. Even before the advent of Hitler to power, he defended a trio of Nazi officers accused of spreading party propaganda in their barracks, and sympathised with the Nazi re-armament programme after he became chief of the General Staff in 1935. He believed, however, that Hitler's rush to war over Czechoslovakia was too precipitate, and resigned following his failure to organise a 'Generals' Strike' in protest in 1938. In retirement he devoted himself full-time to conspiracy and was persuaded of the need to eliminate Hitler physically. Named as head of state in the post-putsch government that would have followed the events of 20 July, he spent the day in the Bendlerblock trying to shore up support for the failing coup, and died in a forced and botched suicide that night.

**Boeslager, Freiherrs Georg von (1915–1944) and Philipp von (1917–2008)**: Scions of an aristocratic Catholic family, the Boeslager brothers were cavalry officers who became involved in various abortive plots to assassinate Hitler associated with Henning von Tresckow at the Army Group Centre headquarters. Georg helped to obtain the explosive used by Stauffenberg in his bomb on 20 July. The following month, Georg was killed in action on the Russian front. Philipp was marching his unit to support the putsch in Berlin on 20 July, standing them down only when he heard of the plot's failure. One of the conspiracy's last survivors, he published his memoirs the year before he died.

**Bussche-Streithorst, Baron Major Axel von dem (1919–1993)**: A highly decorated and much-wounded aristocratic officer, von dem Bussche was horrified when he witnessed the mass shooting of Jewish civilians at Dubno in 1942 and resolved to join the Resistance. He volunteered to blow Hitler up with grenades while modelling an army greatcoat, but the event was cancelled after the coats were destroyed in an Allied air raid. Soon afterwards, von dem Bussche lost a leg in action and was hospitalised for most of the rest of the war.

**Canaris, Admiral Wilhelm (1887–1945)**: A strongly nationalist career naval officer, Canaris became involved in right-wing conspiratorial activity against the Weimar

Republic, and initially sympathised with the Nazi regime. In 1935 he became chief of the Abwehr military intelligence service. Increasingly critical of the Nazis and horrified by Hitler's reckless aggression, he allowed the Abwehr to become a nest of anti-Nazi conspiracy, while appearing to serve his Nazi masters in a risky double game. Oster, Dohnanyi, Bonhoeffer and other Abwehr plotters were arrested in 1943, and Canaris fell under suspicion, finally being sacked in February 1944. Arrested after 20 July, he was executed at Flossenbürg concentration camp in the last days of the war.

**Dohnanyi, Hans von (1902–1945)**: Married to Dietrich Bonhoeffer's sister, Dohnanyi was a lawyer and jurist attached to the Abwehr. He played a leading role in Oster's abortive coup plans in September 1938. He also gathered information on Nazi atrocities and war crimes for use in future prosecutions, and acted as link man between the Abwehr and the military conspirators.

During the war he helped Jews evade Nazi persecution and was arrested, initially for currency offences, in 1943. Brutally tortured, he deliberately infected himself with toxic bacillae in an effort to evade his tormentors. Some of the documents he meticulously assembled were discovered after 20 July and provided damning evidence against his co-conspirators. He was executed in Sachsenhausen concentration camp in April 1945.

**Fellgiebel, General Erich (1886–1944)**: A signals specialist, he was appointed head of the Signals Corps in 1938. A close friend of Beck and Stülpnagel, Fellgiebel's independent views attracted Hitler's suspicion, but the Führer needed his expertise. On 20 July, he was tasked with cutting off the Wolfschanze's communications with the outside world, and met Stauffenberg before the bombing. He was arrested at Rastenburg that night. Bravely defending himself before Judge Freisler in the People's Court, Fellgiebel was condemned on 10 August and executed on 4 September.

**Freisler, Judge Roland (1893–1945)**: As a prisoner of war in Russia in the First World War, Freisler became a Bolshevik. He studied law and switched allegiance to the Nazis in 1925, rising through the Third Reich's legal hierarchy to be appointed president of the People's Court in 1942. Briefed by Hitler to bully and humiliate the defendants, Freisler's conduct of the 'trials' that followed the July plot became notorious thanks to the films made of the early hearings. He delighted in taunting and sadistically sentencing his victims to death, and it seemed to many a judgement of God when he was killed in an Allied air raid in February 1945 while conducting the trial of Fabian von Schlabrendorff.

**Fromm, General Friedrich (1888–1945)**: Chief of the Wehrmacht's armaments until 1944 when he was appointed head of the Reserve Home Army. Mistrusted by Hitler, Fromm knew of the plans being hatched around his office in the Bendlerblock to overthrow the regime, but cynically and deliberately held aloof until the outcome became clear. Briefly detained by the plotters on 20 July, Fromm was freed and had Beck, Stauffenberg, Mertz and Werner von Haeften condemned to death and immediately shot – not least to cover up his own complicity and duplicity. The act angered the Nazis and Fromm too was arrested, tortured, and court-martialled for cowardice and dereliction of duty. He was executed by firing squad – one of Hitler's least mourned victims.

**Gersdorff, Baron General Rudolf Christoph von (1905–1980)**: An intelligence officer at Army Group Centre in 1941, Gersdorff tried unsuccessfully to recruit Field Marshal Manstein to the Resistance. On 21 March 1943 he attempted to blow up Hitler (and himself) in a suicide bombing while guiding the Führer around an exhibition of captured Soviet weaponry at the Berlin Armoury. Undetected, he rose to be Chief of Staff to the Seventh Army in 1944–45 and survived the war.

**Gisevius, Hans Bernd (1904–1974)**: A legal official at the Prussian Police Ministry, Gisevius left the service in disgust after the Night of the Long Knives and devoted himself to conspiracy. He played a leading role in Oster's abortive 1938 coup, becoming an early advocate of assassinating Hitler, and the following year joined Canaris's Abwehr.

From 1940–44, he headed the Abwehr station in Switzerland and made contact with his opposite number Allen Dulles of the OSS (forerunner of the CIA). Gisevius met and quarrelled with Stauffenberg, but he was at the Bendlerblock on 20 July. He managed to escape and went underground, fleeing to Switzerland in disguise. His memoir *To The Bitter End* is an important and rare – but not always reliable – personal account from inside the Resistance.

**Goerdeler, Carl Friedrich (1884–1945)**: An ultra-conservative economist and politician, Goerdeler was mayor of Leipzig from 1930, and commissioner for price control in the dying days of Weimar and the early days of the Nazi regime. He resigned as Leipzig's mayor in 1937 for refusing to remove a statue of the Jewish composer Mendelssohn. Thereafter he became actively opposed to the Nazis, tirelessly travelling at home and abroad in his efforts to build support against Hitler, who had ignored his many memos advising him on policy.

Garrulous, indiscreet and a bad judge of character, Goerdeler was absurdly optimistic about removing Hitler peacefully and always opposed his assassination. He favoured a compromise peace with the West that would allow Germany to keep many of the Nazis' territorial gains – another example of his poor grasp of reality.

He drew up many blueprints for a future post-Nazi Christian Germany and was the conspirators' candidate for chancellor in a post-Nazi regime. Warned of his impending arrest, he went underground just before 20 July, but was recognised and arrested in August. Sentenced to death by the People's Court in September, he was kept alive for five months because he 'named names' in a misguided attempt to show the Nazis how unpopular they were. He was finally hanged in February 1945.

**Haeften, Hans-Bernd von (1905–1944) and Werner von (1908–1944)**: A member of the anti-Nazi Confessing Church and a diplomat, Hans-Bernd von Haeften was Stauffenberg's man in the Foreign Office and would have become Foreign Office state secretary in a post-putsch government. He was hanged in Plötzensee Prison on 15 August. His younger brother Werner, a Berlin legal banker in peacetime, was severely wounded in Russia and joined the Home Reserve Army, where he became Stauffenberg's friend and aide-de-camp in late 1943. He accompanied Stauffenberg to Rastenburg on 20 July, helped him prime the bomb, returned with him to the Bendlerblock and was executed alongside him that night.

**Halder, General Franz (1884–1972)**: Succeeding Beck as chief of the General Staff in 1938, although he shared Beck's view that Hitler's war policy was madness, Halder lacked the resolution to take effective action to stop it. Claiming that he often carried a loaded pistol into conferences with the Führer, Halder showed no sign of using it, and went along with the invasions of France and Russia as a professional soldier. Dismissed in September 1942 for opposing Hitler's military decisions, he took no active part in the July plot, but was arrested anyway, and confined to a concentration camp. He was one of the convoy of 'Prominenten' prisoners who were lucky to survive the war, and gave evidence before the Nuremberg Tribunal. Halder worked with the US Army in post-war Germany, and published both his own wartime diaries and a book attacking Hitler's qualities as a military leader.

**Hase, General Paul von (1885–1944)**: Berlin's military city commandant on 20 July, and a conspirator since 1938, Hase sent Major Otto Remer's *Grossdeutschland* Guards Battalion and other troops to seal off Berlin's government quarter without ascertaining where their true loyalties lay. After Remer's defection, Hase went to see Goebbels to parley and was arrested. He was tried with the first group of conspirators before the People's Court on 8 August and executed that afternoon.

**Heinz, Friedrich Wilhelm (1899–1968)**: A shadowy figure but a born survivor, Heinz was a First World War army officer active in the violently right-wing *Ehrhardt* Freikorps, responsible for assassinating left-wing figures in the Weimar Republic. Heinz joined the early Nazis as a journalist, but – like many ex-Freikorps activists – fell foul of the party and was expelled, joining the nationalist paramilitary Stahlhelm movement. Recruited by Oster to the Abwehr, Heinz was tasked with leading the commando unit attacking the Chancellery and killing Hitler in the abortive September 1938 coup. As an army officer in 1941 he commanded the 4th Regiment of the Brandenburg Division. Once again, he was to have led a task force in Berlin on 20 July, and appeared at the Bendlerblock. He escaped in the aftermath of the putsch's failure and hid out in Berlin until the end of the war. A local politician in Soviet-run East Berlin after the war, he re-emerged in the west to play a mysterious part in West Germany's intelligence service.

**Helldorf, Count Wolf Heinrich von (1896–1944)**: Like Heinz, Helldorf was a former Freikorps fighter and Nazi who fell out with his party. Joining the NSDAP in 1925, he became the SA leader in the Berlin–Brandenburg Gau, and survived the 1934 purge to become Berlin's Police President in 1935. Notoriously corrupt, he took cash bribes from persecuted Jews to get them exit visas. The atrocities of *Kristallnacht* in November 1938, however, proved a pogrom too far and Helldorf joined the opposition. Arrested after 20 July, he was tortured, tried before the People's Court and executed on 15 August.

**Hoepner, General Erich (1886–1944):** Prepared to lend his troops' support to the abortive September 1938 coup, Hoepner took part in the invasion of Russia. However, he seriously annoyed Hitler by disobeying a direct 'Führer-order' not to withdraw his tanks during the battle for Moscow in the winter of 1941/2. He was sacked in disgrace and forbidden to wear his uniform. Embittered, he joined the plot, though probably as much out of personal pique as principle. Appointed by the conspirators to succeed his friend Fromm as commander of the Home Reserve Army, Hoepner arrived at the Bendlerblock with his uniform in a suitcase and changed in Olbricht's office toilet. When the putsch failed he was arrested with the other leading conspirators, but successfully pleaded for his life with Fromm, who reprieved him from the firing squad that killed Stauffenberg and sent him to jail instead. Brutally tortured and possibly drugged, he cut a sorry figure before the People's Court in a shabby cardigan, and was among the first of the conspirators to be hanged on 8 August.

**Hofacker, Colonel Casar von (1896–1944):** A lawyer, a nationalist and a cousin of Stauffenberg, Hofacker was a prisoner of war in France in the First World War, afterwards joining the Stahlhelm paramilitary nationalist group. Called to the colours in 1939 as a Luftwaffe officer, he was posted to Paris where he became personal aide to France's military Governor, Stülpnagel. The main liaison man between the plotters in Berlin and the conspirators in France, Hofacker was at Stülpnagel's side as he vainly tried to persuade Field Marshal Kluge to join the plot on 20 July. He went into hiding but was discovered, arrested and condemned to death by the People's Court. Under prolonged torture, he revealed Rommel's peripheral role in the plot. He was finally hanged on 30 December 1944.

**Kaltenbrunner, Ernst (1903–1946):** An Austrian, hailing from the same area as Hitler, Kaltenbrunner was a lawyer who joined Austria's Nazis and SS in 1932. Imprisoned after the unsuccessful Nazi putsch in Vienna in 1934, he played a prominent part in the *Anschluss* and was promoted by Hitler. A tall, gaunt forbidding figure with a scarred face, Kaltenbrunner succeeded Heydrich as head of the SD after the latter's assassination. He was in overall charge of the investigation into the aftermath of the July plot. Arrested at the war's end, he unconvincingly denied his role in such enormities as the Holocaust and atrocities against prisoners, and was condemned to death and hanged at the Nuremberg Tribunal in October 1946.

**Keitel, Field Marshal Wilhelm (1882–1946):** After a brave but undistinguished early military career, culminating in being Field Marshal Blomberg's office manager, Keitel was plucked from obscurity by Hitler to be chief of the newly created OKW, the Armed Forces High Command. Thereafter he slavishly obeyed his master's every wish, earning the derision of his fellow officers and the nicknames 'Nickesel' ('Nodding Donkey') and 'Lakeitel' ('Lackey') for his supine behaviour. As ever, at Hitler's side when Stauffenberg's bomb exploded, it was the burly Keitel who helped the injured Führer from the devastated conference room, and who told the outside world by phone that Hitler had survived the attack. Keitel was arrested after signing

Germany's military surrender in 1945 – he was tried at Nuremberg for war crimes, condemned to death and hanged.

**Kleist-Schmenzin, Ewald von (the elder) (1890–1945) and Kleist-Schmenzin, Ewald Heinrich (the younger) (1922– ):** Descended from an old and distinguished Prussian family, the Kleist-Schmenzins, father and son, were both outright opponents of Hitlerism. The elder Ewald, a conservative landowner, travelled to London and met British leaders in an abortive effort to enlist support for Oster's September 1938 coup. He remained in the Resistance, supported Stauffenberg's intention to kill Hitler, and would have played a prominent part in a post-putsch government. Arrested after the plot's failure, he was tried and executed.

His son, also named Ewald, was one of the young officers who volunteered – with his father's approval – to kill Hitler. Although at the Bendlerstrasse as an adjutant to the putschists on 20 July, he managed to survive the subsequent purge while serving at the front. At the time of writing he is still alive in Munich – the very last of the July plotters.

**Kluge, Field Marshal Günther 'Hans' von (1882–1944):** Succeeding Bock in command of Army Group Centre in Russia in December 1941, Kluge dithered after coming under pressure from his aide Henning von Tresckow to join the anti-Hitler plot. His career in Russia was brought to an end when he was severely injured in a car crash in 1943. On recovering, he was appointed to succeed Rommel as commander of the Army Group B fighting the Normandy campaign in France in mid-July 1944. On 20 July he again hesitated when asked by Beck to join the putsch, before dramatically coming out against the plot when he realised that Hitler was alive. Mistrusted by Hitler, he was relieved of his command a month later and recalled to Germany to face investigation, being succeeded in Normandy by Field Marshal Walter Model. Like Stülpnagel, Kluge attempted suicide close to the battlefield of Verdun, where both men had fought in the Great War. Unlike Stülpnagel, Kluge succeeded – biting a cyanide capsule during a roadside picnic.

**Mertz von Quirnheim, Ritter Albrecht (1905–1944):** An army friend and contemporary of Claus von Stauffenberg, Mertz soon repented of an early sympathy for the Nazi regime. He succeeded Stauffenberg as Chief of Staff to Olbricht in the Home Reserve Army, by which time he was a convinced conspirator. Mertz was the man who issued the Valkyrie orders from the Bendlerblock. He was arrested by Fromm and executed with Beck, Stauffenberg, Olbricht and Werner von Haeften on the night of 20 July.

**Moltke, Count Helmuth James von (1907–1945):** A descendant of one of Prussia's great military families and with an English mother, Moltke was a lawyer who had practised in London and had many British ties. After war began, he worked as a legal adviser to OKW Intelligence, arguing for the humane treatment of prisoners. His Kreisau estate became the centre of an ever widening circle of dissent, ranging from Social Democrats and trade unionists to conservative aristocrats and churchmen. The Kreisau Circle drew up plans for a non-Nazi post-war Germany and a united Europe, but Moltke refused to approve assassinating Hitler. Arrested in January 1944, he was tried before the People's Court, and after verbally duelling with Freisler, was condemned to death and executed in January 1945. His letters from his cell to his wife Freya are among the most moving documents to have come from the Resistance.

**Nebe, Arthur (1894–1945)**: After serving and being wounded in the First World War, Nebe joined the Berlin police and, in 1930, the Nazi party and the SS. Rising to the rank of SS Gruppenführer, he was appointed head of the Criminal Police and led the investigation into Georg Elser's bombing. But Nebe's attitude was ambiguous in the extreme – he was on the fringes of the Oster conspiracy in 1938, and was finally disillusioned with the regime after witnessing atrocities following the invasion of Russia. At the same time, Nebe himself led the *Einsatzgruppen B* murder squad, responsible for some 45,000 civilian deaths. On 20 July, along with his similarly ambiguous police colleague Count von Helldorf, he was ready to support the putsch, but never received the order from the Bendlerblock to move his men. He went into hiding on a wooded island in Berlin but was betrayed by a mistress, tried and condemned, and executed in March 1945. Reports that he survived the war are apparently groundless.

**Oberg, Carl-Albrecht (1895–1965)**: A failed businessman, his career was rescued by the SS and in 1942 he became senior SS commander in occupied France. As such, he was responsible for deporting French Jews to their deaths and for repression and reprisals against the French Resistance. Briefly arrested by the conspirators on 20 July, Oberg then interrogated Stülpnagel, the man who had ordered his detention, after the latter had blinded himself in a suicide bid. After the war, he was condemned to death in Germany in 1946, and in France in 1954, escaping the extreme penalty on both occasions. His sentence was commuted to life imprisonment in 1958 but he was released on health grounds in 1965, the year of his death.

**Olbricht, General Friedrich (1888–1944)**: A backroom boy, but technically very able, the self-effacing Olbricht used his position as Chief of Staff to Fromm, commander of the Reserve Army, to plan a putsch under cover of the Valkyrie plan for putting down a revolt in the Reich. A convinced opponent of Nazism from the outset, Olbricht visited Stauffenberg in hospital after he was wounded in Tunisia in 1943, and arranged for him to be appointed his Chief of Staff in October 1943. Working together they refined Valkyrie, but made no allowance for Hitler surviving an assassination attempt. On 20 July Olbricht fatally delayed putting Valkyrie into effect until Stauffenberg's return from Rastenburg, although he was happy to approve when Mertz issued the orders. Arrested with Beck, Stauffenberg, Mertz and Haeften, Olbricht was executed on Fromm's orders that night. His widow Eva inaugurated the memorial at the Bendlerblock after the war.

**Oster, General Hans (1888–1945)**: Oster was effectively Canaris's deputy in the Abwehr and a convinced and very active opponent of Nazism, which he regarded as the negation of Germany's Christian traditions. He was chiefly responsible for organising the first serious military conspiracy against Hitler in September 1938, when senior officers feared that Hitler's intentions to risk a war over the annexation of Czechoslovakia would involve Germany in a conflict she could not win. However, the plotters' plans to overthrow Hitler in a putsch and kill him in the confusion, were aborted after the Western Allies caved in to the Führer's demands at Munich. Oster graduated from conspiracy to treason when he informed the Norwegian and Dutch military attaches of Hitler's plans to attack their countries – he was not believed. Oster fell under suspicion and was detained with his aide Dohnanyi in 1943, and placed under house arrest. Picked up on 21 July 1944, he was executed with Canaris, Bonhoeffer and other Abwehr plotters at Flossenbürg concentration camp on 9 April 1945.

**Remer, Major Otto Ernst (1912–1997)**: Remer was a fanatical Nazi soldier, highly decorated and much wounded on the Eastern Front. Appointed commander of the *Grossdeutschland Wach* Battalion, a unit charged with ensuring security in Berlin, on 20 July he received orders from the city commandant, General Paul von Hase, to seal off the central government area with his men. His suspicions fanned by a Nazi education officer attached to his unit, Remer sought out Goebbels, who connected him by phone to Hitler at Rastenburg. Hitler promoted Remer to full colonel on the spot and put him in temporary charge of all troops in Berlin with orders to put down the putsch at any cost. Remer did this, surrounding the Bendlerblock with his men. In the meantime, loyalist Nazi officers inside the Bendlerblock had staged their own counter-coup, arrested Stauffenberg and his closest confederates, and shot them. Eventually reaching the rank of Major-General, Remer fought on the Eastern Front and in the Ardennes with a notable lack of success, his unit incurring heavy casualties for little gain. A prisoner of the US army until 1947, in 1950 he founded a neo-Nazi group, the Socialist Reichs Party, which gained some local electoral successes in Saxony and Bremen before it was dissolved in 1952. Remer regularly spoke out against the July plotters as 'traitors' and was a prominent Holocaust denier. An unrepentant Nazi, he fled to Spain, Syria and Egypt in 1994 to avoid imprisonment for his Holocaust denial in Germany. He died in exile.

**Rommel, Field Marshal Erwin (1891–1944)**: A brave and talented infantry officer on the Italian front in the First World War, Rommel became the most celebrated German commander of the Second, with his élan, dash and mastery of tank tactics. His armoured columns were in the vanguard in the invasion of France in 1940, but his fame reached its height when he was made commander of the Afrika Korps in Libya and Egypt. At first Rommel carried all before him, taking Tobruk and threatening Cairo. However, checked at El Alamein, he was defeated there in 1942, and beat a fighting retreat to Tunisia, where, starved of supplies by Allied air power, he fell sick and was evacuated, leaving his army to be captured. Appointed commander of Army Group B in France, he prepared to meet the Allied invasion, but despaired of victory, and, influenced by his Chief of Staff and fellow Swabian, Hans Speidel, he drafted a letter to Hitler appealing to him to make peace. On leave in Germany on D-day, he returned to the front, only to be seriously injured when his staff car was strafed from the air. He was thus out of action on 20 July. After Casar von Hofacker, under torture, had implicated Rommel in the plot, the Nazis offered him a stark choice between committing suicide and a humiliating People's Court trial and execution. It was announced that he had died of his wounds, since it was thought that putting a popular hero like Rommel through the Freisler experience would be bad publicity. Compelled to swallow a cyanide pill near his home in October, Rommel was buried with full military honours in a funeral attended by his widow and son. The full truth about his death only emerged after the war.

**Schlabrendorff, Fabian von (1907–1980)**: A conservative lawyer before the war, he became Henning von Tresckow's adjutant at Army Group Centre and his first lieutenant in conspiracy. He acted as contact man between the front and the plotters in Berlin and was the key figure in the 'bottle bomb' plot to destroy Hitler in the air. He was arrested after 20 July, then interrogated and tortured at Gestapo headquarters in Berlin. He eventually went on trial at the People's Court. Miraculously, Judge Freisler was killed in an air raid while hearing Schlabrendorff's case. Freisler's successor – also miraculously – acquitted him on the grounds that he had been tortured, but he was immediately re-arrested and held in concentration camps. Incredibly, he survived the war to write one of the earliest histories of the Resistance and resume his legal career. He was a judge of West Germany's constitutional court between 1967 and 1975.

**Schulenberg, Count Fritz-Dietlof von der (1902–1944)**: A lawyer and member of the Nazi party and regional government in the 1930s, Schulenberg was later expelled from the party on grounds of political unreliability. In 1940 he joined the Kreisau Circle and became a contact man between various oppositon groups. A close friend of Stauffenberg, he was arrested after 20 July and hanged on 10 August.

**Stauffenberg, Colonel Count Claus Schenk von (1905–1944)**: With his older twin brothers Alexander and Berthold, he was influenced by the mystical poet Stefan George in his youth, but soon decided on a military career, as suiting his active and dynamic personality, and joined a cavalry regiment. A conservative nationalist in keeping with his aristocratic antecedents, he had high hopes of the Hitler regime but soon became disillusioned with the violence and vulgarity of the 'brown plague'. He took part in the occupation of Czechoslovakia and the Polish and French campaigns where his abilities as a staff officer and charismatic manner won him great respect.

Angry at Hitler's inept conduct of the Russian campaign, he began to voice his opinions among his wide circle of well-connected military family and friends. Transferred to Tunisia in 1943 he was severely wounded when his staff car was strafed from the air, losing an eye and a hand and two of the fingers on his remaining hand. Evacuated, he made a swift recovery and joined the staff of the Reserve Home Army in Berlin with the explicit intention of staging a putsch to eliminate Hitler – telling friends that he was knowingly committing high treason. His energy and charisma re-vitalised the conspirators and plans for the Valkyrie putsch were re-vamped. After attempting to recruit several junior officers as assassins, Stauffenberg decided to do the job himself after his promotion to Chief of Staff to Fromm gave him regular access to the Führer. After two abortive attempts, he succeeded in detonating the bomb at Rastenburg on 20 July, and immediately flew back to Berlin and attempted to launch Valkyrie by telephone. After the failure of the putsch, he was wounded in a gun battle with loyalist Nazi officers and arrested. He and his aide-de-camp Werner von Haeften, along with Generals Beck and Olbricht and his friend Mertz von Quirnheim, were hastily condemned and shot by firing squad in the Bendlerblock's courtyard on the orders of Fromm. Since his death Stauffenberg has become the central icon of the German resistance to Hitler: 'The head, heart and hand of the conspiracy'.

**Stieff, General Hellmuth (1901–1944):** The youngest general in the German army – and also probably the shortest – Stieff won early promotion thanks to his exceptional organisational abilities. Despite Hitler's dislike for him – the Führer called him the '*Giftzwerge*', or 'poison dwarf' – Stieff was attached to his headquarters. A late recruit to the Resistance – he was the unwitting recipient of Schlabrendorff's 'bottle bomb' – Stieff initially agreed to assassinate Hitler after much hesitation – then changed his mind again. Clearly a timid man, he attempted to dissuade Stauffenberg from carrying out the assassination himself.

Arrested on the night of 20 July, he was brutally tortured, but stood up well to his tormentors and to Judge Freisler's bullying in court. He was among the first to be hanged on 8 August. His letters to his wife are a moving record of the Resistance.

**Stülpnagel, General Karl-Heinrich von (1886–1944):** An early veteran of the military conspiracy, he was ready to move against Hitler in 1938 along with his old friend Beck. He succeeded his cousin Otto von Stülpnagel as military commander of occupied France in 1942. Helped by Hofacker, Stülpnagel's Paris command was the only place on 20 July where the Valkyrie putsch was completely successful, and the entire SS and SD staff of Paris were rounded up in a bloodless coup on Stülpnagel's orders. However, after the news of Hitler's survival came through, Stülpnagel failed to persuade his superior, Field Marshal Kluge, to join the putsch and he was compelled to release the SS/SD detainees. Sacked on the spot and recalled to face the music, he attempted to shoot himself near Verdun, where he had fought in the First World War, but only succeeded in blinding himself. He was patched up, tried before the People's Court and hanged on 30 August.

**Tresckow, Brigadier-General Henning von (1901–1944):** This chief conspirator was son-in-law of General Erich Falkenhayn, the commander of Germany's armies in the middle period of the First World War. Like many of his brother officers he initially supported Hitler's regime, but swiftly turned into a bitter and determined opponent. In his key position as Chief of Staff at Army Group Centre's headquarters in Russia he recruited a team of young officers as keen as he to rid the world of Hitler – and made repeated attempts to do so. In 1943, he briefly returned to Berlin and helped Stauffenberg draw up the Valkyrie II plan for a covert coup. Posted again to the Eastern Front, he continued to assert – not least to Stauffenberg – the necessity of killing Hitler for the moral rebirth of Germany. He killed himself with a rifle grenade in the front lines on 21 July after learning of the failure of the putsch.

His body was disinterred by the Nazis when they realised the extent of his plotting and cremated at Sachsenhausen concentration camp before the horrified eyes of his former adjutant Fabian von Schlabrendorff. Now regarded, along with Stauffenberg and Oster, as the most effective and morally focussed of all the conspirators.

**Wagner, General Eduard (1894–1944)**: Quartermaster general of the German army, responsible for supplying the troops on both the Eastern and Western Fronts, Wagner lent his personal plane to Stauffenberg to fly to Rastenburg and make the attempt on Hitler's life on 20 July. After the failure of the plot, expecting arrest, Wagner took his life on 23 July by shooting himself simultaneously with two pistols.

**Witzleben, Field Marshal Erwin von (1881–1944)**: As commander of the Berlin military district in 1934, he approved the bloody purge of the SA, but swiftly recanted and became an outspoken opponent of Hitler, ready to use his troops to support the September 1938 coup attempt. In 1940 he was promoted to Field Marshal and commanded an army group in the invasion of France. From 1941–42 he commanded in France and planned to kill Hitler in Paris, but the Führer never came and Witzleben retired on grounds of ill-health.

Witzleben joined the military conspiracy in Berlin and agreed to put his name to the putsch proclamation, and to head the Wehrmacht under the post-putsch government. He appeared briefly at the Bendlerblock late in the day on 20 July, only to loudly denounce the bungled coup in parade-ground terms. He then went home, where he was arrested the next day. Among the first conspirators to be tried, he was deliberately humiliated by Freisler, who ordered the removal of his dentures, belt and braces, forcing him to hold up his trousers throughout his trial. The first of the plotters to be hanged, he went to his death with dignity and courage.

**Yorck von Wartenburg, Count Peter (1904–1944)**: A cousin of Stauffenberg, Yorck was a lawyer and economist. Unlike other members of the Kreisau Circle, he was an early proponent of the necessity of killing Hitler. Slated to become state secretary in the Chancellery in the post-putsch government, he appeared at the Bendlerblock on 20 July and was arrested there. He was among the first group of conspirators to be tried before the People's Court and executed on 8 August.

# Guide to Sites

The Bendlerblock in central Berlin, on the street now named Stauffenbergstrasse, was the focus of the putsch attempt on 20 July, and the scene of the execution of Claus von Stauffenberg, Friedrich Olbricht, Werner von Haeften, Albrecht Mertz von Quirnheim and the enforced suicide of Ludwig Beck. Although still the headquarters of the German Defence Ministry, it is today also the site of the 'Gedenkstatte Deutscher Widerstand' (GDW), 'Memorial of the German Resistance', an organisation that maintains a permanant exhibition in the second-floor offices where the drama was played out. Additional temporary exhibitions (all in German) are mounted elsewhere in the building complex. The courtyard that was the scene of the executions contains a symbolic statue of a bound and naked male figure and a plaque recording the names of the

The courtyard of Berlin's Bendlerblock, today a memorial site.

Stauffenberg's office
in the Bendlerblock.

five men who died here. Official commemoration ceremonies honouring those executed, attended by leading representatives of the German state and descendants of the conspirators, are held here every 20 July. The GDW has a library of 5,000 photographs relating to the Resistance, and publishes books, biographies and other works on all aspects of the resistance to National Socialism – military, religious, the labour movement and young people. Special tours can be arranged (with a minimum of four weeks' notice) and audio guides in English are also available.

info@gdw-berlin.de                    Tel: +49 30 26 99 50 00.

The GDW also maintains a memorial at Berlin's Plötzensee Gefangnis (Plötzensee Prison) where some 3,000 victims of Nazism were executed – either guillotined or hanged. The victims included, besides some two hundred July plotters, members of the Red Orchestra Communist spy ring and the Czechoslovak Resistance. Although Plötzensee is still used as a jail, the execution chamber is kept as a permanant memorial.

The 'Wolf's Lair' at Rastenburg ('Wolfschanze' – 'Wilczy Szaniec' in Polish), Hitler's East Prussian headquarters, which was the scene of Stauffenberg's bomb on 20 July, is also maintained as a memorial site in today's Poland. Although attempts were made by the Nazis to destroy the complex – ironically with explosives – in November 1944 before the advancing Red Army reached it in January 1945, the concrete fortified bunkers were so massive that the demolition was only partially successful. Explanatory notices on the site guide today's visitors around the overgrown scenes of Hitler's living quarters and Stauffenberg's assassination attempt.

kontakt@wolfschanze.pl  Tel: +48 89 75 24 429.

The homes of the Stauffenberg family, where Claus and Berthold von Stauffenberg spent their childhoods, are still extant at Schloss Lautlingen, in the Swabian Alps south of Stuttgart, where there is a small memorial chapel; and at the Altes Schloss [Old Castle] in Stuttgart's city centre, both of which are open to visitors.

info@landesmuseum-stuttgart.de.  Tel: +49 711 279 34 98.

The picturesque Chateau La Roche-Guyon, Rommel's French head-quarters at the opening of the Normandy campaign until he was suc-ceeded by Field-Marshal Kuge after being severely wounded, and the scene of Stülpnagel's dramatic dinner with Kluge on the evening of 20 July, is open to visitors.

information@chateaudelarocheguyon.fr  Tel: +49 1 34 79 74 42.

# Acknowledgements and Sources

Long before any approach by a publisher, I felt fated to write this book. For as far back as I can remember, I have been fascinated, appalled and frankly obsessed by the tragic and heroic story of the doomed German resistance to Hitler's Nazism. And when, from my teenage years, I began first to visit and finally to live and work in both Austria and Germany, I lost no time in seeking out and listening to those 'ordinary people' who had experienced life in the Third Reich, and surviving participants – alas, all now dead – on both sides of the events of 20 July 1944.

I would, therefore, belatedly like to thank publicly (and sadly, posthumously), and in no particular order, the following for the gift of their memories: the late Ernst Jünger; Otto John; Otto Ernst Remer; Axel, Freiherr von dem Bussche; Leon Degrelle; Hans Bernd Gisevius; Frau Lore Beck; and General Hans Speidel.

My greatest debt in Germany, however, is to General Count Berthold von Stauffenberg, eldest son of Claus, who has been more than generous in enlightening me at length, both in person at his home and by phone and email, on all aspects of his parents, his extensive family and his own experiences both before and after July 1944. As well as granting me his hospitality over an extended interview, Count von Stauffenberg also kindly made available to me his memoir of the ordeal he and his younger siblings went through in the final months of the war, which I have translated – with his amendments and approval – and which is published here for the first time. It is wholly understandable that, after a lifetime of fielding such impertinent enquiries, Count von Stauffenberg now wishes for 'closure' – and a tribute to the nobility of spirit that his name embodies that he bore my quizzing with such grace.

During the writing of this book my gratitude has been particularly owed to friends and family who answered my questions, sought solutions to my problems and generally endured my anxious hand-wringing as an already overdue book elongated exponentially and, seemingly, endlessly. So now it is done, many thanks to friends and fellow historians of Nazism, Roger Moorhouse and Chris Hale, and above all to my publisher and editor, that model of patience, Michael Leventhal, who (I hope) will remain a friend even after all the trials I have put him through.

The literature on the German Resistance in general, and on Claus von Stauffenberg and the July Plot in particular, is enormous and ever growing. I list here only those books and documents that I have myself read and consulted in preparing this book. For an English readership, I have confined myself to books available in English. For translated works I have given their original German or French date of publication first, followed by the date of translation.

Early biographical studies of Stauffenberg by Joachim Kramarz (1967), Christian Mueller (1972) and G. Graber (1973); though useful and informative, have now been entirely superseded by Peter Hoffmann's monumental *Stauffenberg: A Family History 1905–1944* (1992, 1995, 2003). Hoffmann is a German – indeed, like Stauffenberg himself, a Swabian – academic historian, now based at a Canadian university, who has devoted his professional life to the study of the Resistance and to Stauffenberg's biography. And it shows. As the subtitle suggests, Hoffmann sets his subject firmly in the context of his family and his deeply rooted south-west German heritage, giving due, but not excessive, weight to the influence of the Stefan George cult. If, especially in his recounting the minutiae of Stauffenberg's military career, his writing gets somewhat dense, this is balanced by the sheer profundity of his research. Like Martin Gilbert's massive biography of Churchill, this book will not necessarily be read for the felicities of its prose style (German historians as a rule don't do that), but for its unimpeachable authority. It is a definitive treasure house of facts that will be mined by Stauffenberg scholars for many years to come.

The same author's *German Resistance to Hitler* (1988) similarly brings his trademark dogged, wood-rather-than-trees approach to an equally fact-heavy history of the Resistance, which by its sheer accumulation of detail bids fair to be definitive. The late Joachim Fest's *Plotting Hitler's Death: The German Resistance to Hitler* (1994, 1996, 1997) is the best popular account – wide-ranging, comprehensive and fair – although it can be a little dry. It is admiring, but by no means uncritical of these brave men and women. Fest, of course, is also the author – among many distinguished works – of the best German biography of *Hitler* (1973).

More recently, Roger Moorhouse's *Killing Hitler* (2006) is a fluently written, authoritative, detailed yet concise and very readable account of all the serious attempts on the Führer's life – not only those organised by Stauffenberg, Elser, Oster and Tresckow, but those planned by the Russians, the Poles – and even the British too. Highly recommended.

Two books written by active participants in the Resistance who – almost uniquely – survived the experience, and which remain indispensible, despite their antiquity are Fabian von Schlabrendorff's *The Secret War Against Hitler* (1965); and Hans Bernd Gisevius's *To The Bitter End* (1948). Both reflect the personalities of their authors. Schlabrendorff's memoir is that of the judge and jurist: courageous, precise, and shot through with Christian faith and charity – even to those who tortured him. Gisevius, appropriately for one who was long involved in the world of secret service, is cynical, bitter, mocking, ruthless – and unsparing of reputations, particularly that of Stauffenberg himself, with whom Gisevius did not get on, finding him arrogant and impetuous, and whom he unhesitatingly criticises. Despite doubts about Gisevius's credibility – most of those whom he quotes were no longer around to contradict him - his memoir is a useful corrective to an otherwise near-universal chorus of praise for Stauffenberg.

The official post-war federal German government 'white book' *Germans Against Hitler: July 20th, 1944* (1964) published on the twentieth anniversary of the plot, is an exceptionally informative collection of documents and photographs of the infamous People's Court trials and those executed after those obscene hearings. Intensely moving for a government document, it includes statements collected by the Gestapo investigators from witnesses such as Remer and his cohorts, Olbricht's secretary in the Bendlerblock, Delia Ziegler and letters written by the condemned to their loved ones on the eve of execution.

Early accounts of the plot written in English include Guardian journalist Terence Prittie's *Germans Against Hitler* (1964), which covers such resistants as the White Rose group as well as the July Plot, and is perhaps over-anxious to emphasise that not all Germans were Nazis; and the highly ambiguous work of the self-taught historian and diplomat Sir John Wheeler-Bennett: *The Nemesis of Power: the German Army and Politics 1918–1945* (1952). From being a pre-war friend to some of the plotters, Wheeler-Bennett reverted by the time of the plot to a cynical critic, even praising the SS in a Foreign Office memo for making the Allies' post-war task easier by purging the plotters. In this huge book, he critically traces the decisive role of the army in German history from the

Kaiser to the end of Hitler's war. He castigates the army for combining plotting against the benign regime of Weimar with fawning obeisance to Hitler, and comes close to applauding the failure of Stauffenberg's plot. He concludes by warning that rearming Germany risks a repeat of the inter-war years. Well, he was wrong about that. An interesting work, but one deeply flawed by the author's prejudices.

Constantine Fitzgibbon's *The Shirt of Nessus* (1956) was later re-issued as *To Kill Hitler: The Officers' Plot, July 1944* (1994). Considering that it was written barely a decade after the events it describes, it is remarkably accurate, and a fast-moving, journalistic narrative. *The July Plot* (1964) by those tireless Anglo-German chroniclers of the Third Reich, Roger Manvell and Heinrich Fraenkel is, like all these authors' works, brisk, informative and very readable; as is the same authors' *The Canaris Conspiracy: The Secret Resistance to Hitler in the German Army* (1969), which concentrates on the conspirators working inside the Abwehr.

There have been several biographies of Admiral Canaris, reflecting the central but still deeply mysterious and contentious role played by this enigmatic figure throughout the Third Reich. The huge *Canaris* (1976, 1979) by Heinz Hohne – like Fest, a respected German journalist-historian with great expertise on the Nazi period – while respecting the courage and cleverness of the little admiral, is highly critical of his early fostering of violent German nationalism, and his later cynical and duplicitous double gamesmanship. In stark contrast, *Hitler's Spy Chief: The Wilhelm Canaris Mystery* by Richard Bassett (2005) almost deifies this quintessential spymaster as a hero and martyr who conducted a lonely secret war against Hiterism throughout his Abwehr career. American academic Terry Parssinen has written the best available account of the abortive Abwehr/military attempt to overthrow or even assassinate Hitler on the eve of the Munich conference in *The Oster Conspiracy of 1938* (2004), in which he goes into minute, almost microscopic, detail to suggest that this was the most serious threat to Hitler until the advent of Stauffenberg.

If the conspirators themselves are to be believed, the main reason why the Oster conspiracy failed in 1938 was the readiness of the Western powers – especially Britain – to appease Hitler at Munich. The whole sorry story is comprehensively covered by Patricia Meehan in *The Unnecessary War: Whitehall and the German Resistance to Hitler* (1992) which records the desperate – and, alas, unavailing – efforts of the conspirators to secure British support for their plan to oust or eliminate Hitler. Sadly, Whitehall had other plans and priorities. Richard Lamb's

*The Ghosts of Peace 1935–1945* (1987) covers much the same ground – extending the story to the war's end.

The Venlo Incident – the SD 'sting' that coincided with Georg Elser's Munich beerhall bomb in 1939, and fatally innoculated the British authorities against any meaningful dealings with the genuine Resistance thereafter, is covered by one of the participant/victims in Sigismund Payne-Best's *The Venlo Incident* (1950). Fascinating in its detailed account of how it felt to be abducted at gunpoint and then interned throughout the war in Sachsenhausen concentration camp, the book also recounts the author's dramatic race with death at the end of the war when he and other VIP prisoners of the Nazis – including many associated with the July plot – were ferried around a dying Germany by their SS captors, expecting execution at any moment. Another account of Venlo is to be found in Leo Kessler's *Betrayal at Venlo* (1991). The memoirs of the slippery SD spymaster who organised the kidnap and many other dirty deeds are to be found in *The Schellenberg Memoirs* by Walther Schellenburg (1956). To be treated with even more caution than that applied to almost anything written by anyone from the murky world of espionage, but fascinating nonetheless.

One of the moving spirits behind the 1938 plot, and an unyielding opponent of Nazism from first to last, was General Ludwig Beck, sometime chief of the German General Staff, whose tragic story is told in a fine biography by American soldier Nicholas Reynolds: *Treason Was No Crime* (1976). Beck's botched suicide in the Bendlerstrasse on the night of 20 July 1944 was, alas, all too symbolic of the incompetence of the whole plot, which relied too much on wishful thinking, and too little on hard-headed ruthless realism. Beck's successor as Chief of Staff, the wily Franz Halder, although finally arrested and confined in a concentration camp, survived to write his *War Memoirs* (1962, 1976). His colleague in caution, Hitler's one-time economic wizard, Hjalmar Schacht, had the unique distinction of being imprisoned by the Nazis for his suspected opposition, then – much to his outrage – being tried at Nuremberg with other Nazi leaders. He was acquitted and returned to a high-level finance career. His memoirs were published as *My First Seventy-Six Years* (1955).

Popular, journalistic accounts covering the military conspiracy include two American works, *Code Name Valkyrie: Count von Stauffenberg and the Plot to Kill Hitler* by James Forman (1973) and *To Kill Hitler* by Herbert Molloy Mason (1980). Although aimed at a mass audience, with Forman in particular writing in a novelistic style – for instance reproducing verbatim conversations that he can only have imagined – both are serious works containing plenty of authentic detail. The same can hardly be said of *Secret Germany: Stauffenberg and the Mystical Crusade against Hitler* by Michael Baigent and Richard Leigh (1994, 2006). Written by two of the authors of *The Holy Blood and the Holy Grail*, this is an attempt to present Stauffenberg as the front man of a secret cult around the poet Stefan George. While there is no doubt that Stauffenberg was heavily influenced by his youthful intellectual infatuation with George, on which the book is quite informative, this was not the main motive behind his actions; nor, *pace* the authors, were his last words 'Long live secret [*geheim*] Germany', but, as several witnesses attested, 'Long live sacred [*heilige*] Germany.'

The initially entirely successful Paris part of the Valkyrie putsch on 20 July is well covered in several books, of which *Conspiracy Among Generals* (1953, 1956) by Wilhelm von Schramm, one of the surviving plotters, is the earliest, and as an inside account, invaluable. Another plotter, General Hans Speidel, survived to write his memoirs, *Invasion 1944: Rommel and the Normandy campaign* (1950, 1981). This too is an invaluable insider's account, especially important as Speidel was successively Rommel's and then Kluge's Chief of Staff, privy to the vacillations of both Field Marshals as they teetered on the edge of resistance. *Hitler Lives – and the Generals Die* (1981, 1982) by French journalist Pierre Galante covers the entire July conspiracy – including its Paris end – and benefits from Galante's interviews with General Adolf Heusinger, the Wehrmacht's operations chief, who was present in the conference room when Stauffenberg's bomb exploded. Although critical of Hitler's war policy and an intimate friend of some of the plotters, Heusinger was not himself a member of the conspiracy, and was indeed injured by the bomb. Nevertheless, he was arrested in hospital, detained and interrogated by the Gestapo, before being grudgingly released. He was restored to the army, but found himself demoted, and was never fully trusted by Hitler again.

Another general present in the conference room on the fatal day, who was also injured by Stauffenberg's bomb, was Walter Warlimont, Heusinger's deputy, whose memoirs *Inside Hitler's Headquarters* (1962, 1964) give a vivid picture of how it felt to be at the Führer's side as the great tragedy unfolded. Similarly, Nicolaus von Below's *At Hitler's Side* (1980, 2004) offers the memoirs of Hitler's Luftwaffe liaison officer, a loyalist who remained at his post until the Berlin *Gotterdammerung* in 1945. Bernd Freytag von Loringhoven was another young officer –

an aide to General Heinz Guderian – who remained close to Hitler until the last days. His *In The Bunker With Hitler: The Last Witness Speaks* (2005, 2006) contains valuable eye-witness evidence of the aftermath of the plot at Rastenburg – including the author's vain efforts to protect his cousin, one of the conspirators.

*The German Resistance to Hitler* (1966, 1970) is valuable because it is an early work on the Resistance by *German* historians, covering Resistance foreign policy (Hermann Graml); the constitutional plans of the Resistance (Hans Mommsen); resistance in the labour and trades union movement (Hans-Joachim Reichhardt); and the political and moral motives behind the Resistance movement (Ernst Wolf). An even earlier account from a German source is Hans Rothfels's *The German Opposition to Hitler* (1948). *The German General Staff* (1953) by Walter Goerlitz describes the effects of the July plot on Hitler's surviving senior officers.

Biographies of the two central figures in the Confessing Church's resistance to Hitler record the enormous importance of the moral element in the Resistance: the ponderous but immensely detailed and moving *Dietrich Bonhoeffer* by Eberhard Bethge (1967, 1970) is, as one would expect from a close colleague and relative of the pastor and theologian, uncritical – but inspiring and interesting on Bonhoeffer's wartime role as a representative of the Resistance to an uncomprehending Anglo-Saxon world. *Martin Niemöller* by James Bentley (1984) is a concise life of the turbulent pastor who turned from nationalist U-boat commander to one of the sharpest thorns in the sides of Hitler's regime.

Writings by participants in the July plot and its associated offshoots are, for obvious reasons, few and far between, but Dietrich Bonhoeffer's *Letters and Papers From Prison* (1971) is an indispensible text for anyone interested in the life of this modern martyr. *A German of the Resistance* (1948) contains the intensely moving last letters from the cell of the condemned Helmuth von Moltke – the leading figure in the Kreisau Circle – together with a brief biography. Gerhard Ritter was a conspirator, and a German historian who has written a sympathetic biography of his one-time cellmate, Carl Goerdeler, the 'holy fool' of the Resistance: *The German Resistance: Carl Goerdeler's Struggle Against Tyranny* (1956, 1958). Ulrich von Hassell's *The Von Hassell Diaries 1938–1944* (1947) gives a rare insight into the evolution of a conservative mind towards active, subversive opposition to the state he had once faithfully served. *A Mother's War* by Fey von Hassell (1990) is the memoir of Ulrich von Hassell's daughter, detained by the SS after 20 July and forcibly separated from her two small sons. It is one of the most vivid accounts of the Nazis' savage *Sippenhaft* decree, and is all the more remarkable for having been written by a victim.

Other valuable and moving eye-witness accounts of the events surrounding 20 July written by women witnesses related to the plotters by ties of family and friendship are: *The Berlin Diaries 1940–1945* by Marie 'Missie' Vassiltchikov (1985), a White Russian émigré drawn into the plot through her friendship with Adam von Trott zu Solz, and *The Past Is Myself* by Christabel Bielenberg (1968). Adam von Trott zu Solz himself is the subject of a biography, *A Good German* by Giles MacDonogh (1991) and an interesting recent fictional representation in the novel *The Song Before It is Sung* by Justin Cartwright (2007). Another interesting novel – this one about Stauffenberg himself – is Paul West's *The Very Rich Hours of Count von Stauffenberg* (1980).

Finally, *Tapping Hitler's Generals: Transcripts of Secret Conversations*, edited by Sönke Neitzel (2005, 2007) is a very revealing volume detailing the secretly recorded private conversations of senior German officers captured by the British towards the end of the war. This includes their uncensored reactions to the news of Stauffenberg's bomb; their disgust with the SS; disillusionment with Hitler's regime and their assessments of Stauffenberg.

# Picture Credits

# Index